German English Words

GERMAN
ENGLISH
WORDS

A Popular Dictionary
of German Words Used in English

Robbin D. Knapp

ROBBSBOOKS.COM
Capitola, California

1st edition © 2005 by Robbin D. Knapp, published in November 2005 by RobbsBooks.com, an imprint of Robbin D. Knapp.

Ver. 1.02

Printed by Lulu.com in the United States of America.

Library of Congress Control Number: 2005910116
ISBN: 1-4116-5895-7 (paperback: alk. paper)
ISBN-13: 978-1-4116-5895-0 (paperback: alk. paper)
EAN: 9781411658950

This book may be purchased at special discounts when purchased in bulk for educational, business, fund-raising or sales promotional use. Special editions or book excerpts can also be created to specification. For information address robb@robbsbooks.com.

Cover design by Robbin D. Knapp. Depicted are the flags of the countries with the highest numbers of German speakers in order: Germany, Austria, Switzerland, France, USA, Brazil, Argentina, Canada, Luxembourg, Belgium, and Liechtenstein.

For the women in my life,
Gerti, Sylvia and Carina

CONTENTS

INTRODUCTION

According to the 2000 U.S. census, between a sixth and a fifth of the U.S. population (17.3 % or 47.4 million people) considers themselves German Americans, that is, their ancestors came from a German-speaking part of Europe. Included in this number are Americans who reported that they are of German, Austrian, Pennsylvania German, Alsatian, or German Russian ancestry. One was allowed two answers in the ancestry category; both answers are included. Other ancestors such as European, Swiss, Belgian, or Luxemburger may also have spoken German, but these answers were not included in the number above since only a portion of these groups speaks native German. Therefore, the actual number of German Americans is higher. This is an estimate because only a sixth of the households received the long census form including the ancestry questions.

In the 1990 census the number was higher (23.9 % or 59.6 million Americans), but that does not mean there were fewer German Americans ten years later. It is just that more people reported their ancestry as United States or American in 2000. This indicates either a sinking interest in ancestry and genealogy or a rising feeling of being "100 percent American". However, with rising Internet access since 2000, interest in ancestry or genealogy will no doubt further increase due to the relative ease of finding one's ancestors.

The census shows that German Americans form the largest ethnic group in the U.S., before even Irish, English, and African Americans. German immigrants have shaped America's way of life and its language. Thousands of English words come from German, many more than one might think. Most people recognize many of them as German, like *kindergarten* and *Wiener schnitzel*, but one might not know what they mean in English or in the original German. One would not think of many of them as being German at all, such as *masochism*, *Pez*, and the *-ja* part of *Ouija board*. Many others are very recent, like *Infobahn* and *Fahrvergnügen*. In addition, of course, the words for America's favorite foods are German, for example *hamburger*, *frankfurter*, and *wiener*. In 2001, President George W. Bush proclaimed October 6 to be the annual German American Day in order to recognize German Americans for their many contributions to the U.S. About 1.5 million people in the U.S. still speak German, making it the fifth largest German-speaking country in the world behind Germany, Austria, Switzerland and France (Alsace-Lorraine).

Besides coming from immigrants other German words have found their way into English due to events originating in Germany, most notably the two world wars. This has given rise to such words as *Nazi*, *Gestapo*, *blitz*, and *flak*.

This book describes these words and more in dictionary format for the average person. The dictionary entries include the English and German meanings and origin. The numerous, often entertaining, sample sentences from sources like classical and modern literature, magazines, song lyrics, and the Internet show how each word is used in various situations. Often interesting comments are also included in the entries.

At least two authors have estimated about 6000 Germanisms including all German words that have ever been used in English. However, only about ten percent of these are used in everyday life. This book includes about 300 of the most interesting, not necessarily the most common, German words used in English and was inspired by my successful Web site, GermanEnglishWords.com.

Many users of the Web site have made suggestions for entries, many of which have been included. The names of those who made the suggestions are included in the entries. Many thanks to all my faithful and loyal visitors, who have pointed out mistakes and made many suggestions!

Besides German Americans, there are millions of people who learn or teach German or visit German-speaking countries each year. In addition, many people encounter German words in their reading and want to know their meaning or origin.

About two million U.S. tourists visit Germany every year. Another 170,000 come from Canada. These numbers include only tourists staying in accommodations with nine beds or more. They do not include business travelers and emigrants, nor do they include visitors to other German-speaking countries. Therefore, the actual number of visitors to German-speaking countries is higher.

Each year about 355,000 students learn German in grades K-12. Another 89,000 study German at colleges and universities every year. Not included in these numbers are those learning German at language schools, cultural institutions (e.g. the Goethe-Institut), etc. In addition, there are about 12,500 teachers of German in the U.S. in grades K-12 and about 5,000 in colleges and universities. German is the third most popular foreign language at all levels of education, behind Spanish and French. Many of the reactions to the GermanEnglishWords.com Web site are from German teachers looking for ideas for their classes or students looking for ideas for their assignments.

In addition, anyone who reads, listens to music, or watches television or movies will invariably come across German words, many of which cannot be found in common dictionaries. *Fahrvergnügen* is a good example from commercials. Another example is *Ehrenbreitstein*, which occurs in Herman Melville's *Moby Dick*. Melville expects one to know that it is a fortress or figuratively something imposing or hard to penetrate. A book by Michael Crichton contains *Diener*, which means "morgue assistant". I contacted Random House, who informed me that they did not have an example of this word in their dictionary citation files and would add the Crichton citation I noticed. There are also newer forms of words that have not yet made it to dictionaries, such as *zeitgeisty* (from *Zeitgeist*). This word itself seems to be zeitgeisty (trendy), because it is found in magazines and newspapers but in almost no books.

The relative scarcity of information on many of these words is actually the reason I started the Web site in the first place and the reason I wrote this book. I hope you enjoy it.

If you have any suggestions, corrections or comments, please feel free to e-mail me at robb@robbsbooks.com.

ABOUT THIS BOOK

This is a dictionary of some German words used in the English language (**Germanisms**), each with a literal or German meaning, English definition and often actual sample sentences from literature and the Internet.

Some German words like <u>kindergarten</u> are so Anglicized that they are now considered English words borrowed from German. Such words are called **loan words** or **loanwords**. *Loan word* itself is a literal translation of the German *Lehnwort*, making it a **loan translation**, *loan translation* itself being a loan translation of *Lehnübersetzung*. Loan translations are also called **calques**.

Other German words like <u>*Waldsterben*</u> are still considered **foreign words** used in English and often describe a particular technical term. Foreign words are usually italicized in literature.

The entries in this dictionary may sometimes have alternate definitions that are not given here.

I include mostly only entries that are derived from Modern German, although some come to English through Yiddish, in which case the entries are clearly so designated. I include Yiddish words if they are close in meaning to their Modern German cognates.

Yiddish is a High German language written in Hebrew characters that is spoken by Jews and descendants of Jews of central and eastern European origin. Its grammar and much of its vocabulary are Germanic, but it has also borrowed many words from other languages such as Hebrew and Slavic. Yiddish became a separate language between the 9th and 12th centuries, so one cannot say it developed from Modern German, but rather arose about the same time Old High German gave way to Middle High German. In other words, Yiddish is a Germanic language in its own right just as for example German, English, Dutch and Swedish. The word *Yiddish* comes from the Yiddish word *yidish*, which is short for *yidish daytsh* "Jewish German" [< Middle High German *jüdisch diutsch* "Jewish German"].

Another source of German words in the English language is the **Pennsylvania Dutch**, who are comprised of several groups of German emigrants who came from the lower Rhine provinces, Bavaria, and Saxony. They were not from the Netherlands as one might conclude from the name *Pennsylvania Dutch*; the *Dutch* part of the term is related to *deutsch*, which is German for "German".

Since about 1869, many people have preferred the term **Pennsylvania German**.

Of course *Dutch* and *deutsch* are etymologically related [English *Dutch* < Middle English *Ducch, Duch,* Dutch *duits, duitsch* < Middle Dutch *dutsch, duutsch,* Old High German *diutisc* "popular, vernacular (language)", related to Old English *theodisc* "speech"]; [German *deutsch* < Middle High German *diutisch, diutsch, tiutsch, tiusch* < Old High German *diutisc*].

In addition to *Pennsylvania Dutch* another example of *Dutch* used to mean "German" is in *David Copperfield* (1849), an <u>*Entwicklungsroman*</u> by Charles Dickens: "Miss Betsey, looking around the room, slowly and inquiringly, began on the other side, and carried her eyes on, like a Saracen's head in a Dutch clock, until they reached my mother."

Then there is the term *Dutch cheese*, which can refer either to a cheese similar to Edam (therefore no doubt from the Netherlands), or to cottage cheese (<u>schmierkase</u>), in which case it is definitely Pennsylvania German.

3

Any time you see a word or phrase underlined in this book, it is a cross-reference to another entry in this book or to an Internet Web site.

In the sample sentences, I have used the actual spelling and punctuation I encountered.

In the main entries I have included spellings, punctuation and capitalization found in literature. These are not always the currently "accepted" spellings and capitalization.

ABBREVIATIONS AND SYMBOLS

[ ]	etymology (word derivation)
<	derived from (in etymologies)
adj.	adjective
adv.	adverb
interj.	interjection
n.	noun
pl.	plural
sing.	singular
v.i.	intransitive verb
v.t.	transitive verb

A

abseil *v.i., n.*

from *abseilen* "to rope down": to rappel; a descent by rappelling [German *ab-*, "down" + *Seil*, "rope, line"]. *Abseil* is chiefly British and Australian; *rappel* is chiefly American. This is one of the very few English words that come from a German verb. *Abseiling* is now even used in its English form in German to mean specifically the new, trendy sport. This entry suggested by malacalypse the younger.

- "It is also an excellent vantage point from which to watch Samuel L. Jackson, who has taken everyone in a neighbouring building hostage and is fighting off helicopters, while men abseil down the building and a SWAT team opens fire from a barge in the middle of the river." "States and the film industry: Lures and enticements", *The Economist*, Mar. 14, 1998.
- "It [canyoning] involves following a stream from the top of a canyon to the bottom by jumping off low cliffs, abseiling over waterfalls and zipping down natural rock waterslides." Daffyd Roderick, "Travel Watch: Detour", *Time International*, Oct. 18, 1999, p. 8.
- "The boys' companion Tiggy Legge-Bourke, 33, will be on hand (though presumably not for sports outings after her recent blunder in allowing the princes [William and Harry] to abseil--rappeling headfirst down a steep in- cline--without helmets) as will their cousins Zara, 17, and Peter Phillips, 20, Princess Anne's children." Anne-Marie O'Neill et al., "A Lesson In Loss", *People*, Aug. 31, 1998, p. 48.
- "You don't have to abseil down a corporate skyscraper to join in. The World Bank bonds boycott is a campaign to cut World Bank funds off at source, in the spirit of the anti-apartheid movement." "Campaign: Spank the Bank", *New Internationalist*, Sep. 2001.
- "However at the end of last year, Toplis was asked if he was interested in attempting a 140 ft abseil to raise money for the Anthony Nolan Trust." Andrea Kon, "Jumping for Joy", *Vavo*, Jan. 29, 2001.
- "In the 1990s, taking your team to learn to abseil down a cliff face, battle with paint balls or build a raft to cross a river were vaunted as the way to bond teams and get them to work effectively together." Annie Gurton, "An exercise in bonding", *Computer Weekly*, Nov. 9, 2000.
- "The event was managed by youth consultancy Cake, which persuaded Spice Girl Mel C, and Richard Branson to abseil down the front of the store." Sue Levy, "Media expansion tests PR tracking", *Marketing*, Feb. 24, 2000.

affenpinscher *n.*

from *Affenpinscher* "monkey terrier": a breed of dog. See also <u>Doberman pin- scher</u>, <u>pinscher</u>.

- "For the breeders of the 2,620 champion canines (from affenpinschers to Yorkies) competing in American dogdom's Super Bowl, the potential payoff was worth it--not the prize money (there is none) but the bragging rights." "Up Front: Kennel Nation", *People*, Feb. 24, 1997, p. 50.

- "In the unlikely event that Johnny doesn't make it out of his breed, Love predicts a free-for-all among a giant schnauzer (Ch. Skansen's Tristan II), a white standard poodle (Ch. Lake Cove That's My Boy), an Afghan bitch (Ch. Tryst of Grandeur), an English springer spaniel (Ch. Salilyn 'N Erin's Shameless) and her long shot, the affenpinscher Ch. Yarrow's Super Nova." Franz Lidz, "Scorecard/Dogs: Party Animals", *Sports Illustrated*, Feb. 7, 2000, p. R14.
- *Affenpinscher Champions, 1968-1998*, Jan Linzy, 1999.

ahnentafel *n.*

from *Ahnentafel* "ancestor chart": a type of chart used in genealogy that uses a particular numbering system for all ancestors of the main person [German *Ahn, Ahne*, "ancestor" + *Tafel*, "table, chart"]. This entry suggested by G. Victor Paulson.

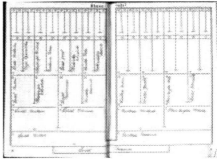

- "Ahnentafel Numbers Are not as Mysterious as they Seem", Anneliese Graebner Anderson, *Missouri State Genealogical Association Journal*, Winter 1995, p. 52-53.

alpenglow *n.*

from *Alpenglühen* "Alpine glow": a reddish-purple glow often seen on mountain tops just before sunrise or after sunset.

- "At length, toward the end of the second day, the Sierra Crown began to come into view, and when we had fairly rounded the projecting headland before mentioned, the whole picture stood revealed in the flush of the alpenglow." John Muir, *The Mountains of California*, 1894.
- "We had heard the heavy detonation of the slide about the hour of the alpenglow, a pale rosy interval in a darkling air, and judged he must have come from hunting to the ruined cliff and paced the night out before it, crying a very human woe." Mary Austin, *The Land of Little Rain*, 1903, p. 130.
- "But no painter ever laid such colours on his canvas as those which are seen here when the cool evening shadows have settled upon the valley, all gray and green, while the mountains shine above in rosy Alpenglow, as if transfigured with inward fire." Henry Van Dyke, *Little Rivers: A Book of Essays in Profitable Idleness*.
- "Alpenglow suffuses many of the photos, from Mono Lake in California's Sierra Nevada Mountains to the Annapurna Range in Nepal to a reflecting pond in Alaska's Denali National Park: eerie almost extraterrestrial pinks, mauves and purples." Robert F. Jones, "Books: Photographer with an Eye for Adventure", *Sports Illustrated*, Dec. 25, 1989, p. 18.
- "A few innocent-looking clouds are sliding in from the west, a nice accent that helps fire the peaks with alpenglow." Steve Howe, "This is no picnic", *Backpacker*, Aug. 1, 1996, p. 64.
- "Because what we'd miss even more than the peaks covered in alpenglow, even more than the sparkle of sun on the waves, is the furious meeting of rock and water, the high drama and often unspeakable beauty the two [man and woman] produce when they stand side by side." Pam Houston, "Why Women Love Men", *Men's Health*, Sep. 1, 1996, p. 132.

- "In fact, Goldie Hawn, Kate Hudson and Catherine Zeta-Jones all owe their alpenglow to [beautician Lily] Garfield." Suzanne Brown, "Beauty Talk/Black Book: Height Of Luxury", *InStyle*, Apr. 1, 2001, p. 324.

alpenhorn *n.*

See alphorn.

alpenstock *n.*

from *Alpenstock* "Alps stick": a strong iron-pointed staff used by mountain climbers. See also Birkenstock.

- "The little boy had now converted his alpenstock into a vaulting pole, by the aid of which he was springing about in the gravel and kicking it up not a little." Henry James, *Daisy Miller*, 1879. *Alpenstock* is used 6 times in this book.
- "It [the smoke] came from the pipe of a young man who had an alpenstock and who looked as if he had climbed to see the sun rise." Frances Hodgson Burnett, *The Lost Prince*, 1914, p. 238.
- "All [the tourist children] carried toy hatchets with a spike on one end built to resemble the pictures of alpenstocks." Stewart Edward White, *The Mountains*, 1904, p. 200.
- "Roofs slope off into the bluffs, houses are built on green ledges of earth, and back yards shoot skyward, so that the vineyards grow at an angle of forty-five degrees, and he who goes to look at his garden must needs take an alpenstock in his hands." Elia Wilkinson Peattie, *After the Storm: A Story of the Prairie*, 1897, p. 403.
- "And as a kind of horrid climax to the purge, a Soviet agent befriended Trotsky in Mexico City, then hacked him to death in 1940 with a steel-bladed alpenstock." Otto Friedrich, "World: Headed for the Dustheap", *Time*, Feb. 19, 1990, p. 36.
- "This rich tradition of mountain guiding and exploration comes to life through archival photos and a period re-creation complete with hemp ropes, alpenstocks, and wool knickers." "Anyplace Wild: Companion Guide to the Public Television Series (Special Supplement to Backpacker Magazine)", *Backpacker*, Jun. 1, 1998, p. S1.

alphorn, alpenhorn *n.*

from *Alphorn* "Alpine horn": a curved, wooden, powerful-sounding horn used by Swiss mountaineers for signaling.

- "Before that, Hans Rudolph Dutschler, an amateur alpenhorn player, covered the debts from his surveying business." Margot Hornblower, "Music", *Time International*, May 28, 1990, p. 52.
- "Another touch of town authenticity resounds from the alpenhorn of Bob Johnson, owner of the Enzian Motor Inn. Wearing traditional Bavarian dress, Johnson plays his 12-foot-long alpenhorn for about 10 minutes each morning from the balcony railing of the Enzian." "Leavenworth: Alpine Authenticity", *German Life*, May 31, 1997.
- "We've even had an alpenhorn player come in and play." Hartley Wynberg, "Glenn Gould Studio: Homage to a Master", *Professional Sound*, Oct. 1, 1999.

8

- "The Pastoral Symphony asks for a solo 'corno pastoriccio', a valveless instrument that some think was an 'alpenhorn'." Carl Bauman, "Mozart, L.: Symphonies", *American Record Guide*, May 1, 1998.
- "Lodging: Alpenhorn Bed and Breakfast. Most rooms have spa tubs and gas fireplaces. From $149. 601 Knight Ave.; 866-5700, (888) 829-6600, or www.alpenhorn.com." "The West's Best Lakes", *Sunset*, Aug. 2001.
- *Alphorn Favorites*, Various Artists, music CD, 1997.
- *Alphorn Concertos*, Leopold Mozart et al., music CD, 1997.

angst, *Angst* n.

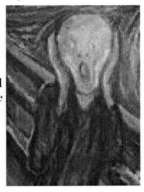

from *Angst* "strong fear": anxiety, anguish, distress, worry, alarm, fright, gloom, depression [< German *Angst* < Middle High German *angest* < Old High German *angust*. *Angst* has the same Indo-European root as English *anxiety, anxious, anguish* and *anger*, and Latin *anxietas, anxius, angustus* "narrow, tight" < *angere* "to press tightly; strangle; distress, anguish, make anxious". Merriam-Webster says, "Danish & German; Danish, from German". Wikipedia says, "Angst is a Dutch and German word for fear or anxiety", and also mentions the Danish word *angst*. All of my other sources only mention the German origin.]

- "In a jewelry shop a black-haired woman wore a sweat-shirt that offered, at least for her, a resolution for cultural Angst. It said, 'Don't Worry, Be Hopi.'" Chris Bolgiano, *Mountain Lion: An Unnatural History of Pumas and People*, 2001.
- "He suffered perpetual auto angst. For weeks his Jaguar had been sputtering to an inappropriate halt at stoplights all over the Valley." Jerry Stahl, *Permanent Midnight: A Memoir*.
- "'Every generation thinks they're uniquely unexceptional,' replied Yukio. 'It's this generational envy thing, happens every twenty-five years. At least be original in your existential angst. This is a long-distance call.'" Christopher John Farley, *My Favorite War*, 1996.
- "'THE TENSION, MOM! YOU KNOW! THE ANGST!!' 'YOU FEEL TENSION AND ANGST??'" Cathy Guiswite, *Cathy* comic strip.
- "The Angst over EMU", Jay Branegan, *Time*, Mar. 17, 1997, p. 22.
- *Woody Allen's Angst: Philosophical Commentaries on His Serious Films*, Sander H. Lee, 1996.
- *Technoscientific Angst: Ethics + Responsibility*, Raphael Sassower, 1997.

angstmeister n.

See angst, -meister.

ansatz n.

from *Ansatz* "statement, formulation; beginning, start": a technical term used by mathematicians and especially by theoretical physicists to describe a solution to a problem which is guessed (usually with some free parameters). This entry and definition suggested by Hilmar R. Tuneke.

- "It is shown that a correct description of the stationary quantum transport in superlattices with field-induced localized eigenstates requires the determination of a time-dependent distribution function from a kinetic equation, which emerges beyond the Kadanoff-Baym Ansatz.", P. Kleinert & V. V. Bryksin, "Quantum Transport in Semiconductor Superlattices Beyond the Kadanoff-Baym Ansatz", *International Journal of Modern Physics B*, 2001, p. 4123.

- "The Bethe-ansatz wave function", Minoru Takahashi, *Thermodynamics of One-Dimensional Solvable Models.*

Anschluss *n.*

from *Anschluß* "annexation": a union; political and economic union (of two countries); the annexation of Austria by Nazi Germany in 1938.

- "And after the Anschluss, he [Kurt Waldheim] waited *two whole weeks* before joining the <u>Nazi</u> Student Union." Bill Bryson, *Neither Here Nor There: Travels in Europe*, 1991, p. 264.
- "Here is an example of exactly such a leap of faith, which legitimizes a startling educationistic Anschluss of a host of traditional and concretely identifiable academic studies: ..." Richard Mitchell, *The Graves of Academe*, 1981.
- "And Hitler sent Bloch loving postcards afterwards with 'yours gratefully, Adolf,' and he became the protector of Dr. [Eduard] Bloch after the 1938 Anschluss." Ron Rosenbaum, *Explaining Hitler: The Search for the Origins of His Evil*, 1999.
- "[Fritz Mandl] appears to have been willing to do business with anyone on any side of any war, and because of that, the <u>Nazis</u> confiscated his factory even before the Anschluss joined Austria to Germany, in 1938." Hans-Joachim Braun, "Advanced Weaponry of the Stars", *Invention and Technology*, Spring 1997, p. 13.
- *Austria Before and After the Anschluss*, David Lehr, 2000.
- *The Anschluss Movement 1931-1938 and the Great Powers*, Alfred Low, 1985.
- *Timor's Anschluss: Indonesian and Australian Policy in East Timor, 1974-1976*, Sue Rabbitt Roff, 1992.

Ausländer, Auslander, auslander *n.*

from *Ausländer* "outlander": citizen of a foreign country, foreigner, alien, outsider [< German *Ausland* "foreign country" < *aus* "out, away" + *Land* "land, country"]. This entry suggested by Wilton Woods.

- "It ['fraki'] means a groundhog, an earthdweller, a dirt dweller, one who never goes into space, not of our tribe, not human, a goy, an auslander, a savage, beyond contempt." Robert A. Heinlein, *Citizen of the Galaxy*, 1982, p. 74.
- "In Ketzin, 10 miles from Berlin, 44 Auslander barely escaped with their lives when the building they inhabited was razed by torch throwers." "German right-wingers spearhead scores of attacks against foreigners", *Time*, Sep. 14, 1992.
- "Putting out the welcome mat represents a 180-degree policy turn for Germany, which has long denied being an immigrant nation, even though loopholes have let in 'guest workers' and political refugees. Those waves of Auslander have pushed the foreign-born population to 9%." Jack Ewing, "International Business: Immigration: HELP WANTED", *Business Week*, Sep. 17, 2001, p. 52.

- "The Bill of Rights is like foreign aid--something we like to talk about, but are too stingy or too indifferent to give to auslanders." Nicholas von Hoffman, "Defending Freedom By Suspending Liberty", *The New York Observer*, Jan. 7, 2002.
- "While the experience varies from employer to employer, veterans say a few lessons should be borne in mind by anyone thinking of working for an auslander. First, be sure your prospective employer knows what it's doing in coming to America." Wilton Woods, "Executive Life: Should You Work for a Foreigner?", *Fortune*, Aug. 1, 1988, p. 123.
- "As much as he [Joseph A. Reaves] loves his native land, particularly that part of it that is Wrigley Field, he sadly concludes that he is yet an auslander. 'I don't know where home is,' he writes. 'I fear I will never know.'" Ron Fimrite, "Books: A Couple of Curveballs", *Sports Illustrated*, Sep. 22, 1997, p. R24.
- *Auslander: A Novel*, Mary Curtner Powell, 2000.

autobahn, Autobahn *n.* [*pl.* **autobahns, autobahnen**]

from *Autobahn* "auto way": (in Germany) superhighway, interstate highway, freeway, expressway, limited access highway [Am.], motorway [Br.] [< German *Auto* "auto", short for *Automobil* "automobile" + *Bahn*, "way, road, track, path"]. This entry suggested by Anne Koth. See also infobahn.

- "The parallel set-up cannot quite compete with the petrol engine in its performance but, with a top speed of 210kph and 150 horsepower, it should be sufficient to satisfy all but the most impatient autobahn driver." *The Book of Visions: An Encyclopaedia of Social Innovations*, edited by Nicholas Albery.
- "Germany, where some locals guard the entitlement to drive 200-plus km/h as though it were a natural right and visitors prize a freedom denied at home, remains the exception: there is only one limit on most of the superhighways, and that is the car's performance. But the days of warp drive on the autobahn may be numbered." Daniel Benjamin Berlin, "Living: Speed Kills -- Right?", *Time*, Apr. 27, 1992, p. 40.
- "The Yankees go through a World Series like a Mercedes on the autobahn." Michael Knisley, "October Best", *The Sporting News*, Nov. 6, 2000.
- "Late in the last century (the 1990s believe it or not), we spoke of the information highway as if we were riding on a high-speed autobahn feeling barely in control and having few exits." Philip R. Jr. Day, "Blind Ride on the Technology Highway" *Matrix: The Magazine for Leaders in Education*, Jun. 2000.
- "Many people still believe that the autobahns in Germany were a National Socialist 'creation', but this is very wide of the mark." Uwe Oster, "The Autobahn myth", *History Today*, Nov. 1996.
- *American Autobahn: The Road to an Interstate Freeway with no Speed Limit*, Mark Rask, 1999.

automat, Automat *n.*

from *Automat* "vending machine": a restaurant in which patrons obtain food from small compartments with doors opened by inserting coins into slots [< German *Automat* "vending machine, self-operating machine", shortened from *Automaton* (*n.sing.*) < *automata* (*n.pl.*) < Greek *autó-matos* "self-moving"].

- "The wall reminded Hall oddly of an automat." Michael Crichton, *The Andromeda Strain*, 1969, p. 140.
- "That he was not succeeding soon became evident when he explained to Ron how to get a free bowl of tomato soup at an Automat." Russell Miller, *Barefaced Messiah: The True Story of L. Ron Hubbard*, p. 65.
- "We must eat in the foreigners' cafeteria where the food ranges from very poor to good. The atmosphere is reminiscent of a cross between an automat and a warehouse." Karen Turner-Gottschang & Linda A. Reed, *China Bound: A Guide to Academic Life and Work in the PRC*.
- "You go a little farther down the street and get it at the Automat or the Crystal Lunch." Christopher Morley, *The Haunted Bookshop*.
- "We had heard about Automats but had never seen one, so we ate a large breakfast at one and then went on a walking tour of Rockefeller Center." W. Carl Ketcherside, *Pilgrimage of Joy: An Autobiography of Carl Ketcherside*.
- "For me, the Smothers brothers are as dated as Chubby Checker, the Automat and a good 10-cent cigar." Rex Reed, "Travolta's Mission: Incomprehensible ... Hollywood on Ecstasy", *The New York Observer*, Jun. 11, 2001.
- "The toughest part is that I don't want to eat in the Automat for the rest of my life." Clement Greenberg, as quoted in: Raphael Rubinstein, "The Harold Letters 1928-1943: The Making of an American Intellectual", *Art in America*, Dec. 2000.

B

Baedeker, baedeker *n.*

a guidebook to countries or a country, a guidebook to places, a guidebook to other things such as restaurants usually for travelers [< Karl Baedeker (1801-1859), publisher of a series of travel guidebooks < Bädeker, Bädker, Bödeker, Böcker, Bäker, the Low German form of the name Böttcher "vat maker", not related to Bäcker "baker"].

- "But as a general thing all the circus folk preferred to roam among the native people and native scenes, and even found some scenes that the Baedeker guidebooks neglected to mention." Gary Jennings, The Center Ring: Spangle #2, 1999, p. 132.
- "When he catches sight through his window of a group of strangers, Baedekers in hand, asking directions of a policeman, he merely hopes that they

won't seek out, through this tangle of streets, the traghetto San Gregorio ...." Ian Littlewood, *A Literary Companion to Venice*, 1995, p. 4.
- "Rimbaud never travelled with a Baedeker and showed no interest in any particular category of art or architecture." Graham Robb, *Rimbaud: A Biography*, 2001, p. 1.
- "This is as good a place as any to say that I am not lost without a Baedeker." James Thurber, *My World and Welcome to It*, 1969, p. 224.
- "The man had already made all the arrangements and now he stood waiting on the platform, smiling cheerfully, red Baedeker guide in hand." Kevin Baker, *Dreamland: A Novel*, 2002, p. 68.

Baedeker Blitz, Baedeker raids *n.*

a series of raids conducted by the German Luftwaffe during World War II on cities of cultural and historical interest in England reputedly chosen from the Baedeker tourist guide to Britain.
- *The Great York Air Raid: The Baedeker bombing attack on York, April 29th, 1942*, Leo Kessler, 1979.

Bauhaus *n.*

from *Bau* "construction, architecture, a building" + *Haus* "a house, a building": an architectural school founded in Germany in 1919, known for its experimental use of metal, glass, etc. in buildings. See also gasthaus, hausfrau and plattenbau.
- "As always, the atmosphere there was chaotic; all the phones were ringing, but there was no receptionist in the little waiting area by the elevators, which was decorated with faded, taped-up posters for a 1929 Bauhaus Exhibition in Berlin and an old science-fiction movie called *The Forbin Project*." Michael Crichton, *Disclosure*, 1993.
- "When the Lovell family Chevy pulled up in front of these blocky, Bauhaus-like structures in the steady drizzle, Marilyn's mood sank." Jim Lovell & Jeffrey Kluger, *Apollo 13*, 1995.
- "Oil paintings of benefactors hung in the lobby of Gilman—'the idiot children of the rich,' said the dean, as he gave me a quick tour—and in the Bush Library, a four-story circular structure, concrete and brick and of a sturdy Bauhaus demeanor, with high beamed ceilings, the stacks dotted with study carrels, the building eerily empty, devoid of students." Garrison Keillor, *Wobegon Boy*, 1997, p. 7.
- *The Dessau Bauhaus Building 1926-1999*, by Margret Kentgens-Craig, 1999.
- *Biedermeier to Bauhaus*, by Sigrid Sangl, Barbara Stoeltie and Rene Stoeltie, 2001.

baum marten *n.*

from *Baummarder* "tree marten": (the brown fur of) the European (Pine) Marten (*Martes martes*)
- "The pine marten (*M. martes*) of European and Central Asian forests is also called baum marten and sweet marten." "marten", Britannica.com.

Beck's *n.*

a brand of beer from Germany [< *Beck, Becke, Becker, Böck, Bäck, Bäcker*, a common German surname, *Bäcker* "baker"].

- "THE MOST FAMOUS GERMAN WORD IN THE ENGLISH LANGUAGE", Beck's beer magazine advertisement, 1984. Wishful thinking, common to advertising copy.
- "He passed out Beck's beer to nearly all the other passengers." Thomas J. Stanley, *Millionaire Women Next Door: The Many Journeys of Successful American Businesswomen*, 2004, p. 198.

berg *n.*

related to *Berg* "mountain": an iceberg: Merriam-Webster says *iceberg* probably comes from Norwegian or Danish *isberg*, but to me German *Eisberg* also seems conceivable. [Middle High German *berc*; Old High German *berg*.] See also <u>burg</u>.

- "Antarctica continually sheds accumulating ice as glaciers calve bergs—some as big as Rhode Island." Eugene Linden, *Time*, May 12, 1997.

***Bildungsroman*, bildungsroman** *n.*

from *Bildungsroman* "education novel": a novel focusing on the moral and spiritual development of the main character, an <u>*Entwicklungsroman*</u>.

- "Lewis' Bildungsroman is an ironic twist on the 19th century romantic novels he studies in his library carrel." Alessandra Stanley, "Quixotic Quest", review of *Lewis Percy* by Anita Brookner, *Time*, Mar. 19, 1990, p. 83.
- *The Way of the World: The Bildungsroman in European Culture*, by Franco Moretti, 2000.
- *The Female Bildungsroman in English: An Annotated Bibliography of Criticism*, by Laura Sue Fuderer, 1991.

Birkenstock *n. usually pl.* **Birkenstocks**

from *Birkenstock* "Birkenstock": brand name of a leather and cork sandal made in Germany by the Birkenstock company, which goes back to Johann Adam Birkenstock in 1774 [< German *Birke* "birch" + *Stock* "stick, staff"]. See also <u>alpenstock</u>.

- "Thin ankles will look like trees stuck in concrete in clumpy shoes such as Birkenstock clogs." Trinny Woodall & Susannah Constantine, *What You Wear Can Change You Life*, 2005, p. 151.
- "The woman was short, small and slender, with curly gray hair cut close to her head, in a loose green sack of a dress, a necklace made of chunky glass beads, and Birkenstocks over black tights." Jennifer Weiner, *Goodnight Nobody: A Novel*, 2005, p. 192.
- "She's stomping around my room in her Mao jacket and Birkenstocks, shaking her glossy curls, her eyes, behind the lenses of her glasses (I guess revolutionaries working to empower the masses don't wear contacts), filled with bitter tears." Meg Cabot, *The Princess Diaries, Volume V: Princess in Pink*, 2004, p. 207.

- "She wears thick baggy clothing and wool socks and Birkenstocks and she wears silver rings on her fingers and a turquoise pendant around her neck." James Frey, *A Million Little Pieces*, 2003, p. 48.
- "Believe it or not, your feet may grow as much as a full size during pregnancy. If all else fails, think Birkenstocks!" Ann Douglas, *The Mother of All Pregnancy Books: The Ultimate Guide to Conception, Birth, and Everything in Between*, 2002, p. 253.
- "One guy went home before the meeting to change into Dockers and a button-down shirt to be more 'appropriate,' only to discover that his associates and a few of the senior staff were attending in T-shirts and Birkenstocks." Bill Gates, *Business @ the Speed of Thought: Succeeding in the Digital Economy*, 1999.
- "He was the first one with Birkenstocks, the first with bell-bottoms, the first with sideburns off, and the first with diversity." Michael Crichton, *Disclosure*, 1993.

blende *n.*

from *blenden* "to blind": an ore especially of certain metallic sulfides, having a fairly bright luster [German *blenden* < Old High German *blenten*, related to Old English *blind*]. See also <u>hornblende</u>.

- "Sphalerite, also known as zinc blende, is a very important zinc ore and is mined in many parts of the world." "Sphalerite", *Microsoft® Encarta® 98 Encyclopedia*.

blitz, Blitz *n., v.t.*

from *Blitz* "lightning": a fast intensive campaign; a <u>blitzkrieg</u>; an air raid; a rush of the passer by the defensive linebackers in American football; a type of chess game in which one has little time to move, similar to rapid and lightning chess. See also <u>Baedeker Blitz</u>.

- "... one of the guests (a famous celebrity who shall remain nameless) got so blitzed on booze, and God knows what else, that she passed out right in the middle of the living room floor." Fran Drescher, *Enter Whining*, 1996, p. 48.
- "Ever since Israel blitzed the Arabs in 1967's Six Day War—taking the Sinai and Gaza from Egypt, the Golan Heights from Syria and the West Bank from Jordan—the concept of 'land for peace' has been the cornerstone of all efforts to negotiate an end to the Arab-Israeli conflict." Christopher Dickey & Daniel Klaidman, "A Blueprint For Peace", *Newsweek*, Apr. 22, 2002, p. 17.
- "Bullock's quest for the truth began, he told me, in the midst of the Blitz." Ron Rosenbaum, "Explaining Hitler", *The New Yorker*, May 1995.
- "Deutsche Telekom goes public with a successful sales blitz." James O. Jackson, *Time*, Dec. 2, 1996.
- "In a blitz of polar air one night they lost thirty head of cattle and chipped them from the ice a week later like the fallen statures of an ancient creed." Nicholas Evans, *The Horse Whisperer*, 1995, p. 128.
- *The Kaizen Blitz: Accelerating Breakthroughs in Productivity and Performance*, by Anthony C. Laraia, Patricia E. Moody & Robert W. Hall, 1991.
- *From the Crash to the Blitz: 1929-1939*, by Cabell B. H. Phillips, 2000.

blitzkrieg *n., v.t.*

from *Blitzkrieg* "lightning war": a swift surprise offensive; <u>blitz</u>.

- "The blitzkrieg to cut Finland in half was to be abandoned after the heavy losses and the Finns could gradually be withdrawn to other fronts." Eloise Engle & Lauri Paananen, *The Winter War: The Soviet Attack on Finland 1939-1940*, 1973, p. 104.
- "Most of the quality were staying an extra day, just to avoid the stampede; but the smaller delegations, co-ops, representatives, and consortia preferred to blitzkrieg the bellhops and crowd the cashier rather than pay for another exorbitant night at the Chateau Hôtel Casino." Dafydd ab Hugh, *Balance of Power (Star Trek: The Next Generation)*, 1995.
- "Just two days after issuing a statement downplaying the suit, AOL—famous for blitzkrieg marketing tactics—reconsidered and announced a full retreat: the company will throttle back efforts to sign up new subscribers and invest $350 million to upgrade its networks." Daniel Eisenberg and Anita Hamilton, *Time*, Jan. 27, 1997.
- *The Path to Blitzkrieg: Doctrine and Training in the German Army, 1920-1939*, by Robert Michael Citino, 1999.
- *Hitler's Blitzkrieg Campaigns: The Invasion and Defense of Western Europe, 1939-1940*, by J. E. and H. W. Kaufmann, 1993.

bratwurst *n.*

from *Bratwurst* "meat sausage": a kind of sausage ideally made of pure pork that is usually fried [< German *Brät, Brat* "finely chopped, raw sausage meat before filling into skins" < Middle High German *brate* < Old High German *brato* "pure meat (not mixed with other ingredients), soft parts" (related to German *Braten* "roast meat", not related to *braten* "to fry" as some dictionaries

state and many German speakers themselves also believe) + *Wurst* "sausage"]. See also <u>wurst</u> and <u>knackwurst</u>.

- "I had seen all of my relatives, eaten a yard of bratwurst, fished for crappies, heard dozens of stories of shame and degradation, and was cured of my fevered thoughts about Jean." Garrison Keillor, *Wobegon Boy*, 1997, p. 105.
- "Half an hour after the plane landed, I was in a south Minneapolis backyard sitting on green grass next to a bed of irises, feasting on sweet corn and bratwurst, drinking green nectar, talking about old times like they were back again." Garrison Keillor, insert in *Lake Wobegon Loyalty Days*, CD, 1989.
- "It says here you exposed yourself in the cafeteria."
  "I was joking with the lunch lady. It was a bratwurst."
  "Bratwurst? Aren't we the optimist?"
  10 Things I Hate About You, starring Heath Ledger, Julia Stiles & David Krumholtz, 1999.
- "'Bratwurst and <u>sauerkraut</u>,' said Marietta, twirling a strand of blond hair between her fingers. '<u>Wiener schnitzel</u> and kreplach.'" Tama Janowitz, *By the Shores of Gitchee Gumee*, 1996, chapter 1.
- "[The bag] looked like a bratwurst and he guessed it weighed about ten pounds." Stephen King, *Desperation*, 1996.

16

Bremsstrahlung, bremsstrahlung *n.*

from *Bremsstrahlung* "braking radiation": in physics, the electromagnetic radiation produced by the sudden retardation of a charged particle in an intense electric field (as of an atomic nucleus); the process that produces such radiation [German *bremsen* "to brake" < *Bremse* "a brake" < Late Middle Low German *bremse* "nose clamp for horses" < Middle Low German *premse, premese* < *pramen* "to press" + *Strahlung* "radiation" < *strahlen* "to radiate" < *Strahl* "ray" < Middle High German *stral, strale* < Old High German *strala* "arrow, stripe"]. This entry suggested by Georg Kreyerhoff.

- "We can study along the same lines [as Thomson scattering] classical bremsstrahlung, i.e., radiation by a charge suddenly accelerated." Claude Itzykson & Jean-Bernhard Zuber, *Quantum Field Theory*, 1986, p. 39.
- "The power radiated in Bremsstrahlung (*B*) and radiative recombination (*R*) is also shown." Martin V. Zombeck, *Handbook of Space Astronomy and Astrophysics*, 1990, p. 280.
- *Polarization Bremsstrahlung (Physics of Atoms and Molecules)*, V. N. Tsytovich & I. M. Oiringel, 1993.
- "The unique construction of thin layered lead encapsulated in acrylic completely attenuates Beta emission and errant Bremsstrahlung." *Cone Instruments Nuclear Medicine Supplies and Accessories*, hospital supply catalog, 2001/2002.
- "Phosphorus-32 produces Bremsstrahlung, a high energy secondary photon radiation." *Radiation Safety*, scientific supply catalog, 2002.

Buba, BuBa *n.*

See <u>Bundesbank</u>.

bund, Bund, *often pl.* **bunds** *n.*

a German government bond denominated in <u>deutschemarks</u> [< *Bund-* ("federation") in <u>Bundesbank</u>, influenced by English *bond*]. This entry suggested by Josef Weidacher.

- "However, as the rapid convergence of Eurozone bond yields shows, monetary union has greatly reduced what investors call country risk, so that all Eurozone members' bonds are now regarded as being (almost) as good as the old German bunds." Niall Ferguson, *Colossus: The Price of America's Empire*, 2004, p. 232.
- "Once you've learned the ropes, consider moving up to stock index futures or the futures on the German Bund, both among the favorite vehicles of professional day-traders." Alexander Elder, *Come Into My Trading Room: A Complete Guide to Trading*, 2002, p. 145.
- "In the United States, it [the safest bond] had to be the thirty-year Treasury; in Germany, the ten-year Bund." Roger Lowenstein, *When Genius Failed: The Rise and Fall of Long-Term Capital Management*, 2001, p. 145.
- "For example, consider a trader who is active in the Bund option market, and who is trying to find a simple way to integrate a volatility skew into his theoretical pricing model." Sheldon Natenberg, *Option Volatility & Pricing: Advanced Trading Strategies and Techniques*, 1994, p. 408.

Bundesbank, Deutsche Bundesbank, Buba, BuBa *n.*

"Federal Bank": the German central bank [< *Bundes-* "federal" + *Bank* "bank"].

- "In contrast, the Deutsche Bundesbank controlled policy without government interference (Schaling 1995; 95-6)." Kelly H. Chang, *Appointing Central Bankers: The Politics of Monetary Policy in the United States and the European Monetary Union*, 2003, p. 1.
- "The French seldom disagreed with the BuBa's 'sound money' policies." John Gillingham, *European Integration, 1950-2003: Superstate or New Market Economy?*, 2003, p. 234.
- "Buba Knows Best?" Daniel Yergin & Joseph Stanislaw, *The Commanding Heights: The Battle for the World Economy*, 2002, p. 345.
- "What if he asks me a question about interest rates? What if he wants to talk about the Bundesbank or American growth prospects? But all he says is 'Harrods, please,' to the driver." Sophie Kinsella, *Confessions of a Shopaholic*, 2001, p. 152.
- "One time, I had a really large position in Deutsche marks when the Bundesbank came in and decided to punish the speculators." Jack D. Schwager, *Market Wizards: Interviews with Top Traders*, 1993, p. 36.
- "Hans Zietmeyer, the high priest of the Bundesbank, chimed in just solemnly." Jordan Bonfante, "A German Requiem", *Time*, July 6, 1998.

bunds *n.pl.*

See bund.

burg, -burg *n.*

related to *Burg* "castle, fortress": city, town. Actually comes from Middle English *burg, burgh, burch,* Old English *burg,* Anglo-Saxon *burg, burh, buruh,* related to Old High German *burg* "fortified place (on a hill)". Probably also related to Old English *beorg* "hill" and Old High German berg "hill, mountain". The meaning has therefore changed from "hill" to "fortress on the high" to "walled town" to "town". Thus the place-name endings *-berg, -burg, -burgh, -boro,* etc. are basically only spelling variants.

- "'Just let me check here—this one house—and then this burg is history,' he said, and turned into the driveway of a small ranch-style home on the left side of the street." Stephen King, *Desperation*, 1996.

burger, -burger *n.*

See hamburger.

C

Capellmeister *n.*

See Kapellmeister.

CJD *n.*

See Creutzfeldt-Jakob disease.

cobalt *n., adj.*

from *Kobalt*: a metal, element and nutrient; cobalt blue [German *Kobalt* < *Kobold*, so-called because kobolds supposedly stole the more valuable silver and

18

replaced it with cobalt]. See also <u>kobold</u>, <u>nickel</u> and <u>quartz</u>. See further example under <u>zinc</u>.

- "The grinning Bea brought down-stairs a pile of soft thick sheets of paper with designs of lotos blossoms, dragons, apes, in cobalt and crimson and gray, and patterns of purple birds flying among sea-green trees in the valleys of Nowhere." Sinclair Lewis, *Main Street*, 1920, p. 78.
- "The Inspector-General of State Hospitals (whose maintenance is a charge upon the Gould Concession), Official Adviser on Sanitation to the Municipality, Chief Medical Officer of the San Tomé Consolidated Mines (whose territory, containing gold, silver, copper, lead, cobalt, extends for miles along the foot-hills of the Cordillera), had felt poverty-stricken, miserable, and starved during the prolonged, second visit the Goulds paid to Europe and the United States of America." Joseph Conrad, *Nostromo: A Tale of the Seaboard*, 1904, p. 504.
- "When a man once knows that he has done justice to himself, let him dismiss all terrors of aristocracy as superstitions, so far as he is concerned. He who keeps the door of a mine, whether of cobalt, or mercury, or <u>nickel</u>, or plumbago, securely knows that the world cannot do without him." Ralph Waldo Emerson, *English Traits*, 1849, p. 868.
- "I mean, if a couple of hundred million people all decide that their national honour requires them to drop cobalt bombs upon their neighbour, well, there's not much that you or I can do about it." Helen Broinowski Caldicott, *A Desperate Passion: An Autobiography*, 1996.
- "This is England, but Spain and Italy have coloured the dishes and displayed their bowls and plates upon the wooden dresser, adding their cobalt Mediterranean blues and their hot mustard yellows." Margaret Drabble, *The Witch of Exmoor*, 1997.
- "In terms of energy, iron-56 lies at the bottom of a valley, with lighter nuclei, including those of oxygen, carbon, helium and hydrogen, up one side and heavier nuclei, including cobalt, <u>nickel</u>, uranium and plutonium, up the other side." John Gribbin, *The Search for Superstrings, Symmetry, and the Theory of Everything*, 1998.
- "This day it is a deep blue-green, a combination of green earth and ultramarine, and the sky above is cobalt blue and the moon still visible above the horizon: there, *there*." Nicholas Delbanco, *What Remains*, 2000.

coffee clutch, coffee-klatsch, coffee klatsch, coffee klatch *n.*

See <u>kaffeeklatsch</u>.

Commerzbank *n.*

"Bank of Commerce".

- "'The <u>deutsche mark</u>'s most important role, though, was in imposing a [*sic*] entire "stability culture",' says Commerzbank economic research director Jürgen Pfister." Jordan Bonfante, "A German Requiem", *Time*, July 6, 1998, p. 21.

Concertmeister, Concert-Meister *n.*

See <u>Konzertmeister</u>.

Creutzfeldt-Jakob disease, CJD, Creutzfeldt-Jakob syndrome, Jakob-Creutzfeldt disease, Jakob-Creutzfeldt pseudosclerosis, Jakob's pseudosclerosis *n.*
from *Creutzfeldt-Jakob-Krankheit, Creutzfeldt-Jakobsche Krankheit* "Creutzfeldt-Jakob disease": a disease of the human central nervous system, associated with bovine spongiform encephalopathy (BSE, mad cow disease), named for Hans Gerhard Creutzfeldt (1883-1964) and Alfons Maria Jakob (1884-1931), German neurologists [German *Creutz, Kreuz* "cross" + *Feldt, Feld* "field" + *Jakob* "Jacob, James"].

- "One [reason] was the developing theory that a mysterious kind of protein, tentatively described as a prion and readily transmitted from beef to beef eaters in Europe, was causing a fatal brain disease known as Creutzfeldt-Jakob disease." Dale Peterson, *Eating Apes*, 2003, p. 87.

- "Creutzfeldt-Jakob Disease (CJD) may not yet have gotten much public attention in the United States, but in England this obscure but terrifying illness has become a household word because of its association with that country's epidemic of mad cow disease." Sheldon Rampton & John Stauber, *Mad Cow U.S.A.: Could the Nightmare Happen Here?*, 1997, p. 1.

- "The individuals were diagnosed with a variant strain of Creutzfeldt-Jakob disease (CJD), a rare syndrome that ordinarily strikes people in middle age." Kathleen Hart, *Eating in the Dark: America's Experiment With Genetically Engineered Food*, 2002.

- "The rapid spread of the illness [BSE], which likely resulted from feeding cattle meat and bonemeal from animals that already had the disease, was linked with more than a hundred cases of deadly Creutzfeldt-Jakob brain disease in humans who had consumed the infected meat." Jennifer Ackerman, "Food: How Safe?", *National Geographic*, May 2002, p. 23.

- "Because some experts say BSE can be transmitted to humans in the form of Creutzfeldt-Jakob Disease (CJD), a fatal neurological disorder that has increased more than 100 percent in England." Amy Rosenbaum Clark, "When stiff upper lips are quivering: a by-the-numbers look at Britain's 'mad cow' crisis", *Vegetarian Times*, Sep. 1996.

- "Over the past several years, numerous Brits have been diagnosed with the human equivalent of mad cow disease, known as Creutzfeldt-Jakob Disease (CJD)." Jon Geller, "When Man's Best Friend Isn't", *Mother Earth News*, Sep. 1996.

- "Creutzfeldt-Jakob disease comes in two forms, one old and one new, both terrible and both rare." Josie Glausiusz, "Case closed", *Discover*, Jan. 1998.

crimmer *n.*
See <u>krimmer</u>.

D

dachshund *n.*

from *Dachshund* "badger hound": a small dog of a breed of German origin originally used to hunt badgers. In German-speaking countries dachshunds are more often called *Dackel* nowadays, but also *Dachsel* and *Dachser*.

- "On the carpet in front of the fire, a pretty little dachshund was curled up asleep with its nose tucked into its belly." Roald Dahl, "The Landlady", *Kiss Kiss*, 1959, p. 10.
- "Who ever heard of a German without a dachshund?" Christopher Morley, *The Haunted Bookshop*, 1918.
- "I'm raising a dachshund now—by your methods." Robert A. Heinlein, *Starship Troopers*, 1959.

das ist gut

"this/that is good": a phrase used in English-language media without translation because it is easily understood while still sounding very German.

- "Does he have DAS?"
  "DAS what?"
  "Das ist gut."
  "Damage Avoidance System."
  A.I. - Artificial Intelligence, directed by Steven Spielberg, 2001.
- "'Das ist gut.' 'Die Engel-kinder!' cried the poor things, as they ate, and warmed their purple hands at the comfortable blaze." Louisa May Alcott, *Little Women*, 1869, p. 14.
- "It was given to men of square determined stature with grim reliability and efficient ways to work and tend these slopes and gather the harvest. God saw das ist was gut and he rested." Ralph Steadman, *The Grapes of Ralph: Wine According to Ralph Steadman*, 1996, p. 78. This is intentional horrible grammar. Correct German would be, "Gott sah, dass es gut war ...."

deaner *n.*

See *diener*.

delicatessen, deli *n.*

from *Delikatessen (-laden, -geschäft)* "(shop of) delicacies": ready-to-eat, often unusual or foreign foods; a shop where such foods are sold [German *Delikatessen, Delicatessen* "delicacies" < *Delikatesse, Delicatesse* "delicacy" < French *délicatesse* "delicacy" < Old Italian *delicatezza* "delicacy" < *delicato* "delicate" < Latin *delicatus*; the notion that *Delikatessen* comes from German *delikat* "delicate, fine" + *Essen* "food" is a folk etymology and therefore incorrect].

- "In order to do this, many pathologists have taken to describing diseased organs as if they were food, earning themselves the name, delicatessen pathologists." Michael Crichton writing as Jeffery Hudson, *A Case of Need*, 1968.
- "The Porsche jumped the curb, plowed through a stack of black plastic garbage bags, and crashed through the plate glass window of a small delicatessen that was closed for the night." Janet Evanovich, *Eleven on Top (A Stephanie Plum Novel)*, 2005, p. 69.

- "The place [the Bagel Bin on Little Santa Monica] was New Age Deli: glass cases of smoked fish and meat and all the right salads, but the stainless-steel/vinyl ambience was autopsy room." Jonathan Kellerman, *Rage (An Alex Delaware Novel)*, 2005, p. 176.
- "Though they had few servants, yet with gas stoves, electric ranges and dish-washers and vacuum cleaners, and tiled kitchen walls, their houses were so convenient that they had little housework, and much of their food came from bakeries and delicatessens." Sinclair Lewis, *Babbitt*, 1922.
- "At one point a thirty-minute meal break was called and three or four of our company hurried across the street to a small restaurant-deli." Steve Allen, *Dumbth: The Lost Art of Thinking, With 101 Ways to Reason Better and Improve Your Mind*, 1998, p.101-2.
- "The stories are not those I expect to hear, of people getting sick from drinking unpasteurized milk or eating deviled eggs left too long in the hot sun at a picnic, but tales of peopled sickened by contaminated parsley and scallions, cantaloupes, leaf lettuce, sprouts, orange juice, and almonds; refrigerated potato salad, eggs, chicken, salami, and beans; hot dogs, <u>hamburgers</u>, deli meats." Jennifer Ackerman, "Food: How Safe?" *National Geographic*, May 2002, p. 9.

Der Freischütz n.
  See *Freischütz, Der*.
der Führer n.
  See Führer.
Der Kindestod n.
  See Kindestod, Der.
Der Weihnachtsbaum n.
  See *Weihnachtsbaum, Der*.
Deutsche Bundesbank n.
  See *Bundesbank*.
deutsche mark, deutschemark, Deutsche mark, Deutschemark, D-mark, DM, DEM n. [pl. Deutschemark, Deutsche-marks]
  from *deutsche Mark* "German mark". See further examples under <u>Commerzbank</u> and <u>Wirtschaftswunder</u>.

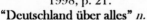

- "In the '50s and '60s the deutsche mark went on to serve as anchor of Germany's economic miracle." Jordan Bonfante, "A German Requiem", *Time*, July 6, 1998, p. 21.

"Deutschland über alles" n.
  "Germany over everything": also known as the *Deutschlandlied* "Germany song", the national anthem of Germany, sung to the tune of the Emperor's Hymn or *Austria*, the Austrian national anthem from 1797 to 1918, composed by Haydn. The controversial first verse referring to *über alles* was replaced in 1950 with the third verse referring to unity, justice and freedom. Nowadays *Deutschland über alles* is a nationalist slogan. This entry suggested by Wilton Woods.
  See also *über-*.

According to Daniel Molkentin:

"The [phrase] 'Deutschland über alles' had a completely different meaning before Hitler started abusing it.

Back when the hymn was composed, Germany was just a loose association of states which had their own borders and no central government or emperor. That was a major drawback compared to England or France, because among other things the economy was hopelessly inefficient through all the different taxes and currencies inside Germany.

So the Germans had the wish to get some central government/emperor in place. The first verse tried to express that in the sense of, 'Put all your energy into (a united) Germany; it's more important for us to achieve that than anything else' ('anything else' being 'the world', you probably say 'the universe' today).

The first to abuse that in the way of, 'Germany is better [than] every other nation in the world', were Adolf Hitler and the <u>Nazis</u>, just as they made other stuff fit with their *Weltanschauung* (another German word, funny :)."

- "Just as the Prussian military caste had its slogan 'Deutschland ueber Alles!' so the Knights of Slavery have their slogan: 'Make America Catholic!'" Upton Sinclair, *The Profits of Religion: An Essay in Economic Interpretation*, 1918, p. 126.

- "Other fun bumper stickers can say things like, BEER DRINKERS GET MORE HEAD; SUCK MY TAILPIPE; HONK IF YOU'RE HORNY; HOORAY FOR THE KKK; or DEUTSCHLAND UBER ALLES." George Hayduke, *Getting Even: The Complete Book of Dirty Tricks*.

- "The virtuous German had been advancing heroically with the double desire of enlarging his country and of making valuable gifts to his offspring. 'Deutschland uber alles!' But their most cherished illusions had fallen into the burial ditch in company with thousands of comrades-at-arms fed on the same dreams." Vicente Blasco Ibanez, *The Four Horsemen of the Apocalypse*.

Die Hand die Verletzt *n.*

See <u>Hand die Verletzt, Die</u>.

diener, deaner *n.*

from *Diener* "servant": a man-of-all-work in a laboratory (*Dorland's Illustrated Medical Dictionary*), morgue attendant, pathology or autopsy assistant. (Special thanks to all the helpful medical transcriptionists in <u>sci.med.transcription</u>.)

- "While the pathologist is doing this, the deaner cuts the scalp open, removes the scullcap, and takes out the brain if permission for brain removal has been obtained .... Deaner is a traditional term for a man who takes care of the dissecting room. It is an ancient term, dating back to the days when anatomy dissections were done by horse gelders and butchers. The deaner keeps the rooms clean, cares for the corpses, and aids in the dissection." Michael Crichton writing as Jeffery Hudson, *A Case of Need*, 1968.

- "Immediately before the autopsy, the body is removed from the cooler by a morgue attendant who will help with the autopsy. This individual is called a **diener** (DEE-nur), which is German for 'servant.' Most dieners do not realize the derivation of this word and would probably object to being called 'diener' if they did. Dieners are not formally trained, but many have some background of employment in the funeral industry. For some reason, in the southern U.S. anyway, about ninety per cent of dieners (my estimate) are African-American. I would estimate that less than ten per cent of dieners are female. Dieners tend to work at their job for decades. I think this is because 1) management types don't know what goes on in the morgue, and would not care to mess around with its staffing come belt-tightening time, and 2) dieners are pretty much left alone by management and enjoy a much greater degree of autonomy than most workers at their pay grade and level of education. My own impression of the 'diener personality' is that they are somewhat secretive and cliquish, and one gets the idea that they have a lot more going on in their lives than they tend to let on .... For fiction writers, I think there is a lot of character development potential for dieners ...." Ed Uthman, "The Routine Autopsy", www.neosoft.com/~uthman/Autop.html.

- "Works under the technical and administrative direction of a pathologist. Obtains approval and instructions to begin autopsy, insures correct identification, via I.D. wristband, lays out standard autopsy instruments and apparel for the pathologist. Labels specimen jars, fills formalin containers, prepares tissue cassettes, bunsen burner together with Petri dishes for cultures as requested ...." "Hospital Autopsy Support (Diener) Services", Glossary, 1800autopsy.com.

Diesel, diesel *adj., n.*

from *Diesel*: pertaining to a type of internal-combustion engine in which ignition is caused by heat due to air compression instead of due to an electric spark as in a gasoline engine; Diesel engine or motor; Diesel fuel; Diesel automobile or other vehicle; named for Rudolf Diesel, 1858-1913, German inventor [< South German *diesel* "well, healthy" or short for *Matthiesel*, diminutive of *Matthias, Matthäus* "Matthew"].

- "Champ is the salt of the earth but somehow I can't imagine him joining you in symbolic dancing, or making improvements on the Diesel engine." Sinclair Lewis, *Main Street*, 1920, p. 155.
- "The compression-ignition, or diesel, engine differs in several ways from the spark-ignition engine, although it is based on the same two- or four-stroke cycle." Committee on Fuel Economy of Automobiles and Light Trucks, *Automotive Fuel Economy: How Far Should We Go?*, 1992, p. 33.
- "The cold diesel turned over instantly, coughing a bit uneasily but then rumbling powerfully, and a corner of his mind congratulated himself for having had it overhauled before he left port." David Weber, *The Apocalypse Troll*, 1999.
- "This is the point in the infomercial where the guy wearing the CAT Diesel cap asks, 'Do I need a college education to build one of these here multiple-truth Web sites?'" Philip Greenspun, *Philip and Alex's Guide to Web Publishing*, 1999.
- "One of the Diesel engines broke down in the morning, and while we were working on it, the forward port diving-tank commenced to fill." Edgar Rice Burroughs, *The Land That Time Forgot*.
- "This usage is usually found in metaphors that treat computing power as a fungible commodity good, like a crop yield or diesel horsepower." Eric S. Raymond, *The New Hacker's Dictionary*.

24

- "... the town's sole gas station refused to sell them diesel for their tractors." Stefan Thiel, "Old <u>Stasi</u> Never Die", *Newsweek*, Dec. 10, 2001, p. 39.

diktat *n.*

from *Diktat* "dictation, something dictated": a harsh settlement unilaterally imposed (as on a defeated nation); decree, order [< New Latin *dictatum* < Latin *dictatus* < *dictare* "to dictate"]. This entry suggested by Alastair Lack.

- "Weary Iraq accepts UN diktat", Dominic Evans, *The Economic Times*, June 20, 1998.
- "Democracy is not the diktat of one armed party." Mesfin Wolde-Mariam, "The Ethiopian Human Rights Council and Human Rights", *Ethiopia on the Web*, July 1996.
- "Investment by government diktat" Robert McKee, *World News Magastories.*
- "SEBI diktat on trading with CRB-linked firms", *The Financial Express*, July 8, 1997.
- "It is for that reason that we want to replace the Diktat, and repair the damage to the Union." David Trimble, "Speech by David Trimble at the Annual General Meeting of the Ulster Unionist Council", *CAIN Project*, Mar. 23, 1996.

dirndl *n.*

from *Dirndl* "dirndl; girl": a woman's dress with a close-fitting bodice and full skirt, commonly of colorful and strikingly patterned material, fashioned after Tyrolean or Alpine peasant wear; a full, gathered skirt attached to a waistband or hip yoke; any skirt with gathers at the waistband. [German short for *Dirndlkleid* "traditional woman's dress" < Bavarian and Austrian German dialect *Dirndl* "girl", diminutive of *Dirne* "girl" < Middle High German *dierne* < Old High German *diorna, thiorna* + *Kleid* "dress".] See further example under <u>yodel</u>.

Genuine modern Austrian dirndls ...

- "It is a handsome thoroughfare and well worth an amble, so long as you don't let your gaze pause for one second on any of the scores of shop windows displaying dirndls and <u>lederhosen</u>, beer mugs with pewter lids, peaked caps with a feather in the brim, long-stemmed pipes and hand-carved religious curios." Bill Bryson, *Neither Here Nor There: Travels in Europe*, 1991, p. 250.

... and Sandra Bullock wearing an intentionally <u>kitschy</u> one in *Miss Congeniality.*

- "Elvira Wallner, daughter of the pastry chef in St. Wolfgang, wears a dirndl dress and carries an heirloom handbag." George W. Long, "Occupied Austria, Outpost of Democracy", *National Geographic*, Jun. 1951, p. 777.
- "On Thursday nights in north Scottsdale, the hills are alive with the sound of music—not Julie-Andrews-twirling-around-in-a-dirndl music, but the kind of music that makes your feet want to get up and dance." Kurt Repanshek, "A

new generation in Yellowstone, western history gets a new home, revisiting Mount St. Helens", *Sunset,* Jun. 1995.

- "After all, I'd tried on one of those Laura Ashley dresses, the ones with puffy short sleeves and wide dirndl skirts in tiny floral prints." Gina Barreca, "The Power of an 18-year-old with Hungry Red Lips", *The Hartford Courant,* Jan. 29, 2001.

Doberman pinscher, Doberman, pinscher *n.*

from *Dobermannpinscher* "Dobermann's terrier": a breed of dog first bred by Ludwig Dobermann, 19th century German dog breeder. See also pinscher.

- "No one sat at the bar except a Doberman on the end stool." Barbara Holland, *Bingo Night at the Fire Hall: The Case for Cows, Orchards, Bake Sales and Fairs,* 1997.

dollar *n.*

See taler.

doppelganger, doppelgänger, *Doppelgänger*, doubleganger, double-ganger *n.*

from *Doppelgänger* "double goer": the ghost or wraith of a living person; a double; alter ego; a person who has the same name as another. See further example under eigen-.

- "Mullin discussed several aspects of individual stories in *Strange Meeting*: the title story, in which a mysterious doppelgänger abducts a scholar obsessed with Dante's *Inferno*, 'The Lord of Close Vicinity,' a meditation on the return of Columbus to the Old World, 'The History of London,' in which someone tries to records everything that happened in a single day in that city." David Czuchlewski, *The Muse Asylum*, 2001, p. 13.
- "The two women are either related – twins, even – or they're lookalikes. Well, that's obvious, Doppelgangers." Martha Grimes, *The Stargazey: A Richard Jury Mystery*, 1998, p. 147. This quote suggested by Volker Knopp.
- "Ghostly horror by Stephen King's doppelganger." from a review by the *San Francisco Chronicle* in Stephen King writing as Richard Bachman, *Desperation*, 1996, p. 548.
- "The spells resorted to get rid of his supposed delusions are alternative that of turning the cloak – (recommended in visions of the second-sight or similar illusions as a means of obtaining a certainty concerning the being which is before imperfectly seen*) –- and that of exorcising the spirit with a cudgel which last, Corbett prudently thinks, ought not to be resorted to unless under an absolute conviction that the exorcist is the stronger party.
  * double-ganger. [footnote]" Sir Walter Scott, *Letters on Demonology and Witchcraft*, 1884, p. 148.
- "A species of apparition, similar to what the Germans call a Double-Ganger, was believed in by the Celtic tribes, and is still considered as an emblem of misfortune or death." Walter Scott, *A Legend of Montrose.*
- "I could scarcely believe that it was I,--that figure whom they called a Consul,--but a sort of Double Ganger, who had been permitted to assume my aspect, under which he went through his shadowy duties with a tolerable show of efficiency, while my real self had lain, as regarded my proper mode of being and acting, in a state of suspended animation." Nathaniel Hawthorne, *Our Old Home: A Series of English Sketches*, 1883.

- "And she will *never* allow Slitscan to run that footage of your doppelgänger." William Gibson, *Idoru*, 1997, p. 363.

Doppler *adj.*

referring to the <u>Doppler effect</u> or <u>Doppler radar</u>, e.g. *Doppler shift* or *Doppler ultrasound.*

- "An associate of Sarno's listened to her symptoms and asked her what no other medical doctor had thought to ask: 'Have you had a Doppler flow test?'" Fran Drescher, *Cancer Schmancer*, 2002, p. 58.

to doppler *v.i.*

to display the <u>Doppler effect</u>.

- "Zona, the only one telepresent who'd ever seen anything like a real jungle, had done the audio, providing birdcalls, invisible but realistically dopplering bugs, and the odd vegetational rustle, artfully suggesting not snakes but some shy furry thing, soft-pawed and curious." William Gibson, *Idoru*, 1997, p. 13.
- "His words were lost in the scream of a ship, dopplering in at the spaceport behind him." Robert A. Heinlein, *Citizen of the Galaxy*, 1982, p. 6.

Doppler effect, Doppler *n.*

from *Doppler-Effekt*: the effect named for Austrian physicist Christian Johann Doppler (1803-1853), which explains why things sound higher pitched when moving toward the observer than when moving away, and also why stars with different relative speeds to the earth apparently show different colors [< Middle High German *topeler* "dice player, dice maker" < *topelstein* "a die, *pl.* dice"].

- "Smythe unveiled the next lot, a stereographic sensor array that purported to be able to detect even cloaked vessels by the Doppler effect they produced in the subspace continuum." Dafydd ab Hugh, *Balance of Power (Star Trek: The Next Generation)*, 1995, p. 208.
- "'There was a Doppler effect to his scream as he flew over us,' a witness reported, 'followed by a loud thud.'" Wendy Northcutt, *The Darwin Awards*, 2000, p. 124.

Doppler radar, Doppler *n.*

a radar system that uses the Doppler effect for measuring velocity. This is the radar police use to measure the speed of cars.

- "NAW. MY MOM'S PARTY DOPPLER PICKED IT UP IMMEDIATELY." Jerry Scott & Jim Borgman, *Zits* comic strip, Sep. 5, 2004.
- "They didn't have satellite trucks or Doppler radar, or anything flashy for that matter." David Haynes, *Live at Five*, 1996.

doubleganger, double-ganger *n.*

See <u>doppelganger</u>.

drang *n.*

See <u>sturm and drang</u>.

dreck, drek *n.*

related to *Dreck* "dirt, filth, mud", also fig.: to quote Steve Hawley: "Detritus. Useless garbage." [Yiddish *drek*; German *Dreck* < Middle High German *drec*; related to Old English *threax* "rubbish"].

- "... and suddenly I was in a gloopy passage about public radio as a telephone in a dark forest whereby the brave exchange their messages (*Where did this dreck come from?* I thought), and I felt thoroughly ashamed to be giving a speech this dumb and wasting everyone's time, I felt bitter shame rise in my throat, I was choking on it." Garrison Keillor, *Wobegon Boy*, 1997, p. 121.

- "Damn women writers write about drivel and dreck and people fawn over them." Garrison Keillor, "Address to the National Federation of Associations Convention, Minneapolis, June 12, 1993", *The Book of Guys*, 1993, p. 4.

dummkopf *n.*

from *Dummkopf* "dumb-head": stupid person, dumbbell, blockhead, fool, oaf, dolt [< German *dumm* "stupid, dumb" + *Kopf* "head"]. This entry suggested by Wilton Woods.

- "Who ever doubted it but a *Dummkopf*?" George Gissing, *The Emancipated*.

Durmstrang *n.*

See *Sturm und Drang*.

E

echt *adj.*, **echt-** *prefix*

from *echt* "real, true, pure, genuine, authentic, natural": authentic, genuine, real, typical, the opposite of <u>ersatz</u> [High German *echt* < (Middle) Low German *echt* "genuine, legal" < Middle Low German *chacht, chaft* "legal" < Middle High German *e* < Old High German *ewa* "law, marriage (contract)"]. This entry suggested by Christiane Leißner. See further example under <u>Gasthaus</u>.

- "Stylish she likes they should be, and echt Amerikanisch." Edna Ferber, *Dawn O'Hara, the Girl who Laughed*, p. 134. *Amerikanisch* means "American".
- "Take your pencil and begin marking individual lines or passages which strike you as echt-Shakespearean." George Steiner, "Seen the new Shakespeare yet?" review of *King Edward III* by William Shakespeare, *The Observer*, May 10, 1998.
- "In recipes that emphasize the realizable over the echt, she combines components of popular cuisines of the past decade (Thai green curry paste, Mexican ancho chile essence) and fashionable cooking techniques, and gives them her own innovative twist (slow roasting duck for five hours, tenderizing lamb roast with a paste of crushed olives, garlic, lemon peel and herbs)." Corby Kummer, "Cooking", review of *A New Way to Cook* by Sally Schneider, *The New York Times*, Dec. 2, 2001.
- "For the gourmet alone, there is tiramisu at the Burger King in Kyoto, echt angel-hair pasta in Saigon and enchiladas on every menu in Nepal." Pico Iyer, "The Global Village Finally Arrives", *Time*, Dec. 2, 1993, p. 86.
- "The final evening's final act echt-L.A. band the Red Hot Chili Peppers, may have fanned the flames or perhaps just got stuck with the check Durst left, but it was while they played that the fires started, trucks toppled and bones broke." Rj Smith, "Days of Rage", *Los Angeles*, Oct. 1999.

- "In London, a city whose theater is not overly versed in such things, the echt-Jewishness of the text – with its references to Kaddish and the mitzvah -- may set 'Howard Katz' apart." Matt Wolf, "Howard Katz", *Variety*, Jun. 25, 2001.

edelweiss *n.*

from *Edelweiß* "edelweiss": *Leontopodium alpinum*, alpine European plant with white woolly leaves and flowers [German *edel* "noble" + *weiß* "white"].

- "Made into a wreath and worn, edelweiss confers invisibility." Scott Cunningham, *Cunningham's Encyclopedia of Magical Herbs*, 1985, p. 107.

- "Charge a dozen linen handkerchiefs embroidered with edelweiss to her father's account." Susanna Moore, *In the Cut*, 1999, p. 123.

- "The women were freckled, hatted with alpines, in which edelweiss – artificial, I think -- flowered in abundance; they sported severely plain flannel shirts, bloomers of an aggressive and unnecessary cut, and enormous square boots weighing pounds." Stewart Edward White, *The Mountains*, 1904, p. 200.

- "Wandering about gathering edelweiss, while he is alone and wretched!" Rebecca Harding Davis, *Frances Waldeaux*, 1897, p. 94.

- "Edelweiss, Edelweiss, every morning you greet me, small and white, clean and bright, you look happy to meet me.", Richard Rogers & Oscar Hammerstein, Jr., "Edelweiss", film music, *The Sound of Music*, starring Julie Andrews, 1965.

Ehrenbreitstein *n.*

from *Ehrenbreitstein* "Ehrenbert's or Ehrenbrecht's rock or mountain": a fortress above the Rhine River in Koblenz, Germany; figuratively something imposing or impenetrable, like the Rock of Gibraltar [German *Ehrenbert, Ehrenbrecht* "honor" + "bright" + *Stein* "stone, rock"]. See also <u>Frankenstein</u>, <u>stein</u>, <u>steinbock</u>.

- "Figure 32. is a rude sketch of the arrangement of the whole subject; the old bridge over the Moselle at Coblentz, the town of Coblentz on the right, Ehrenbreitstein on the left." John Ruskin, *The Elements of Drawing*, 1876, p. 172.

- "Yes, for replenished with the meat and wine of the word, to the faithful man of God, this pulpit, I see, is a self-containing stronghold—a lofty Ehrenbreitstein, with a perennial well of water within the walls." Herman Melville, *Moby Dick*, 1851, p. 55.

- "They need not be as ceremonious with strangers as the Dutchmen are at Ehrenbreitstein and Verona." Theodore Winthrop, *John Brent*, 1864, p. 82.

- "On some great point where Honor takes her stand,—/The Ehrenbreitstein of our native land,—/See, in the front, to strike for Freedom's cause,/The mailed Defender of her rights and laws!" James Thomas Fields, *Poems*, 1849, p. 20.

- "The post-chaise was now at the door, and Flemming was soon on the road to Coblentz, a city which stands upon the Rhine, at the mouth of the Mosel, opposite Ehrenbreitstein." Henry Wadsworth Longfellow, *Hyperion*.

eigen- *prefix*

from *eigen, eigen-* "own": proper, characteristic; used in technical terms in physics and mathematics, for example in *eigenfrequency, eigenvector, eigenvalue, eigenfunction, eigenspace, eigenstate.* See further example under <u>ansatz</u>.

- "Then the system uses the database to create 73 ghostly, digital <u>doppelgängers</u> called eigenfaces, like the one above." David Shenk, "Watching You: The World of High-tech Surveillance", *National Geographic*, Nov. 2003, p. 18.
- "Built-in spectral-analysis procedures include FFT, autoregressive, moving average, ARMA, complex exponential modeling, minimum variance methods, eigen analysis, frequency estimation, and wavelets." Joseph Desposito, "New Software Automates Signal Analysis Completely", *Electronic Design*, Aug. 9, 1999.
- "That was usually the way in Hollywood, and the formula tended to be even more rigid, in the case of software agents—*eigenheads*, their features algorithmically derived from some human mean of proven popularity." William Gibson, *Idoru*, 1997, p. 229.
- "Energy eigenvalues of the Hamiltonian and the partition function", Minoru Takahashi, *Thermodynamics of One-Dimensional Solvable Models.*

Entenmann's, Entenmann *adj.*

from *Entenmann* "duck man": a brand of bakery products, named for William Entenmann, who immigrated from Germany to the U.S. in 1898 [< German *Ente* "duck" + *Mann* "man"].

- "For example, when Dr. Ira urges Ms. Lavin's despondent Marjorie Taub, 'You need food, real food .... I'm cutting you off a square of this Entenmann's,' the piece of cake that Mr. Roberts offers is, at present, a slice of store-purchased Entenmann's All-Butter Loaf." Amy Berkowitz, "Tale of Allergist's Entenmann's: Lavin Flips for All-Butter Loaf", *The New York Observer*, Feb. 19, 2001.
- "Weakness: Entenmann's chocolate doughnuts", Brad Goldfarb, "Tim Byres", *Interview*, Mar. 2001.
- "6 1-inch-thick slices fat-free chocolate pound cake (like Entenmann's)", Victoria Abbott Riccardi, "Light desserts: These recipes are the perfect finish to a holiday meal", *Shape*, Dec. 2001.
- "This one guy loves Entenmann's doughnuts, so we'd leave a box of them on his desk." Melina Gerosa, "Diet like a man", *Ladies' Home Journal*, Oct. 1998.
- "AND TO THE RIGHT ARE OUR POPULAR NEW THEME HOUSES—SEGA, ENTENMANN AND EROS!", Garry Trudeau, *Doonesbury*, Mar. 1, 2002.

Entwicklungsroman *n.*

"development novel": a <u>Bildungsroman</u>, class of novel in German literature that deals with the formative years of an individual.

- "Verteidigung der Kindheit offered a fascinating Entwicklungsroman reminiscent of the Parsifal theme; now instead we discover a medium-high-level state-government official from Wiesbaden (Hessen's capital) named Stefan Fink, a man in his late fifties at the novel's outset whose six-year legal battle against his own bosses in order to clear his name and find due justice is recounted in gruesome detail." Erich Wolfgang Skwara, "World Literature in Review: German", *World Literature Today*, Jan. 1, 1997.

Erkling *n.*

See *Erl King*.

erlking, Erlking, Erl King, Erl König, Erl-König *n.*

from *Erlkönig, Erlenkönig* "alder king": an evil spirit in Germanic folklore, which is malicious especially toward children [German *Erle* "alder (tree)" + *König* "king", Herder's mistranslation of Danish *ellerkonge, elverkonge* "king of the elves"].

- "Erkling: [Joanne K.] Rowling has transposed a few letters in the name of the Erl King or Erl König ('elf king') of German legend. Otherwise her description holds true. It is an evil creature in the Black Forest of Germany that tries to snatch children." David Colbert, *The Magical Worlds of Harry Potter: A Treasury of Myths, Legends and Fascinating Facts*, 2001, p. 40.

- "Opposite my writing-table hangs a quaint German picture, illustrating Goethe's ballad of the Erlking, in which the whole wild pathos of the story is compressed into one supreme moment; we see the fearful, half-gliding rush of the Erlking, his long, spectral arms outstretched to grasp the child, the frantic gallop of the horse, the alarmed father clasping his darling to his bosom in convulsive embrace, the siren-like elves hovering overhead, to lure the little soul with their weird harps." John Fiske, *Myths and Myth-Makers: Old Tales and Superstitions Interpreted by Comparative Mythology*, 1872, p. 31.

- "I might indeed say the Phuca is a Celtic superstition, from which the word Pook or Puckle was doubtless derived; and I might conjecture that the man-in-the-oak was the same with the Erl-König of the Germans; and that the hellwain were a kind of wandering spirits, the descendants of a champion named Hellequin, who are introduced into the romance of Richard sans Peur." Sir Walter Scott, *Letters on Demonology and Witchcraft*, 1885, p. 150.

ersatz *n., adj.*

from *Ersatz, Ersatz-* "substitute": imitation or substitute, usually inferior; artificial; opposite of <u>echt</u>. In English *ersatz* connotes "artificial, inferior or fake", which it does not in German, e.g. *Ersatzreifen* ("spare tire"), *Ersatzteile* ("spare parts").

- "One of the women duped by Matlock met the ersatz cowpoke in the little cafe in Pearl, Oklahoma, where she worked as a waitress." M. Allen Henderson, *How Con Games Work*, 1986.

- "When another of Gail's friends telephoned Professor Savant's wife to do her duty and tell the 'wronged' woman about the 'other' woman, the ersatz lover suddenly dropped all contact with the bewildered academic." George Hayduke, *Getting Even: The Complete Book of Dirty Tricks*, 1981.

- "Months after we reached our mercenary agreement—and the honeymoon check cleared—my ersatz intended and I actually started hanging out." Jerry Stahl, *Permanent Midnight: A Memoir*, 1998.

- "The ersatz they served in Berlin/Made a once-buxom lady so thin/That when she essayed/To drink lemonade/She slipped through the straw and fell in." Bennet Cerf, Ed., *Laughing Stock*, 1945, p. 195.

- "As in any real launch, this ersatz one was being monitored at both the Cape and at the Manned Spacecraft Center in Houston." Jim Lovell & Jeffrey Kluger, *Apollo 13*, 1995, p. 15.
- "If some undiscerning tourists are fooled, taking snapshots (for a price) of warbonnet chiefs beside ersatz tepees, the Cherokee are not." Geoffrey Norman, "Two Nations, One People: The Cherokee", *National Geographic*, May 1995, p. 82.
- "I don't want any ersatz soldiers, dragging their tails and ducking out when the party gets rough." Robert A. Heinlein, *Starship Troopers*, 1959, p. 109.
- "'All right,' he agreed, flashing an ersatz smile." Dafydd ab Hugh, *Balance of Power (Star Trek: The Next Generation)*, 1995, p. 100.
- "So was the small chemical unit that blew scented ersatz air-freshener into the room, giving it a phony pinewoods odor." Michael Crichton writing as Jeffery Hudson, *A Case of Need*, 1968, p. 66.

F

Fahrenheit, F., Fah., Fahr. *n.*

a scale of temperature, named for Gabriel Daniel Fahrenheit (1686-1736), the German physicist who devised it (in German-speaking countries Celsius is now used exclusively).

- "Engine parts operated at a temperature of 2500 degrees Fahrenheit, well above the melt temperature of most alloys, which turned to soup at 2200 degrees." Michael Crichton, *Airframe*, 1996, p. 127.
- "A Fahrenheit's thermometer, in a mahogany case, and with a barometer annexed, was hung against the wall, at some little distance from the stove, which Benjamin consulted, every half-hour, with prodigious veneration." James Fenimore Cooper, *The Pioneers*, p. 66.
- "This man bathed for the space of five minutes, and without any injury to his sensibility or the surface of the skin, his legs in oil, heated at 97° of Réaumur (250 degrees of Fahrenheit) and with the same oil, at the same degree of heat, he washed his face and superior extremities." Harry Houdini, *Miracle Mongers and Their Methods: A Complete Expose*, 1920, p. 39.
- "On this very 2nd of October he had dismissed James Forster, because that luckless youth had brought him shaving-water at eighty-four degrees Fahrenheit instead of eighty-six; and he was awaiting his successor, who was due at the house between eleven and half-past." Jules Verne, *Around the World in Eighty Days*, 1873, p. 5.

- "I'm burning through the sky, 200 degrees, that's why they call me Mr. Fahrenheit." Queen, "Don't Stop Me Now", *Jazz*, audio CD.
- "He recently lost fifty-two pounds by refusing to eat anything that says 'nonfat' on it, and is working on his next film, titled *Fahrenheit 9/11*." Michael Moore, *Dude, Where's My Country?*, 2003, p. 251.
- *Fahrenheit 451*, by Ray Bradbury.

Fahrvergnügen, Fahrvergnugen *n.*

from *Fahrvergnügen* "driving pleasure": used by Volkswagen in an advertising campaign in the U.S., no doubt in order to emphasize European quality [< German *fahren* "to drive" + *Vergnügen* "pleasure"]. This entry suggested by Bernhard Heger. See also Vorsprung durch Technik.

- "THE OTHER DAY, I LEARNED that Fahrvergnügen—the clever-sounding German slogan that Volkswagen has been using for years—is a real word, not just a creation of the folks who brought us the New Beetle." Andrew Gore, "Experience iBookgruven" *Macworld*, Jul. 2001.
- "The majority were attracted by a difficult-to-define driveability—perhaps the quality that, back in the dark days, VW sold as 'Fahrvergnugen.'", "Volkswagen Jetta: Close to groovin'" *AutoWeek*, Jun. 28, 1999.
- "Already television viewers in the U.S. have seen signs of a heightened linguistic confidence on the part of the Germans. One example: a Volkswagen ad campaign that centers on the word Fahrvergnugen, or joy in driving--however mispronounced it may be in the commercials. Only a few years ago, the use of a German word in an advertisement in English would have been avoided, if only because the sound of German was associated with the bad guys in World War II movies. Today Fahr--and other Vergnugen--may be here to stay." Daniel Benjamin, "And Now for Sprachvergnugen" *Time*, Jan. 9, 1990, p. 79.

faltboat *n.*

from *Faltboot* "folding boat": a light, collapsible boat made like a kayak, foldboat.

feldspar, felspar *n.* **feldspathic, feldspathose, felspathic** *adj.*

from *Feldspath, Feldspat* "field spar": any of several crystalline minerals made up mainly of aluminum silicates, usually glassy and moderately hard, found in igneous rocks.

- "Its minerological constitution is not simple; in some parts the rock is of a cherty, in others of a felspathic nature, including thin veins of serpentine." Charles Darwin, *The Voyage of the Beagle*, 1836.

Felsenmeer *n.*

"sea of rocks": chaotic, block-like assemblage of fractured rocks or rock surfaces.

- "The result is mile upon mile of jagged, oddly angled slabs of stone strewn about in wobbly piles known to science as *Felsenmeer* (literally, 'sea of rocks')." Bill Bryson, *A Walk in the Woods*, 1997.

felspar *n.*

See *feldspar*.

-fest, fest *n.*

from *Fest* "festival celebration": festive occasion, as in *songfest*, (slang) bout, session as in *gabfest*; (slang) an occasion with much, as in *slugfest* [< Middle High German *fest, vest* < Latin *festum*

"festival", related to English *feast* and French *fête*]. This entry suggested by Alexandra Schepelmann. See also <u>festschrift</u>.

- Annual Autofest at Spindles Auto Club, <u>spindlescarclub.tripod.com</u>.
- "The menopause one [documentary] was a lulu, a marathon gripefest, an orgy of self-pity, women moaning and grousing about their sad lives and the uncomprehending world around them, and then some of those women showed up on the mercury-poisoning one too—the symptoms of *that* (forgetfulness, fatigue, depression, achiness) being symptoms of menopause as well." p. 14, "They talked about what a shoozefest the conference was, compared to other years, and my face burned." p. 122, "WSJO was in the midst of a major screamfest, Wagner or the Berlioz Requiem or something, Amazons with their heads thrown back and their mouths open wide as grapefruit, their harpy hair stuck out, their spears in hand." p. 125, "She went every morning to her exercise group and enjoyed a long lunch and a bridge game and a gabfest with her cronies and then a nap." p. 218, Garrison Keillor, *Wobegon Boy*, 1997.
- "Far from the integrated love fest of the 1960s, the Gombe chimpanzees were now more like the Carrington family of television's *Dynasty*." Jonathan Marks, *What It Means to Be 98% Chimpanzee*, 2003, p. 164.
- "One of the livest banquets that has recently been pulled off occurred last night in the annual Get-Together Fest of the Zenith Real Estate Board, held in the Venetian Ball Room of the O'Hearn House." Sinclair Lewis, *Babbitt*, 1922.
- "Time for some serious flamefesting!", "eoff (end of flame fest :-)" Chris DiBona et al., *Open Sources: Voices from the Open Source Revolution*, 1999.
- "They even allowed BATF spokesperson David Troy get in on the slugfest; Troy declared that Koresh was just a 'cheap thug who interprets the Bible through the barrel of a gun.'" Carol Moore, *Davidian Massacre: Disturbing Questions About Waco Which Must Be Answered*, 1996.
- "All's quiet along the Potomac. Those Beecher natives are having some sort of a songfest, though." Victor Appleton, *Tom Swift in the Land of Wonders*, 1917.

festschrift, Festschrift *n.* [*pl.* **Festschriften, festschrifts**]
from *Festschrift* "celebration writing": commemorative volume, collection of writings usually by different authors especially in honor of a scholar. See also <u>fest</u>.

- "In a multiauthor book, such as a festschrift or the proceedings of a symposium, it is often desirable to list the contributors separately, with only the editor or editors appearing on the title page (see 1.7)." *The Chicago Manual of Style*, 1993, p. 27.
- "This was a few days earlier, when I received a Festschrift, a publication in which grateful pupils had commemorated the jubilee of their teacher and laboratory director." Sigmund Freud, *The Interpretation of Dreams*, 1911.
- "This book is presented as a sort of *Festschrift* - a tribute to Cornell University as it enters the second quarter-century of its existence, and probably my last tribute." Andrew D. White, *A History of the Warfare of Science With Theology in Christendom*, 1896.

flak, flack *n.*

from *Flak* "antiaircraft gun": antiaircraft guns; the bursting shells fired from flak; criticism, opposition [German *Fliegerabwehrkanonen* < *Flieger*, "flyer, airplane" + *Abwehr*, "defense" + *Kanonen*, "canons, guns"]. This entry suggested by M. Larson.

- "'I hope you don't get too much flak when you change the format,' I said. 'These classical music fans get pretty sour when you take away their station.'" Garrison Keillor, *Wobegon Boy*, 1997, p. 278.
- "Many years ago, Police Explorers were shown a training video called *Flack Vest Testing by a Fool.*" Wendy Northcutt, *The Darwin Awards*, 2000, p. 180.
- "Real IRA threat forces RUC into flak jackets", Henry McDonald, *Observer*, Oct. 22, 2000.

flehmen, flehming *n.*, **to flehm, to flehmen** *v.i., v.t.*

from *flehmen* "to flehm": a behavioral response of many male mammals, for example deer, antelope and cats, consisting of lip curling and head raising after sniffing a female's urine, also called lip curl. This word is often capitalized, perhaps due to a mistaken notion that it is named for someone [German *flehmen* "to twist one's mouth"]. This entry suggested by Ekkehard Dengler.

- "The flehmen response and liquid-borne compounds (non-volatile to low volatility) are generally assumed to be involved in vomeronasal sensory perception (e.g., see Wysocki et al. 1980)." George Waring, *Horse Behavior*, 2002, p. 29.
- "Males that flehmen or flehm have a Jacobson's organ." Raymond J. Corsini, *The Dictionary of Psychology*, 2002, p. 381.
- "The male smells and licks the female's vulva; then he holds his head out and curls his lip up, in a behavior known as a Flehmen response." Carol Ekarius, *Small-Scale Livestock Farming: A Grass-Based Approach for Health, Sustainability, and Profit*, 1999, p. 52.
- "The smell they [the cats] tasted, flehming and growling, was the stink of human death." Shirley Rousseau Murphy, *Cat in the Dark: A Joe Grey Mystery*, 1999, p. 188.
- "Another characteristic expression [of the Feral Horse] is the flehmen, in which the neck is extended and the upper lip curled, exposing the teeth...." John O. Whitaker Jr., *National Audubon Society Field Guide to North American Mammals*, 1996, p. 811.
- "When the [Jacobson's] organ is in use the cat will appear to be grimacing with his mouth half open. This is called a *flehmen* reaction (a German word with no English translation)." Pam Johnson-Bennett, *Twisted Whiskers: Solving Your Cat's Behavior Problems*, 1994, p. 9.
- "R. F. Ewer once had a tame male suricate (a small burrowing animal native to Africa) who flehmed in response to sherry, but the normal context is sexual." Muriel Beadle, *The Cat: A Complete Authoritative Compendium of Information About Domestic Cats*, 1979, p. 60.

flugelhorn, *Flügelhorn,* **fluglephone** *n.*

from *Flügelhorn* "wing horn": a brass-wind instrument like the cornet in design but with a tone like that of the French horn, sometimes considered to be a type of trumpet.

- "CHUCK MANGIONE: Flugelhorn, Electric Piano", from CD insert, *Feels So Good,* Chuck Mangione, 1977.
- "In music, you have fluglephones (like Chuck Mangione), and the normal trumpets like the ones used by Louis Armstrong, Maynard Ferguson and Herb Alpert." Brad Bilsland, *What It Means to Be in a Marching Band: A Band Geek Perspective for the Musically Challenged,* 2004, p. 12.
- "Concerto for Flugelhorn and Winds", *Night, Again,* composed by Daron Hagen, 1999.

foehn, föhn *n.*

from *Föhn:* a warm, dry wind blowing down the side of a mountain, especially in the Alps [Middle High German *phönne;* Old High German *fonno;* Late Latin *faunjo* < Latin *Favonius,* "west wind"]. In German *Föhn, Fön* also means a hot-air dryer (for hair).

- "Then why not turn your back to the Foehn and go to Lucerene or-- ?" Elizabeth Robins, *The Mills of the Gods,* 1898.
- "It seems to us that at certain times the easterly winds in Greenland show a similar character to the 'Foehn' in Switzerland; and since the second German Polar Expedition discovered very high mountain-ranges in the eastern part of this arctic continent, we do not hesitate to pronounce such winds as described hereafter to be true Foehns." United States Navy Department, *Scientific results of the U.S. Arctic expedition ...,* 1876, p. 55.
- "Ashbery has explicitly addressed closure as a site of authorial strategy in an interview when he was asked whether he ever played a joke on his readers. Ashbery replied:
  A gag that has probably gone unnoticed turns up in the last sentence of the novel I wrote with James Schuyler [A Nest of Ninnies]. Actually, it's my sentence. It reads: 'So it was that the cliff dwellers, after bidding their cousins good night, moved off towards the parking area, while the latter bent their steps toward the partially rebuilt shopping plaza in the teeth of the freshening foehn.' Foehn is a kind of warm wind that blows in Bavaria that produces a fog. I would doubt that many people know that. I liked the idea that people, if they bothered to, would have to open up the dictionary to find out what the last word in the novel meant." John Vincent, "Reports of looting and insane buggery behind altars: John Ashbery's queer politics", *Twentieth Century Literature,* Summer 1998.
- "If on a certain day you find that many people scowl at you and are unusually edgy, the phenomenon would probably be better explained in meteorological rather than in psychological terms. It is Föhnwetter, caused by the warm southern wind, föhn (a term used in German and French-speaking Switzer-

land; 'foehn' in English)." Marcel Bucher, "Headache Wind", *Swiss News*, Jan. 2, 2001.

foosball *n.*

probably from *(Tisch-) Fußball* "(table) football": a table soccer game in which the ball is moved by manipulating small figures attached to rods, also called table soccer, table football, babyfoot (the French term), and gettone. This word is often capitalized, perhaps due to a mistaken notion that it is a trademark. [German *Fußball* (transliterated *Fussball*) "football, soccer" < *Fuß* "foot" + *Ball* "ball"]. This entry suggested by Christian Heldt.

- "Sometimes Demo Karafilis took us downstairs to play Foosball, and, moving among the heating ducts, spare cots, battered luggage, we would tunnel through to the small room Old Mrs. Karafilis had decorated to resemble Asia Minor." Jeffrey Eugenides, *The Virgin Suicides*, 1994, p. 171.
- "Apart from the restaurant, which has decent food (though the pizza is a cheesy bomb), it has a bar with a pool table, darts and *foosball*." Carolina Miranda & Paige Penland, *Lonely Planet Costa Rica*, 2004, p. 365.
- "She'd use the same self-discipline she used for studying in college, marching off to the library while the rest of us procrastinated over foosball and beer." Lolly Winston, *Good Grief*, 2004, p. 150.
- "'You want to come back to the house for a game of foosball?' Foosball, for those of you who lack a basic education, is that tabletop bar game with the soccer-type men skewered on sticks." Harlan Coben, *No Second Chance*, 2004, p. 89.
- "The judge was in his customary booth near the Foosball machines." Carl Hiaasen, *Strip Tease*, 2004, p. 66.
- "Have your BOSS run tournaments out of your day room (pool, foosball, ping-pong, darts, etc)." Nate Allen & Tony Burgess, *Taking the Guidon: Exceptional Leadership at the Company Level*, 2001, p. 152.
- "On dates, I'd feigned interest in all sorts of nonsense—trout fishing, Civil War reenactments, foosball." Susan Jane Gilman, *Hypocrite in a Pouffy White Dress*, 2005, p. 239.

to fotz around *v.i.*

probably from *Fotz, Fotze* "(vulgar) vagina": to mess around, fool around, (vulgar) fart around. Due to this last meaning and the similar spelling some think *to fotz* means "to fart". [< Middle High German *vut* "vagina". (In Austria and Bavaria *Fotze, Fotzen* is dialectal slang for "mouth, face" and by extension "a slap in the face, box on the ear". *Fotzhobel* is a humorous term for "mouth organ", literally "a carpenter's plane for the mouth". In Austria *Fotze* does not have the vulgar meaning it does in Germany)]. This entry suggested by Volker Knopp.

- "I don't want to have to fotz around with all this nonsense and still not end up with real system synergy." Chip Stern, Equipment Report, *Stereophile*, Jan. 2001, p. 108.

frank *n.*

See frankfurter.

Frankenstein, Frankenstein's monster, Dr. Frankenstein, Franken- *n.*

from *Frankenstein* "stone of the Franks": pertaining to the monster in the 1818 novel *Frankenstein* by Mary Wollstonecraft Shelley or to the doctor who created it; figuratively, any horrific creation that gets out of control and becomes evil

and/or destroys its creator. Frankenstein was inspired by a dream Shelley had
while visiting the poet Lord Byron's villa in Switzerland on a dark and stormy
night where ghost stories were read [the name *Frankenstein* was apparently invented by Shelley, but has the elements of a genuine German place name < German *Franken* "the Germanic tribe of the Franks" + *Stein* "stone, mountain"]. See
also Ehrenbreitstein, stein, steinbock.

- "Then there is the Frankenstein of [trom-] bones, the double-bass bone."
  Brad Bilsland, *What It Means to Be in a Marching Band: A Band Geek Perspective for the Musically Challenged*, 2004, p. 18.
- "Apparently he was to be the recipient of one of her laboratory failures, in the
  way of Dr Frankenstein bestowing upon him a poorly functioning hand."
  Martha Grimes, *The Stargazey: A Richard Jury Mystery*, 1998, p. 75.
- "He had also a superabundance of the discordant, ear-splitting, metallic laugh
  common to his breed -- a machine-made laugh, a Frankenstein laugh, with
  the soul left out of it." Mark Twain, *Life on the Mississippi*, 1906.
- "When it was my turn to watch over Billy or to comfort him at night I would
  think – I am some Frankenstein's monster with a defective brain which sometimes wants to cast what it might love into a river like the petals of a flower:
  but since I know this, then might not this be some new growth in a not totally
  defective brain – do you hear me, Billy!" Nicholas Mosley, *Children of
  Darkness and Light*, 1997.
- "In 1998, incensed by regulatory failures that allowed mad cow disease to
  become a multibillion-dollar catastrophe, Europeans protested the 'Franken-
  foods' entering their markets." Jennifer Ackerman, "Food: How Altered?",
  National Geographic, May 2002, p.49.
- "The fish came to light this summer after several snakeheads were found in a
  Maryland pond. The so-called Frankenfish were dumped there by a local
  resident who had initially imported them to make soup." Reuters, "Snake-
  head fish found in seven U.S. states", *CNN.com*, Jul. 23, 2002.
- *Frankenstein or the Modern Prometheus*, by Mary Shelley, 1818.

frankfurter, frank, frankfurt, frankforter, frankfort *n.*
from *Frankfurter (Wurst)* "Frankfurt (sausage)": a
kind of sausage used in hotdogs, wiener. Residents
of the German city of Frankfurt call them *Wiener*,
while residents of the Austrian city of Vienna
(*Wien*) call them *Frankfurter*.

- "He had in his pocket a small loaf of bread and
  two frankfurters, and he heard the splashing
  ripple of a brook." Mary Eleanor Wilkins Freeman, *The Copy-Cat*, p. 243.
- "So he gorged himself with beer and frankfurter sausages plastered with German mustard." Frank Norris, *McTeague; A Story of San Francisco*, p. 145.

Frau, frau, Fr. *n.* [*pl.* **Frauen, Fraus**]
from *Frau* "woman, wife, Mrs.": a married (German or German-speaking)
woman, Mrs., Ms., Madam, a wife [< Middle High German *vrowe* < Old High
German *frouwa* "mistress, lady"]. See also Fräulein, hausfrau.

- "THEN--COMES IT VISITING HOUR--ENTER HIS FRAU, ANNOYA--AND--EXIT HIS HUMOR--LISTEN TO OUR HERO--" Al Scaduto, *They'll Do It Every Time* comic strip, Jun. 26, 2004.
- "There was a moment of breathless staring on the part of the respectable middle-class Frauen at the other tables.'" Edna Ferber, *Dawn O'Hara, the Girl who Laughed*, p. 129.

Fräulein, fräulein, Fraulein, fraulein, Frl. *n.* [*pl.* **Fräulein, Fräuleins**]
from *Fräulein* "young or unmarried woman, miss, Miss, waitress": an unmarried or young German (-speaking) woman, Miss, [chiefly Br.] a German governess [< German *Frau* + *-lein* diminutive form]. See also Frau. This entry suggested by Hans-Michael Stahl and Bastian Sick.

- "She is not my maid. She is Fraulein Arpent." Rebecca Harding Davis, *Frances Waldeaux*, 1897, p. 21.
- "Shortly after, with a good deal of rustling and bustling Fräulein Rottenmeier appeared, who again seemed very much put out and called to Heidi, 'What is the matter with you, Adelheid? Don't you understand what breakfast is? Come along at once!'" Johanna Spyri, *Heidi*, before 1891, p. 105.
- "Toward the end of last year, I spent a few months in Munich, Bavaria. In November I was living in Fraulein Dahlweiner's PENSION, 1a, Karlstrasse; but my working quarters were a mile from there, in the house of a widow who supported herself by taking lodgers." Mark Twain, *Life on the Mississippi*, 1870.
- "No wonder, then, that the good Frau Professorin gathered her Fraulein under her wing, and resented the attentions of such a mauvais sujet." Arthur Conan Doyle, *The Captain of the Polestar and other Tales*, 1894, p. 86.
- "Me, I could never have warred with that Fraulein who served us -- so haughty she was, nicht?" Edna Ferber, *Dawn O'Hara, the Girl who Laughed*, p. 144.
- "After having been engaged to an American actor, a Welsh socialist agitator, and a German army officer, Fraulein Furst at last placed herself and her great brewery interests into the trustworthy hands of Otto Ottenburg, who had been her suitor ever since he was a clerk, learning his business in her father's office." Willa Sibert Cather, *The Song of the Lark*, 1915, p. 144.
- "She had not believed in Him at the time, but because she was frightened after she had stuck the scissors into Fraulein she had tried the appeal as an experiment." Frances Hodgson Burnett, *T. Tembarom*, 1913, p. 274.

Frauleinwunder *n.*
from *Fräuleinwunder* "young woman wonder": a spectacular young German woman [< German *Fräulein* + *Wunder* "wonder, miracle"]. See also Fräulein, Wirtschaftswunder and wunderkind. This entry suggested by Hans-Michael Stahl.

- "The SPD and the Second 'Frauleinwunder'", Eva Kolinsky, *Political Culture in France and Germany: A Contemporary Perspective*, 1991.
- "Cold War diplomats in tracksuits - the 'Frauleinwunder' of East German sport", Gertrud Pfister, *Militarism, Sport, Europe: War Without Weapons*, 2003.

Der Freischütz, Der Freischutz *n.*
from *Der Freischütz* "The Free Shooter": a German romantic opera written by Carl Maria von Weber in 1821.

39

- "The party altogether closely resembled the devils which come on the stage in plays like Der Freischutz." Charles Darwin, *The Voyage of the Beagle*, 1836.

Freudian *adj., n.*, **Freudianism** *n.*

from *Freudsche, freudsche, Freud'sche, Freudianer* "Freudian": of or according to Freud or his theories and practice; a person who believes in Freud's theories or uses his methods in psychoanalysis; after Sigmund Freud, 1856-1939, Austrian physician and psychiatrist [< German *Freude* "joy, happiness" < Middle High German *vröude* < Old High German *frewida, frouwida*]. This entry suggested by Wilton Woods.

- "It's just a fantasy, and it fits you like a Freudian glove." Michael Crichton, *Travels*, 1988, p. 337.
- "But their work was largely forgotten when the early mutations-are-everything geneticists turned their backs on Darwin and the psychologists became so enamored of the behaviorist and Freudian extremes that they could tolerate no other way of looking at things." William H. Calvin, *The Ascent of Mind: Ice Age Climates and the Evolution of Intelligence*, 1990.
- "EXCITATION AND INHIBITION have a range of connotations, even Freudian ones, but to neurophysiologists they mean something close to addition and subtraction, or deposits and withdrawals." William H. Calvin & George A. Ojemann, *Conversations With Neil's Brain: The Neural Nature of Thought and Language*, 1994.
- "And so they wind up with separate departments of thinking, feeling, and willing (translated into Freudian terminology: ego, id, and superego)." William H. Calvin, *The Cerebral Symphony: Seashore Reflections on the Structure of Consciousness*, 1989.
- "In the language of medical psychology, to suggest to the President that the treaty was an abandonment of his professions was to touch on the raw a Freudian complex." John Maynard Keynes, *The Economic Consequences of the Peace*, 1919.
- "Such imagery is very bold – what the Freudians could make of it!" Dorothy Day, *On Pilgrimage*, 1999.
- "And we know from the Freudian teachings what suppressions in the root-instincts necessarily mean." Edward Carpenter, *Pagan and Christian Creeds: Their Origin and Meaning*, 1920, p.189.

fritz, fritz out, be on the fritz, go on the fritz *v.i.*

perhaps from *Fritz*, diminutive of *Friedrich* "Frederick": to be or become broken or inoperable

- "The captain's pocket watch was on the fritz, and John said, 'I can fix watches,' so he went to work on it." Garrison Keillor, *Wobegon Boy*, 1997, p. 96.
- "Simply put, this is the theory that sooner or later all our entertainment and communication appliances (computer, TV, radio, home stereo, VCR, telephone, answering machine, toaster, etc.) will slowly coalesce into one big digital doohickey, a stunning technological advance which will present consumers

with the unprecedented opportunity to have absolutely every gadget we own go on the fritz simultaneously." Evan Morris, *The Book Lover's Guide to the Internet*, 1998, p. 31.

Fritz *n.*

from *Fritz* "Fred", diminutive of *Friedrich* "Frederick": [Slang] a German (soldier): sometimes offensive [< German *Friedrich* "peaceful ruler" < German *Friede* "peace" < Middle High German *vride* < Old High German *fridu* + Middle High German *rich, riche* < Old High German *rihhi* "ruler"]. See also <u>Heinie</u>.

- "A French Gun Much Respected by Fritz" caption of a picture of a cannon in Edward R. Coyle, *Ambulancing on the French Front*, 1918.
- "In other places a large party would be seated on the ground-I do not say because they could not get up, though one of the Fritzes slyly insinuated something of the kind, but because they could not get a big barrel around which they were seated up with them; they therefore preferred to be near the faucet; and it made one thirsty on that warm day to see how eagerly they held the long glasses under the steady flow of the golden-colored liquid, and how, with sparkling eyes, they put it to their lips, as if Paradise lay in the bottom of the mug." W. W. Wright, *Doré. By a stroller in Europe*, 1857, p. 248.

Führer, *Führer,* Fuehrer, der Führer, führer, fuehrer *n.*

from *(der) Führer* "(the) leader, guide": (the) leader, applied to Adolf Hitler [< Middle High German *vüerer* < *vüeren* "to lead, bear" < Old High German *fuoren* "to lead"; related to Old English *faran* "to go"]. Since *der Führer* is often connected with Hitler in German too, one sometimes uses *Leiter* to mean "leader" instead. See further examples under <u>Reich</u> and <u>Schutzstaffel</u>.

- "Herr Gröpenfuhrer! Herr Gröpenfuhrer!" reporters clamoring for Arnold Schwarzenegger's attention, alluding to his alleged groping and Hitler statements, Garry Trudeau, *Doonesbury*, Oct. 22, 2003.
- "While the formal charge against Wasner was 'maliciously slandering the Führer,' the actual crime for which he faced beheading was his embarrassing explanation of Hitler." Ron Rosenbaum, "Explaining Hitler", *The New Yorker*, May 1995.
- "Indeed, the despotic Führer, who prohibited any kind of satirically disrespectful treatment of himself and his policies, would be extremely annoyed if he read the contentious comic book, *Adolf, the <u>Nazi</u> Pig*, which is currently raising laughter, eyebrows and hackles in Germany." Ursula Sautter, "Can Der Führer Be Funny?", *Time*, Aug. 17, 1998.
- "'I'm not opposed to the fact that he [John William King] killed a black guy,' says Davis Wolfgang Hawke, a college student who says his ambition is to be the first führer of the United States.", "At school he's [Davis Wolfgang Hawke] a pariah, but on the Web he's the führer reincarnate.", Matt Bai & Vern E. Smith, "Evil to the End", *Newsweek*, Mar. 8, 1999.

G

ganzfeld *n.*

from *Ganzfeld* "whole field": a type of experiment used in researching psychic experiences [< German *ganz* "complete, whole, perfect" < Middle High German *ganz* < Old High German *ganz* + *Feld* "field" < Middle High German *veld* < Old High German *feld*].

- "I am, in fact, the subject of a ganzfeld experiment. *Ganzfeld*, German for 'whole field,' refers to the boundless void in which I seem to be afloat." Kenneth Miller, "Phychics: Science or Séance?" *Life*, June 1998.

Gasthaus, gasthaus *n.* [*pl.* **Gasthäuser**]

from *Gasthaus* "guest house": a small inn or hotel in German-speaking countries [< German *Gast* "guest" + *Haus* "house"]. See also <u>Bauhaus</u>, <u>Gasthof</u> and <u>hausfrau</u>. This entry suggested by Christiane Leißner.

- "For me there will always be one gasthaus in Niessen: the Niessener Hof." John Wray, *The Right Hand of Sleep*, 2001.
- "They went into the little Gasthaus and got some black bread and sausage and some milk." Francis Hodgson Burnett, *The Lost Prince*, 1941, p. 245.
- "There were fences to cling to, and leading from the railway station to the Gasthaus a little path of cinders had been strewn for the benefit of the wedding guests. The Gasthaus was very festive." Katherine Mansfield, *In a German Pension*.
- "Three taverns, bearing the sign of 'The Pig and Whistle,' indicated the recent English, a cabaret to the Universal Republic, with a red flag, the French, and the Gasthaus zum Rheinplatz, the Teutonic contributions to the strength of our nation." Frederick Law Olmsted, *The Cotton Kingdom: A Traveller's Observations on Cotton and Slavery in the American Slave States: Based upon Three Former Volumes of Journeys and Investigations*, 1861, p. 295. The name of the inn, *Gasthaus zum Rheinplatz*, means "Inn on Rhine Square".
- "Every night, in the course of his rambles, his highness the Sultan (indeed, his port is sublime, as, for the matter of that, are all the wines in his cellar) sets down with an iron pen, and in the neatest handwriting in the world, the events and observations of the day; with the same iron pen he illuminates the leaf of his journal by the most faithful and delightful sketches of the scenery which he has witnessed in the course of the four-and-twenty hours; and if he has dined at an inn or restaurant, gasthaus, posada, albergo, or what not, invariably inserts into his log-book the bill of fare." William Makepeace Thackeray, *Early and Late Papers Hitherto Uncollected*, 1867, p. 1.
- "An example of this kind occurs near the Bernina Gasthaus, about two hours from Pontresina." John Tyndall, *Hours of exercise in the Alps*, 1871, p. 226.
- "Not far from there is a GASTHAUS whose stucco and half-timber construction would look <u>echt</u> in Innsbruck." John Skow, "World Without Walls", *Time*, Aug. 13, 1990, p. 70.

Gasthof, gasthof *n.* [*pl.* **Gasthöfe, gasthofs**]

from *Gasthof* "guest court": a hotel in German-speaking countries, usually larger than a <u>Gasthaus</u> [< German *Gast* "guest" + *Hof* "court, yard, courtyard"]. This entry suggested by Christiane Leißner.

- "Should I walk back to the village, go to the Gasthof, write a letter craving permission to call on my cousins, and wait there till an answer came?" Elizabeth von Arnim, *Elizabeth and Her German Garden.*

gedanken experiment *n.*

from *Gedankenexperiment* "thought experiment": in physics, an experiment which is only described but not made in reality as it is not possible or was not possible as someone thought of it for the first time. This entry and definition suggested by Hilmar R. Tuneke.

- *Gedanken Fictions: Stories on Themes in Science, Technology, and Society,* Thomas A. Easton, 2000.

Geiger counter *n.*

from *Geigerzähler* "Geiger counter": an instrument for detecting and counting particles ionized by radiation that pass through it, named for Johannes Wilhelm (Hans) Geiger, 1882-1945, German physicist [German *Geiger* < Middle High German *gîger* "violinist" < *gîge* "violin"]. This entry suggested by Wilton Woods.

- "A rad-lab technician came in and checked for leakage from the plutonium with a Geiger counter." Michael Crichton, *Terminal Man*, 1988, p. 80.
- "An important difference between chemical toxins and radionuclides is that radioactive contamination is readily detected by relatively inexpensive Geiger counters, while the TCDD isomer of dioxin, like many other toxic compounds, can only be determined by use of a gas chromatograph coupled to a mass spectrometer; the cost of the latter instruments are in the range of $100,000 to $500,000." John W. Birks & Sherry L. Stephens, "Possible Toxic Environments Following a Nuclear War", *The Medical Implications of Nuclear War*, 1986.

Geiger tube *n.*

a tube filled with gas that is ionized by passing charged particles, producing within the tube an electric charge indicative of a particular particle, named for Johannes Wilhelm (Hans) Geiger, 1882-1945, German physicist.

Geltung *n.*

from *Geltung* "validity, recognition": personal standing, recognition, acceptance, esteem, influence [< German *gelten* "to have value, be worth, be valid, hold good" < Middle High German *gelten* < Old High German *geltan*, related to German *Geld* "money" + *-ung* "-ing"].

- *Showing Off: The Geltung Hypothesis*, by Philip L. Wagner, 1995.

gemeinschaft, Gemeinschaft, *Gemeinschaft* *n.*

from *Gemeinschaft* "community, communion, partnership, association, intercourse, fellowship": a social relationship characterized by strong reciprocal bonds of sentiment and kinship within a common tradition, a community or society characterized by this relationship, a fellowship [< German *gemein* "(in) common, general" < Middle High German *gemein, gemeine* < Old High German *gimeini* + *-schaft* "-ship" < Middle High German *-schaft* < Old High German *-scaf*. See also <u>gesellschaft</u>. This entry suggested by Richard W. Hartzell.

- "Their [the communitarian Progressives'] theories echoed distinctions articulated by contemporaneous social theorists from Europe—Sir Henry Maine's status versus contract, Ferdinand Tönnies's Gemeinschaft versus Gesellschaft, Emile Durkheim's mechanical versus organic solidarity, and Georg Simmel's comparison of town and metropolis, all expounded between 1860 and 1902." Robert D. Putnam, *Bowling Alone: The Collapse and Revival of American Community*, 2001, p. 380.

- "In his seminal study in social anthropology *Community and Society (Gemeinschaft and Gesellschaft)*, the nineteenth-century sociologist Ferdinand Toennies concluded that the requisites of traditional blood and clan communities tended inevitably to yield to the requisites of voluntary and contractual societies in an evolution that pointed only forward...." Benjamin Barber, *Jihad vs. McWorld: How Globalism and Tribalism Are Reshaping the World*, 1996, p. 161.

- "I see the willingness to believe in an epidemic as resulting in part from a *Gemeinschaft-Gesellschaft* fallacy that demonizes industrial or post-industrial society and romanticizes the supportive nature of communities in prior eras." Peter D. Kramer, *Against Depression*, 2005, p. 313.

- "Perhaps it is our guilt that has directed our attention to these areas of crass 'pseudo-*gemeinschaft*,' for there is hardly a performance, in whatever area of life, which does not rely on the personal touch to exaggerate the uniqueness of the transactions between performer and audience." Erving Goffman, *The Presentation of Self in Everyday Life*, 1959, p. 50.

- "All EU member states strive toward achieving a European *Gemeinschaft* without anticipating a particular political framework such as a federation, confederation or European commonwealth." David Huang, translated by Wang Hsiao-Wen, "EU-style integration offers hope", *Taipei Times*, Jun. 9, 2004, p. 8.

- "The network phenomenon offers proof that the earlier antinomies posited by modern sociology—*Gemeinschaft* vs. *Gesellschaft*, traditionalism vs. modernity, informal vs. formal—do not hold." Roger Waldinger, *How the Other Half Works: Immigration and the Social Organization of Labor*, 2003, p. 90.

gemütlich, gemuetlich, gemutlich *adj.*

from *gemütlich* "cozy, comfortable, easy-going, good-natured": congenial, agreeable [German *gemütlich* < Late Middle High German *gemüetlich* "concerning the disposition, pleasant, agreeable" < Middle High German *gemüete* "disposition, nature, feelings, mood" and separately < Old High German *gimuati* "of the same nature, pleasant, agreeable"]. This entry suggested by Christiane Leißner.

- "Everybody is at least plump in this comfortable, *gemutlich* town, where everybody placidly locks his shop or office and goes home at noon to dine heavily on soup and meat and vegetables and pudding, washed down by the inevitable beer and followed by forty winks on the dining room sofa with the German *Zeitung* spread comfortably over the head as protection against the flies." Edna Ferber, *Dawn O'Hara, The Girl Who Laughed*, p. 89. *Zeitung* means "newspaper".

- "This get-together after Midnight Mass in the Christmas Room, which is filled with that indescribable 'Christmas smell'--compounded of wax candles,

'Lebkuchen' and balsam fir--has such a very special quality that even the word 'gemutlich' becomes inadequate." Maria Augusta Trapp, *Around the Year with the Trapp Family.*

- "I reviewed Gatti's first Mahler Symphony recording, the Fifth in glowing terms (July/Aug 1998) and am also delighted with this lovely, gemutlich Fourth." Gerald S. Fox, "Mahler: Symphony 4; 4 Early Songs", *American Record Guide*, Mar. 2000.
- "With its open core and rotunda, it is like a fetching little gemutlich miniature of the vertiginous main hall." Kurt Andersen, "Finally Doing Right By Wright: After years of fuss and furor, the great but inhospitable Guggenheim gets a splendid overhaul", *Time*, Jul. 6, 1992, p. 64.
- "And then there was Francis Coppola, the gemutlich Godfather at age 59, back from visiting his daughter, Sofia, on location of a movie she is directing and buzzing about new entrepreneurial adventures for his beloved, if battle-scarred, Zoetrope company." Peter Bart, "'George and Francis show' returns", *Variety*, Jul. 27, 1998, p. 64.
- "The woman was visiting Le Pain Quotidian--among the more gemutlich of bakeries--when she decided that it wouldn't be imprudent to park her child's $200 Concorde MacLaren X267 stroller in the vestibule." Ralph Gardner, Jr., "The Crime Blotter", *The New York Observer*, Mar. 4, 2002.
- "At the height of her success, [Julia] Child could boast a clutch of bestselling cookbooks and a *gemütlich* TV show shot on a single set." Margaret Talbot, "Les Très Riches Heures de Martha Stewart", *<boldtype>*, Oct. 1997.

gemütlichkeit, gemutlichkeit, Gemutlichkeit *n.*

from *Gemütlichkeit* "congeniality": warm friendliness, amicability [< German *gemütlich*].

- "Since I have lived in this pretty town I have become a worshiper of the goddess Gemutlichkeit." Edna Ferber, *Dawn O'Hara, The Girl Who Laughed.*
- "The lodge is friendly, unpretentious and full of tropical Gemutlichkeit." Robert Hughes, "Blissing Out in Balmy Belize", *Time*, Apr. 22, 1991, p. 92.
- "In her youth she adored eating, drinking and singing in the beer halls of Munich, and this German enclave at 2015 New Highway (391-9500), owned by Privatbrauerei Hoepfner Brewery in Karlsruhe and its American partners, recreates the gemutlichkeit of its European counterpart." Richard Jay Scholem, "A La Carte; Cars, Very New and Very Old", *The New York Times*, Oct. 11, 1998. *Privatbrauerei* means "private brewery".

gesellschaft, Gesellschaft, *Gesellschaft* n.

from *Gesellschaft* "companionship, association, company, society, fellowship, club": a rationally developed mechanistic type of social relationship characterized by impersonally contracted associations between persons, a community or society characterized by this relationship [< German *Geselle* "apprentice" < Middle High German *geselle* "friend, companion, comrade, consort, mate" < Old High German *gisello, gisellio* + *-schaft* "-ship" < Middle High German *-schaft* < Old High German *-scaf*. See also gemeinschaft.

- "Know your place, said/The leader, which is together,/And clubbed the errant back,/Giving it the Gesellschaft." John M. Burns, "Conform", *BioGraffiti: A Natural Selection*, 1981.

gestalt, Gestalt, *Gestalt n.* |*pl.* **Gestalts, Gestalten,** *n.* **gestaltism, gestaltist|**

from *Gestalt* "form, figure, shape, frame, stature": in Gestalt psychology, a synthesis of separate elements of emotion, experience, etc., that constitutes more than the mechanical sum of the parts.

- "But if you look more carefully, you might observe that the general gestalt of the [DNA] sequences is roughly the same." Jonathan Marks, *What It Means to Be 98% Chimpanzee*, 2003, p. 25.
- "Understand the gestalt in this easy-to-remember history." Wendy Northcutt, *The Darwin Awards II*, 2001, p. 1.
- "During these years, Robert also participated in a long menu of psychotherapies: group therapy, family therapy, multifamily group therapy, Gestalt therapy, psychoanalytically oriented psychotherapy, goal-oriented therapy, art therapy, behavioral therapy, vocational rehabilitation therapy, milieu therapy, et al." Jay Neugeboren, *Imagining Robert: My Brother, Madness and Survival: A Memoir*, 1998.
- "His photographs came to be a distinctive element of hundreds of album covers, which helped to define the unique Blue Note gestalt." M. Cuscuna, C. Lourie and O. Schnider, *The Blue Note Years: The Jazz Photography of Francis Wolf*, 1995.
- "Similarly, group dynamics was perceived as old-fashioned, a field that had seen its heyday in the Gestalt encounter groups and corporate brainstorming procedures of the early 1970s but now was dated and passé." Michael Crichton, *Sphere*, 1987, p. 13.
- "We need a new political gestalt in America: an expansion of the political arena to more accurately reflect not only what we do, but who we are and are becoming." Marianne Williamson, *The Healing of America*, 1997.
- "Much more an enormous pig than a sort of horse,/Hippo lives, as a matter of course,/Both in water—still or running, fresh or salt—/And on adjacent land, where its Gestalt/Takes fifty pounds (dry weight) of grass per night." John M. Burns, "*Hippopotamus amphibious*" *BioGraffiti: A Natural Selection*, 1981.

Gestapo *n.*

short for *Geheime Staatspolizei* "Secret State Police": the terrorist political police of the <u>Nazi</u> regime.

- "You can't scare me with this Gestapo crap." Keanu Reeves as Neo in *Matrix*, 1999.
- "William Casey, an Allied Intelligence officer, later recalled being told in early May 1945 that the Werewolf organisation was in process of formation and that it was to be built on the framework of the Gestapo and other Nazi security services." Ada Petrova & Peter Watson, *The Death of Hitler: The Full Story With New Evidence from Secret Russian Archives*, 1996.
- "Even in the early decades of the twentieth century, telescoped words and phrases had been one of the characteristic features of political language; and it had been noticed that the tendency to use abbreviations of this kind was most marked in totalitarian countries and totalitarian organizations. Examples were such words as <u>*Nazi*</u>, *Gestapo*, *Comintern*, *Inprecorr*, *Agitprop*. In the

beginning the practice had been as it were instinctively, but in Newspeak it was used with a conscious purpose." George Orwell, *1984*, 1949, p. 252.

- "Tainted evidence about his relations with the Gestapo had been fabricated." Hella Pick, *Simon Wiesenthal: A Life in Search of Justice*, 1996.

gesundheit, Gesundheit, *Gesundheit* *interj.*

from *Gesundheit* "healthiness": used to wish someone good health specially to one who has just sneezed. (As a kid I always thought *gesundheit* literally meant "bless you" in German.)

- "Whether you call it pop or soda, bucket or pail, baby carriage or baby buggy, scat or gesundheit, the beach or the shore—all these and countless others tell us a little something about where you come from." Bill Bryson, *The Mother Tongue: English and How it Got that Way*, 1990, p. 99.

Gleichschaltung *n.*

from *Gleichschaltung* "equalization": the standardization of political, economic, and social institutions in authoritarian states [< German *gleich* "same, equal" + *Schaltung* "switching" < *schalten* "to switch"]. This entry suggested by Christiane Leißner.

- "Simultaneously, the 'Gleichschaltung' (equalization) started; that is to say that the personnel of all offices and institutions of the Government or under Government control became subject to substitution by reliable members of the German National Socialist Party." Gabor Baross, *Hungary and Hitler*, 1964.

- "The findings of this study are not dramatically new, but they provide a nicely nuanced outline of both the complexity of the time and the diversity of the individual actors and their disillusionment as they came face to face with the full implications of Gleichschaltung, which gradually demonstrated an unanticipated authority and discomfiting militancy and brutality." Larry Thornton, "*On the Road to the Wolf's Lair: German Resistance to Hitler*", review of the book by Theodore S. Hamerow, *Historian*, Fall 1999.

- "Throughout these first years of the Third Reich, Hitler imposed a process that the Nazis called Gleichschaltung, which means standardization or making things the same." "Road to War", *Time*, Aug. 28, 1989, p. 40.

- "Not much comfort here, then, for those now busily intent upon a historical Gleichschaltung of all Irish 'traditions'." K. Theodore Hoppen, "An Ascendancy Army: The Irish Yeomanry, 1796-1834", *English Historical Review*, Jun. 1999.

- "This remarkable gathering at Germany's most hallowed literary shrine, the town of Schiller and Goethe, was in fact a tradition that had survived Nazi Gleichschaltung." Gerwin Strobl, "Shakespeare and the Nazis", *History Today*, May 1997.

- "In the name of modernization, Reza Shah mounted one of the most frightful manifestations of fascist statism in modern history, eliminating all autonomous centers of voluntary association, generating a Gleichschaltung program very similar to Hitler's agenda in the contemporary Germany." Hamid Dabashi, "The End of Islamic Ideology", *Social Research*, Summer 2000.

- "Axel Goodbody, Dennis Tate, and Ian Wallace refute a simplistic equation of the German Democratic Republic with the NS-politics of Gleichschaltung, or mass control through ideological uniformity, by charting criticism internal to that state." Karen H. Jankowsky, "*German Cultural Studies: An Introduction*", *Criticism*, Winter 1998.

glitz *n., v.t.,* **glitzy** *adj.*

related to *Glitzer, glitzern* "glitter, to glitter": extravagant showiness, glitter [perh. < Yiddish, perh. < German *glitzern* "to glitter" < Middle High German *glitzen* "to glitter"].

- "Behind the glitz and silliness of the 'multimedia extravaganza' view of the Net touted by the mass media, this 'old Internet' is still chugging along, growing every day." Evan Morris, *The Book Lover's Guide to the Internet,* 1998, p. 12.
- "My enchantment with new things, my vulnerability to the hopeful glitz of even garish packaging has really not diminished." Alan Shapiro, *The Last Happy Occasion,* 1996.
- "Clouded by event, and stripped of glitz, this year's Toronto Film Festival let the movies shine through", Richard Corliss, "An Unfestive Festival", *Time,* Oct. 8, 2001, p. 65.
- "If a person's into glitz, Rico's not for them." Dave Hill, in Carol Horner, "ZipUSA: Rico, Colorado", *National Geographic,* Mar. 2001, p. 128.

glockenspiel *n.*

from *Glockenspiel* "bell play": a percussion instrument.

gneiss *n.*

from *Gneis* "gneiss": a rock resembling granite, consisting of alternating layers of different minerals, such as feldspar, quartz, mica, and hornblende [probably from Middle High German *gneist, ganeist* "a spark" and Old High German *gneisto* "a spark" due to the luster of some of the components]. See further example under quartzite.

- "It has been remarked, with much truth, that abruptly conical hills are characteristic of the formation which Humboldt designates as gneiss-granite." Charles Darwin, "Rio de Janeiro", *The Voyage of the Beagle,* 1836.
- "You sprawl face down on a sloping pavement of gneiss, pressed to the rock by the weight of your pack, and lie there for some minutes, reflecting in a distant, out-of-body way that you have never before looked this closely at anything in the natural world since you were four years old and had your first magnifying glass." Bill Bryson, *A Walk in the Woods,* 1997.

götterdämmerung, Götterdämmerung, *Götterdämmerung, Die Götterdämmerung* *n.*

from *Götterdämmerung* "twilight of the gods": in Germanic mythology, the destruction of the gods and of all things in a final battle with evil powers resulting in the end of the world, also called Ragnarok in Scandinavian mythology; the final opera of Richard Wagner's *The Ring of the Nibelung* on this theme; a collapse (as of a society, regime or institution) marked by catastrophic violence and disorder [< German *Götter* (plural of *Gott* "god") + *Dämmerung* "twilight" < erroneous translation of Old Icelandic *Ragnarök* "fate of the gods" misunderstood as *Ragnarökkr* "twilight of the gods"]. This entry suggested by Wilton Woods.

- "She died. Almost a month ago. I guess she'd been ill, and she thought she didn't have long, so she treated herself to a steak dinner and took all her cats and went and sat in her Cadillac in the garage and turned on the engine while her CD player was doing the immolation scene from *Die Götterdämmerung.*" Garrison Keillor, *Wobegon Boy,* 1997, p. 269.
- "There were, she told him, rehearsals not only for 'Walkure,' but also for 'Gotterdammerung,' in which she was to sing *Waltraute* two weeks later." Willa Silbert Cather, *The Song of the Lark,* p. 470.
- "The War Department in Washington had taken up this notion on 12 February 1945, warning that a man like Hitler would require his Gotterdammerung." Ada Petrova, *The Death of Hitler: The Full Story with New Evidence from Secret Russian Archives.*
- "Even the Hudson and the Susquehanna–perhaps the Potomac itself--had often risen to drown out the gods of Walhalla, and one could hardly listen to the 'Gotterdammerung' in New York, among throngs of intense young enthusiasts, without paroxysms of nervous excitement that toned down to musical philistinism at Baireuth, as though the gods were Bavarian composers." Henry Adams, *The Education of Henry Adams.*
- "The Ring consists of four plays, intended to be performed on four successive evenings, entitled The Rhine Gold (a prologue to the other three), The Valkyries, Siegfried, and Night Falls On The Gods; or, in the original German, Das Rheingold, Die Walkure, Siegfried, and Die Gotterdammerung." George Bernard Shaw, *The Perfect Wagnerite: A Commentary on the Niblung's Ring.*

grosswetterlage, Grosswetterlage *n.*

from *Großwetterlage* "general weather situation": the sea-level pressure distribution averaged over a period during which the essential characteristics of the atmospheric circulation over a large region remain nearly unchanged [German *groß* "large, great" + *Wetter* "weather" + *Lage* "situation, position"]. This entry suggested by Volker Landgraf.

- "They found that the synoptic-scale flow pattern characterized by the Grosswetterlage (greater synoptic situation, e.g. Baur 1957) does not provide a good indication of the likelihood of storm genesis." Maria Peristeri et al., "Genesis conditions for thunderstorm growth and the development of a squall line in the northern Alpine foreland", Jul. 10, 1999.

H

Hallstatt *adj.*

from the Austrian village of *Hallstatt* "salt place": relating to an early stage of the Iron Age in central and western Europe and the Balkans.

- "The knowledge of iron as well as bronze in Europe, centres around the area occupied by the Alpines in the eastern Alps and its earliest phase is known as the Hallstatt culture, from a little town in the Tyrol where it was first discovered." Madison Grant, *Passing of the Great Race, Or, The Racial Basis of*

European History, 1916. Hallstatt is not in the modern-day Austrian province of Tyrol but rather in the province of Upper Austria.

hamburger, burger, -burger, hamburg *n.*

from *Hamburger* "of Hamburg": (uncooked) ground beef; (cooked) Hamburg steak; ground-beef patty sandwich. The hamburger on a bun was invented in America, but the hamburger patty was brought to America by German immigrants, who called it *Hamburger.* Interestingly the hamburger patty is no longer called *Hamburger* in Germany but rather *Frikadelle, Frikandelle* or *Bulette*, originally Italian and French words. And a hamburger on a bun in Germany is called a *Hamburger*, just like almost everywhere else in the world, being a re-import from America.

- "IS HAMBURGER MEAT MADE OUT OF PEOPLE FROM HAMBURG?" Bill Watterson, *Calvin and Hobbes* comic strip, Oct. 22, 1993.
- "The diet sheet that had been sent by the Smeltings school nurse had been taped to the fridge, which had been emptied of all Dudley's favourite things – fizzy drinks and cakes, chocolate bars and burgers – and filled instead with fruits and vegetables and the sorts of things that Uncle Vernon called 'rabbit food'." J. K. Rowling, *Harry Potter and the Goblet of Fire* (Book 4), 2000, p. 30.
- "A week before Christmas 1992 Lauren Beth Rudolph ate a cheeseburger from a Jack in the Box restaurant in California." Jennifer Ackerman, "Food: How Safe?" *National Geographic*, May 2002, p. 15.

Hamburg steak, hamburger steak *n.*

ground beef patty, Salisbury steak.

hamster *n.*

from *Hamster* "hamster": a short-tailed, stout-bodied, burrowing rodent of the subfamily Cricetinae native to Europe and Asia and having large cheek pouches in which it carries food; the species used as a pet or laboratory animal is the golden or Syrian hamster (*Mesocricetus auratus*); the fur of this animal; [computers] a tailless or cordless mouse (input device) [< German < Middle High German *hamastra* < Old High German *hamastro, hamustro* "corn-weevil" < Old Saxon *hamstra* "weevil" < Slavic, related to Old Russian *chomestoru* "hamster", related to Avestan *hamaEstar* "oppressor"]. This entry suggested by Jens Schlatter.

- "At birth, the dog's brain reaches approximately 8% of its mature weight, the hamster 8%, the rat 15%, the mouse 22%, humans 24%, and the monkey 60% (Himwich, 1973˜)." National Academy Press, *Pesticides in the Diets of Infants and Children*, 1993.
- "'Can we get a bunny?' she asked. 'No.' 'I'd take care of it.' 'You have a hamster.'" David Carkeet, *The Error of Our Ways: A Novel*, 1997.
- "The imagination of children never fails to stagger me. Once they put a hamster on my chest, and when I bolted upright (my throat muscles paralyzed with fright) they asked, 'Do you have any alcohol for the chemistry set?'" Erma Bombeck, *Forever, Erma: Best-Loved Writing from America's Favorite Humorist*, 2000.
- "He is a gentleman of limitless patience who sits like a large hamster in a nest of papers." Quentin Crisp, *Resident Alien: The New York Diaries*, 1998.

- "In our family even the hamster was thin." Sarah Dunant, *Under My Skin: A Hannah Wolfe Mystery.*

Die Hand die Verletzt *n.*

from *Die Hand die Verletzt* "The hand that harms": the title of season 2, episode 14 of the TV series *The X-Files* [< German *die* definite article + Hand "hand" + *die* relative pronoun + *verletzen* "to harm"]. This entry suggested by CauNo.

hasenpfeffer, hassenpfeffer *n.*

from *Hasenpfeffer* "peppered hare, also slang for rabbit droppings": jugged hare, a stew of marinated rabbit meat, a dish Elmer Fudd was always trying to make Bugs Bunny into. The *Pfeffer* probably doesn't refer to pepper, although pepper-corns can be used in the marinade, but rather to the chopped meat or the blood used to thicken the sauce. [< German *Hase* "hare", colloquial "rabbit" + *Pfeffer* "pepper"]. This entry suggested by Laura L. B. Schulz. Thanks also to Sigi Rabenstein and Ulrich Wolff. See also <u>Pez</u>.

- "Burch even shares some of his favorite game recipes—including such classics as Hasenpfeffer and Brunswick stew." from the dust jacket of *Field Dressing and Butchering Rabbits, Squirrels, and Other Small Game: Step-By-Step In-structions, from Field to Table,* by Monte Burch, 2001.
- "... since I didn't teach then, but the Greytons had brought by a couple of rabbits, and that was Marygay's specialty, hassenpfeffer." Joe Haldeman, *Forever Free,* 2000, p. 11.
- "Peter had an ambition to become as rich as his neighbor, Hugo Heffelbauer, who smoked a meerschaum pipe three feet long and had wiener schnitzel and hassenpfeffer for dinner every day in the week." O. Henry, *41 Stories by O. Henry,* 1991, p. 236.
- "When Fritz came home in the early blue twilight the snow was flying faster, Mrs. Kohler was cooking Hasenpfeffer in the kitchen, and the professor was seated at the piano, playing the Gluck, which he knew by heart." Willa Cather, *The Song of the Lark,* 1915, p. 73.
- "'Schlemiel, schlimazel, Hasenpfeffer Incorporated!' Tonight on ABC, Laverne & Shirley: Together Again. Bring Squiggy, por favor. [WABC, 7, 8 p.m.]", Jason Gay, "Jerry Nachman Roars Back With MSNBC", *The New York Observer,* May 6, 2002. The quote is the opening lines of the theme song to the TV show *Laverne and Shirley.* The first two words are Yiddish, not German.
- "The audience also follows [Israeli Prime Minister Ariel] Sharon into the kitchen where, in the series premiere, he shares his recipes for beef Welling-ton, autumn squash polenta and his signature dish, Mediterranean hasenpfef-fer." Ashwini K. Chhabra, "Must-see TV", *salon.com,* Sep. 13, 2002.
- "Hasenpfeffer of Rabbit, Grain Mustard Spaetzle, Sweet and Sour Red Cab-bage and Dill Oil $28", menu of the Zealous restaurant in Chicago, Winter 2002, p. 8. Of course, *Hasenpfeffer of Rabbit* is redundant. *Spaetzle* is a side dish made of wheat flour that comes from the Swabian region of Germany. It literally means "little sparrows".

hausfrau *n.* [*pl.* **hausfraus, hausfrauen**]

from *Hausfrau* "house wife, house woman": housewife. See also <u>Bauhaus</u>, <u>Frau</u> and <u>Gasthaus</u>.

- "There's the insecure self-doubter, the self-described 'genius' and the cake-baking hausfrau [Roseanne Barr]", James Poniewozik, "A Rose Without Thorns?" *Time*, Aug. 4, 2003, p. 61.
- "He saw a face whose mild blue eyes and undetermined mouth he still swore by as the standard by which to try all her inferior sisters, and a figure whose growing *embonpoint* yearly approached the outline of his ideal hausfrau." J. Storer Clouston, *Count Bunker*, 1905, p. 8.
- "Civilisation has done away with curl-papers, yet at that hour the soul of the Hausfrau is as tightly screwed up in them as was ever her grandmother's hair; and though my body comes down mechanically, having been trained that way by punctual parents, my soul never thinks of beginning to wake up for other people till lunch-time, and never does so completely till it has been taken out of doors and aired in the sunshine." Elizabeth von Arnim (Marie Annette Beauchamp), *Elizabeth and her German Garden*.
- "And the German Hausfrau, once so innocently consecrated to Kirche, Küche und Kinder, is going the same way." H. L. Mencken, *In Defense of Women*, 1922. *Kirche, Küche und Kinder* means "church, kitchen and children".

Heimlich maneuver *n.*

from *heimlich* "familiar, confidential, secret": named for Henry Jay Heimlich (1920-) American surgeon, a firm embrace with clasped hands just below the rib cage, applied from behind to force an object from the trachea of a choking person [< Middle High German *heimlich, heimelich* "familiar" < Old High German *heimilich* "of the home, familiar" < Old High German *heim* "home"].

- "Another patron grabbed him and started doing the Heimlich maneuver while the rest of us sat dumbfounded." Fran Drescher, *Cancer Schmancer*, 2002, p. 150.
- "Sorry Bob. Your 'Heimlich maneuver' request was reviewed and denied ..." Luckovich, in a cartoon in *Newsweek*, July 27, 1998, p. 8.

heinie, Heinie, Heine *n.*

from *Hein, Heine*, diminutive of *Heinrich* "Henry": [slang] a German (soldier): term of contempt used especially in World War I (not related to *heinie* meaning "buttocks").

- "... so we'd keep clipping him until we had him cut right down to the stubble, pretty much, kind of a dog heinie." Garrison Keillor, "Tomato Butt" *News from Lake Wobegon: Summer*, 1987.

Herr, Mein *n.*

See Mein Herr.

Herrenvolk, herrenvolk *n.*

from *Herrenvolk* "master race": the German nation characterized by the Nazis as born to mastery; a group regarding itself as naturally superior [< German *Herr* "lord, master, Mr." + *Volk* "folk, people, race, nation"]. This entry suggested by CauNo. See also Mein Herr.

- "He turned up as the herrenvolk had solemnly entered the church, top hats on arms, and set up a soapbox newsstand with a saucer full of coppers, and the banner headline **Hitler Assassinated** – needless to say, with no papers to

back it." Albert Meltzer, *I Couldn't Paint Golden Angels: Sixty Years of Commonplace Life and Anarchist Agitation*, 1996.
- "Herrenvolk", season 4, episode 1, *The X-Files.*

hertz, Hz *n.* [*pl.* **hertz, hertzes**]

from *Hertz* "hertz": a unit of frequency equal to one cycle per second, named for Heinrich Rudolph Hertz, 1857-1894, German physicist [< German *Hertz, Herz* "heart" < Middle High German *herz, herze* < Old High German *herza*; or the name *Hertz, Herz* related to German *Hirsch* "deer" < Middle High German *hirz* < Old High German *hirz, hiruz* "antlered animal"]. This entry suggested by Wilton Woods.
- "EMFs are characterized by their wavelength (expressed in meters) and their frequency (expressed in hertz)." National Research Council, *An Evaluation of the U.S. Navy's Extremely Low Frequency Communications System Ecological Monitoring Program*, 1997, p. 21.
- "Sometimes it shows up as a lot more wiggles in the higher frequency range, up around 25 to 70 Hertz." William H. Calvin & George A. Ojemann, *Conversations With Neil's Brain: The Neural Nature of Thought and Language*, 1994.

hinterland *n.*

from *Hinterland* "hinder land": inland or remote region.
- "Your idea of the best in music includes a bunch of hinterland artists with minimal, perhaps questionable, talent." Carl Widing, in a letter to *Time*, Jan. 20, 1997, p. 5.
- "The ruses that are used to lure and retain the workers from desperately poor hinterlands of neighboring countries like Mali and Burkina Faso are just as tried and true." Howard W. French, "On Ivory Coast Farms, Echoes of Slavery", *International Herald Tribune*, June 24, 1998, p. 8.

hopfgeist *n.*

from *Hopfen + Geist* "hops + ghost, spirit": no doubt made up by the author of the following example. See also poltergeist, zeitgeist.
- "There's a smoking-tavern called the Half-way House. The hopfgeist is friendly." Iain M. Banks, *Feersum Endjinn*, 1994, p. 78.

hornblende *n.*

from *Horn* "horn" + *blenden* "to blind": a certain mineral. See also blende.

hornfels, hornfelz *n.*

from *Hornfels* "horn rock": a fine-grained rock produced by the action of heat especially on slate.
- "And the thump it made coming down—tons and tons of skarn and hornfels— set off another [cave-in], deeper in." Stephen King, *Desperation*, 1996, p. 422.

howitzer, hauwitzer *n.*

from *Haubitze* "howitzer": cannon with medium-length barrel and high angle of fire [< Dutch *houwitser, houvietser* < German *Haubitze* < Middle High German *haufnitz* < Czech *houfnice* "catapult, slingshot, sling"].
- "On the stroke of 8:00 A.M. the air was suddenly filled with the whistle of shells, the echo of their detonation, the deeper boom of the howitzers and the muffled roar of the heavies." Eloise Engle & Lauri Paananen, *The Winter War: The Soviet Attack on Finland 1939-1940*, 1973, p. 15.

- "They had found several Krupp howitzers left over from the Bulgarian war and had installed them on concrete foundations." Henry Morgenthau, *Ambassador Morgenthau's Story*, 2000.
- "Look! you can see from this window my brazen howitzer planted/High on the roof of the church, a preacher who speaks to the purpose,/Steady, straightforward, and strong, with irresistible logic,/Orthodox, flashing conviction right into the hearts of the heathen." Henry Wadsworth Longfellow, *The Courtship of Miles Standish and Other Poems*, 1858.
- "The barbers snatched steaming towels from a machine like a howitzer of polished nickel and disdainfully flung them away after a second's use." Sinclair Lewis, *Babbitt*, 1912.

I

infobahn, I-bahn *n.*

from *Infobahn* "infobahn": information superhighway [< *information* + *autobahn*].

- "Most public attention in the last few years has focused on the flashy stretch limo of the infobahn, the World Wide Web with its glamorous graphics." Evan Morris, *The Book Lover's Guide to the Internet*, 1998, p. 51.

J

-ja

See Ouija.

jaeger, jäger *n.*

from *Jäger* "hunter": one of the bird family Stercorariidae, which harasses other sea birds and steals their prey, called skuas in England and *Raubmöwen* ("predatory gulls") in German. *Jaeger* is the correct spelling of *Jäger* when one cannot represent the umlaut on the particular system one is using.

- "Gulls and jaegers are best known for their habit of forcing smaller birds to drop their food, but C. M. Arnold observed a House Sparrow following a robin about and snatching earthworms before it could carry them off to waiting youngsters (Bent)." Roland H. Wauer, *The American Robin*, 1999, p. 75.
- "Jaegers and skuas are most often seen robbing other seabirds of fish." Chandler S. Robbins et al., *Birds of North America*, 1966, p. 130.
- "Where the Churchill River enters the immense expanse of Hudson Bay, you will see arctic terns and parasitic jaegers feeding on the fish stirred up by pods of beluga whales that congregate here." Tim Fitzharris, *Wild Wings: An Introduction to Birdwatching*, 1992, p. 178.

- "Other offshore species include Pomarine Jaegers, Black-legged Kittiwakes, and Red Phalaropes." Laird Henkel, "Birding Hotspots: Monterey Bay, California", *Birder's World*, Dec. 1997, p. 59.

jäger, jaeger, Jaeger, yager *n.*

from *Jäger* "hunter": a hunter; a rifleman in the old Austrian and German armies.

- "In contrast, he was also a graduate of the 27th Jaeger Battalion in 1915, the War Academy in France, and had earlier distinguished himself in the Rautu battles of the Independence War." Eloise Engle & Lauri Paananen, *The Winter War: The Soviet Attack on Finland 1939-1940*, 1973, p. 33.
- "I shouldn't have minded it so much in any other country, but I thought men who wore Jaeger underclothing and women's petticoats for a national costume might have excused so slight an eccentricity as knickerbockers." Richard Harding Davis, *The Princess Aline.*
- "But my punishment was swift to follow, for within the hour the bell rang imperiously twice, and there was Dr. Theobald on our mat; in a yellow Jaeger suit, with a chin as yellow jutting over the flaps that he had turned up to hide his pyjamas." Ernest William Hornung, *Raffles: Further Adventures of the Amateur Cracksman*, 1901.
- "The area thus costumed ceased at the waist, leaving a Jaeger-like and unmedieval gap thence to the tops of the stockings." Booth Parkington, *Penrod*, 1914.
- "One particular body of the subsidiary troops were included in this arrangement, and the Hessian yagers were transformed into a corps of heavy and inactive horse." James Fenimore Cooper, *The Spy: A Tale of the Neutral Ground.*

Jakob-Creutzfeldt disease, Jakob-Creutzfeldt pseudosclerosis, Jakob's pseudosclerosis *n.*

See Creutzfeldt-Jakob disease.

Junker, Junkerdom, Junkerthum, Junkerism *n.*

from *Junker*: (a member of) the East Prussian aristocracy, noted for its harsh, militaristic attitudes [German < Old High German *juncherr, juncherro* < *junc* "young" + *herro* "honorable"; see also Herrenvolk]. This entry suggested by Christiane Leißner.

- "Why, we know the very names of the prelates with whom the master-cynic of the Junkerthum made his 'deal.'", Upton Sinclair, *The Profits of Religion: An Essay in Economic Interpretation*, 1918, p. 153.
- "It was Miles Bjornstam who said, 'I can't figure it out. I'm opposed to wars, but still, seems like Germany has got to be licked because them Junkers stands in the way of progress.'", Sinclair Lewis, *Main Street*, 1920, p. 239.
- "An upstart and a *junker*, like so many others!", Anton Checkov, *The Party*, 1917, p. 25.
- "There was not a word about the marriage, however, but the story was adorned with generals, colonels and kammer-junkers, while Zverkov almost took the lead among them.", Fyodor Dostoyevsky, *Notes from the Underground*, p. 108. *Kammer* means "chamber".
- "'He was a light-headed fellow,' said Johann Helm, 'but he knew how to get the confidence of the old *Junkers*.'", Bayard Taylor, *Beauty and the Beast, and Tales of Home*, 1872, p. 167.

- "Only the Turkish mind, however—and possibly the Junker—could regard it as furnishing an excuse for the terrible barbarities that now took place.", Henry Morgenthau, *Ambassador Morgenthau's Story*, 1918.
- "I assure you that our most pan-Germanic Junker is a sucking dove in his feelings towards England as compared with a real bitter Irish-American.", Sir Arthur Conan Doyle, *The Adventures of Sherlock Holmes.*

kaffeeklatsch, kaffee klatsch, coffee-klatsch, coffee klatsch, coffee klatch, coffee clutch, klatsch, klatch *n.*

from *Kaffeeklatsch* "coffee gossip": informal conversational gathering where coffee is served [< German *Kaffee* "coffee" < French *café* < Italian *caffè* < Turkish *kahve* < Arabic *qahwa* "coffee, wine" + *Klatsch* "gossip, clapping noise" < *klatschen* "to gossip, to clap"]. This entry suggested by Wilton Woods.

- "We sat thus for an hour—an unexpected type of *Kaffee Klatsch* for such an outpost of civilization." Theodore Roosevelt, *A Book-Lover's Holidays in the Open*, 1916.
- "Her clothes always smelled of savory cooking, except when she was dressed for church or *Kaffeeklatsch*, and then she smelled of bay rum or of the lemon-verbena sprig which she tucked inside her puffy black kid glove." Willa Cather, *The Song of the Lark*, 1915, p. 171.
- "Mr. Schultz downplays his formidable business skills, but makes sure to mention his health-care kaffeeklatsch with Bill Clinton." Andrew Stuttaford, "Food & Drink: Mug's Game", *National Review*, Dec. 7, 1998.
- "The oldest coffee-house on the street, Koffee Klatsch (778 Higuera; 544-1228), has been around for 15 years." David Lansing, "The new face of San Luis Obispo", *Sunset*, May 1996.
- "Lazio's ethnic good looks and ready Ultra-Brite smile could land him in the cast of Friends, but he is far more disciplined and determined than the coffee-klatsch crowd at Central Perk." Kate O'Beirne, "New York: The Anti-Hillary Hope - Rick Lazio in the arena", *National Review*, Jun. 19, 2000.
- "And while it can reflect the coffee klatsch of the industry, it often relies on blind items: it was responsible for the WMA rumors, as well as posting copies of internal e-mails sent by Jim Wiatt and Dave Wirtschafter to staffers when they each left ICM for WMA." Marc Graser, "Geek Gab Freaks Film Biz", *Variety*, Oct. 18, 1999.
- "At one point, an aged white businessmen -- member of an informal coffee klatch called 'Bubbas in Training' – casually admits that he's never thought of the word 'nigger' as demeaning or offensive." Joe Leydon, "Two Towns Of Jasper", *Variety*, Jan. 28, 2002.

kaiser, Kaiser *n.*

from *Kaiser* "emperor": emperor; title of the Holy Roman Emperors or the emperors of Austria or Germany until 1918; person who exercises or tries to exercise absolute authority; autocrat [German < Middle High German *keiser* < Old High German *keisar* < Latin *Caesar*, related to Greek *kaisar*].

- "A herd of zebras grazed where once the German kaiser may have reviewed his troops." Edgar Rice Burroughs, *The Lost Continent*, 1916, p. 95.
- "To suppose in these days that one has literally to give all to the poor, or that a starved English prisoner should literally love his enemy the Kaiser, or that because Christ protested against the lax marriages of His day therefore two spouses who loathe each other should be for ever chained in a life servitude and martyrdom – all these assertions are to travesty His teaching and to take from it that robust quality of common sense which was its main characteristic." Arthur Conan Doyle, *The Vital Message*, 1919, p. 24.
- "Every ascendant monarch in Europe up to the last, aped Cæsar and called himself Kaiser or Tsar or Imperator or Kasir-i-Hind." H. G. Wells, *The World Set Free*, 1914, p. 21.

kaiser roll, kaiser *n.*

from *Kaisersemmel* "kaiser roll": a round, raised, unsweetened, crusty, yeast roll often sprinkled with poppy or sesame seeds and used for sandwiches, also called Vienna roll [< German dialectal *Kaisersemmel* < German *Kaiser* "Kaiser" + German dialectal *Semmel* "roll"].

- "She had spent the afternoon in Seneca Falls, at the Elizabeth Cady Stanton house, and come back with steaks for dinners, which I had grilled—strip sirloins, very rare, with a thin slice of raw white onion, in a kaiser roll, with barbecue sauce, and beans on the side—and we had finished a bottle of Barolo and I was about to open another." Garrison Keillor, *Wobegon Boy*, 1997, p. 70.
- "The Judge forgot about his corned beef on kaiser." John Grisham, *The Testament*, 1999, p. 361.

Kapellmeister, Capellmeister *n.*

from *Kapellmeister* "band leader": musical director in a royal chapel, choir-master [< German *Kapelle* "chapel, choir or band that once played in a prince's chapel" < Middle High German *kapelle, kappelle* < Old High German *kapella* < Middle Latin *capella, cappella* "small house of God, small building where the coat of Saint Martin of Tours was kept, small coat" < *cappa* "a kind of head covering, coat with hood" + *Meister*, see -meister].

- "Her master at Mrs. Lemon's school (close to a county town with a memorable history that had its relics in church and castle) was one of those excellent musicians here and there to be found in our provinces, worthy to compare with many a noted Kapellmeister in a country which offers more plentiful conditions of musical celebrity." George Eliot, *Middlemarch: A Study of Provincial Life*, 1871, p. 167.
- "And, with the exception of Mr. Paine, we know of no American hitherto who has shown either the genius or the culture requisite for writing music in the grand style, although there is some of the Kapellmeister music, written by

our leading organists and choristers, which deserves honourable mention." John Fiske, *The Unseen World, and Other Essays*, 1876, p. 266.

- "If without this you have a fancy for quavers and demi-semi-quavers, practise for yourself and by yourself, and torment not therewith the Capellmeister Kreisler and others." Henry Wadsworth Longfellow, *Hyperion*, p. 161.

- "Humanity may well tremble for the future if again resounds under this archway the tramp of boots following a march of Wagner or any other Kapellmeister." Vicente Blasco Ibanez, *The Four Horsemen of the Apocalypse.*

- "This last was sanctified by the spirit of Joseph Haydn, for so many years Kapellmeister to the Esterhazy family." Henry J. Coke, *Tracks of a Rolling Stone.*

kaput, kaputt *adj.*

from *kaputt* "broken": utterly defeated, finished, destroyed; hopelessly outmoded [< French *capot* "not having made a trick at piquet"].

- *Kaput!*, by Stevan Eldred-Grigg, 2000.

- *K-Rations, Kilroy, KP, & Kaputt: One GI's War*, by Henry K. Davis, 1995.

karst *n.*, **karstic** *adj.*

from *Karst*: an irregular limestone region with sinks, underground streams and caverns.

- "So [wild and free] were those who once survived off this rugged karst land—from trappers and loggers to farmers coaxing crops from rocky soil." Lisa Moore LaRoe, "Ozarks Harmony", *National Geographic*, Apr. 1998.

Karst *n.* (also **Kras** or Italian **Carso**)

a limestone mountain range in eastern Italy, western Croatia and western Slovenia [< Serbo-Croatian *Kras* and *krs*].

- "The eastern third of the republic lies within the Karst, a barren limestone plateau broken by depressions and ridges." "Slovenia" *Microsoft® Encarta® 96 Encyclopedia.*

katzenjammer *n.*

from *Katzenjammer* "hangover": hangover; distress; discordant clamor; made famous by The Katzenjammer Kids, a cartoon strip which was based on Wilhelm Busch's Max und Moritz from Germany [< German *Katze* "cat" + *Jammer* "wailing, distress"]. See also to yammer.

- "Bourgeois revolutions like those of the eighteenth century storm more swiftly from success to success, their dramatic effects outdo each other, men and things seem set in sparkling diamonds, ecstasy is the order of the day- but they are short-lived, soon they have reached their zenith, and a long Katzenjammer [crapulence] takes hold of society before it learns to assimilate the results of its storm-and-stress period soberly." Karl Marx, *The Eighteenth Brumaire of Louis Napoleon*, 1852.

- "Alas! as I was to learn at a later period, intellectual intoxication too, has its katzenjammer." Jack London, *John Barleycorn*.

kibitz, kibbitz *v.i., v.t.,* **kibitzer** *n.*

related to *kiebitzen, Kiebitz* "kibitz, kibitzer": to look on and interfere or give unwanted, meddlesome or intrusive comments, advice or criticism, especially during a card game; to chat, converse [< Yiddish *kibetsn* < German *kiebitzen* < German thieves' jargon *kiebitschen* "to examine, search, look through, go through", influenced by German *Kiebitz* "any of several birds called pewits" (imitative)].

- "So I marched myself back into the technician's area, where the Nordic nurse was already kibitzing with one of the doctors." Fran Drescher, *Cancer Schmancer*, 2002, p. 226.
- "I let most of the staff off so they wouldn't kibitz while I was cooking." Katherine Neville, *The Eight*, 1995, p. 212.

kindergarten, K *n.*

from *Kindergarten* "kindergarten". A *Kindergarten* in German-speaking countries would actually be the equivalent of a preschool in the U.S. A U.S. kindergarten would be *Vorschule* in German. A **kindergartner** would be a *Kindergartenkind* while a **kindergarten teacher** would be a *Kindergärtner* (male) or *Kindergärtnerin* (female) [< German *Kinder* "children" + *Garten* "garden"].

- "I haven't been so embarrassed since a very unfortunate incident in kindergarten, even though Captain Jorgenson acted as if nothing had happened." Robert A. Heinlein, *Starship Troopers*, 1959.
- "After all, entire kindergarten classes had come unglued." John Irving, *The Fourth Hand*, 2001, p. 20.
- "McPherson himself always seemed to have a kindergarten quality about him, and a boundless optimism." Michael Crichton, *Terminal Man*, 1988, p. 30.
- "I knew I had to tell him that, otherwise I would get a call from his kindergarten teacher about his uncle the abortionist." Michael Crichton writing as Jeffery Hudson, *A Case of Need*, 1968.
- "I've heard it said that kindergartners already know how to sing and dance and paint." Scott Adams, *The Joy of Work: Dilbert's Guide to Finding Happiness at the Expense of Your Co-workers*, 1999.
- "'Kindergarten might be a good term for this place [nesting colony],' he says." Rick Gore, "Dinosaurs", *National Geographic*, Jan. 1993.
- *Kindergarten Cop*, starring Arnold Schwarzenegger, 1990.

Kinderscenen, Kinderszenen *n.pl.*

from *Kinderscenen, Kinderszenen* "Scenes of Childhood": set of 13 short piano pieces by Schumann, Opus 15, composed 1838 [< German *Kinder* "children" + *Scenen, Szenen* "scenes" (*Scenen* is an older German spelling.)].

- "Then another Schumann, another of his gay ones – *Kinderscenen*." Roald Dahl, "Edward the Conqueror", *Kiss Kiss*, 1959, p. 167.
- "Thea studied some of the *Kinderszenen* with him, as well as some little sonatas by Mozart and Clementi." Willa Silbert Cather, *The Song of the Lark*, 1915, p. 174.

Der Kindestod *n.*

from *der Kindstod* "(the) child death": the name of the monster in season 2, episode 18 ("Killed by Death") of the TV series *Buffy the Vampire Slayer* [< German *Kind* "child" + *Tod* "death", *plötzlicher Kindstod* is the German term for "SIDS, Sudden Infant Death Syndrome"]. This entry suggested by CauNo.

kirsch, kirschwasser *n.*

from *Kirsch, Kirschwasser* "cherry brandy": a dry colorless brandy distilled from the fermented juice of the black morello cherry, especially in Germany, Switzerland and Alsace, France; cherry <u>schnapps</u> [< German *Kirsche* "cherry" + *Wasser* "water"]. See also <u>schnapps</u>. This entry suggested by Michael Kiermaier.

- "Kirschwasser, a clear cordial, is often used in bakeshops and kitchens." Culinary Institute of America, *The Professional Chef*, 2001, p. 159.
- "In our eight years together we'd had exactly one fight: something to do with kirschwasser and a cheese fondue." Michael Chabon, *Wonder Boys: A Novel*, 1995, p. 226.
- "The Swiss offered cigars, and coffee was brought, along with small glasses of Kirschwasser." Frederick Forsyth, *The Dogs of War*, 1982, p. 152.
- "Kirsch or Kirschwasser is made in the Rhine Valley from black cherries and takes its unique flavoring from the cherry pits and skins." Christopher Egerton-Thomas, *How to Manage a Successful Bar*, 1994, p. 26.
- "Teddy glanced at the sideboard and saw that the princess had put out two chipped crystal glasses and a much depleted bottle of *Kirschwasser* from the Black Forest." Barbara Taylor Bradford, *Women in His Life*, 1991, p. 277.
- "I bent over and smelled his breath: a strong odor of kirschwasser was present; the odor of cherries could conceal many other substances." Quinn Fawcett, *Against the Brotherhood: A Mycroft Holmes Novel*, 1998, p. 227.
- "Similarly, the American food writer M F K Fisher categorises trifles as 'innocent', or made with plain bottled fruit, and 'not innocent' -- doused with Kirschwasser or brandy." Bee Wilson, "A trifle guilty: on how teetotallers get drunk on boxing day", *New Statesman*, Dec. 17, 2001.

kitsch *n.*

from *Kitsch* "gaudy trash": something appealing to popular or lowbrow taste [prob. < German dialect *kitschen* "to spread, smear, scratch together, slide"].

- "Normal media are distributed far beyond the reaches of kitsch." Adilkno (Foundation for the Advancement of Illegal Knowledge), *Media Archive*, 1998.
- "In all the years that they lived here, the apartment was never redecorated and the only change was in the quantity of ornaments and kitsch decorations which gathered here in ever greater amounts." Steven Kelly, *Invisible Architecture*.
- "'All yours,' said the mustachioed guard smoothly; he had definitely not been the oaf that Tunk chewed out about dropping pieces of kitsch in the corridor." Dafydd ab Hugh, *Balance of Power (Star Trek: The Next Generation)*, 1995.

klatsch, klatch *n.*

See <u>kaffeeklatsch</u>.

kletterschuh, klett *n.* [*pl.* **kletterschuhe, kletterschuhs**]

from *Kletterschuh* "climbing shoe": a lightweight climbing boot [< German *klettern* "to climb" + *Schuh* "shoe"]. This entry suggested by Claus Günkel.

- "Relying on pitons hand forged by Yvon Chouinard in the Camp 4 parking lot and Austrian kletterschuhs, Bridwell and his cohorts practiced a ground-up ethic that outlawed previewing, hang-dogging, or resting on gear." Peter Potterfield, *Over the Top: Humorous Mountaineering Tales*, 2002, p. 91.
- "Yet I continued to hesitate short of the real plunge—learning to climb with rope and piton and carabiner and the tight-fitting special footgear called *kletterschuhe*." David Roberts, *True Summit: What Really Happened on the Legendary Ascent on Annapurna*, 2002, p. 39.
- "I did not possess a rope of my own, but a pair of *kletterschuhe* or proper climbing shoes were my pride and joy." Anderl Heckmair, *My Life: Eiger North Face, Grand Jorasses, & Other Adventures*, 2002, p. 18.

klieg *n.*
See klieg light.

Klieg eye, Klieg's eye *n.*
a condition marked by conjunctivitis, edema of the eyelids, tearing, and photophobia due to exposure to intense lights (Klieg lights), cinema eye.

klieg light, klieg lamp, klieg *n.*
an intense light used in producing motion pictures, the center of public attention [< brothers John H. Kliegl (1869-1959) & Anton Tiberius Kliegl (1872-1927), German-born American lighting experts. The last letter *l* of their name apparently became fused with the word *light* in the term *klieg light*.].
- "The idea was he would take her in September to Hollywood and arrange a tryout for her, a bit part in the tennis-match scene of a motion picture based on a play of his—*Golden Guts*—and perhaps even have her double one of its sensational starlets on the Klieg-struck tennis court." Vladimir Nabokov, *Lolita*, 1989, p. 276.
- "Klieg lights were turned on for the newsreel cameras." David McCullough, *Truman*, 1993, p. 262.
- "I sat on the chair's edge in a soaking sweat, as though each of my 1,369 bulbs had every one become a klieg light in an individual setting for a third degree with Ras and Rinehart in charge." Ralph Ellison, *Invisible Man*, 1995, p. 13.
- "And even if he were as good as Tiger, he couldn't/wouldn't handle the klieg lights pouring on his face at all times." Rick Reilly, *Who's Your Caddy?: Looping for the Great, Near Great, and Reprobates of Golf*, 2003, p. 121.
- "He looked around at the photographers, the crowd, the dazzling kliegs, the long black limousines at the curb, and she could see that it excited him." Michael Chabon, *The Amazing Adventures of Kavalier & Clay*, 2001, p. 357.
- "The combination of Magellan's rapidly increasing size and fame's klieg light took its inevitable toll." William J. Bernstein, *The Four Pillars of Investing: Lessons for Building a Winning Portfolio*, 2002, p. 92.
- "Bosch felt his skin go hot, as if klieg lights had been turned on him, and that everyone in the courtroom was staring at him." Michael Connelly, *The Harry Bosch Novels: The Black Echo, The Black Ice, The Concrete Blonde*, 2001, p. 602.

Klieg's eye *n.*
See Klieg eye.

knackwurst, knockwurst *n.*

from *Knackwurst* "knackwurst": a short, thick sausage [< German *knacken* "to crack or crackle" + *Wurst* "sausage"]. See also wurst.

- "But on an older guy, gloominess looks like indigestion. People think you had too much knockwurst for lunch." Garrison Keillor, *Wobegon Boy*, 1997, p. 44.

- "4 fully cooked knockwurst or other mild-flavored sausage", Carla Waldemar, recipe for "Sauerkraut and Sausage Rolls", "Comforts from the kitchen", *Better Homes & Gardens*, Feb. 1996.

- "I had been preparing for publication, a directory, and in the progress of the work, called upon an honest German up Walnut street, who was extensively engaged in the manufacture of bratwurst, knackwurst, leber wurst, and sourkrout." Charles Cist, *Sketches and statistics of Cincinnati in 1851*, 1851, p. iv.

- "The food at Cole's is what in some cities is referred to as hofbrau-style. You take a tray, and push it down a rail, ordering items like knockwurst and beans, beef stew, kielbasa, macaroni and cheese, and turkey drumsticks from the people, behind the steam tables." Merrill Shindler, "History in the Tasting (Los Angeles restaurants)", *Los Angeles Business Journal*, Nov. 6, 2000.

- "He had epicanthic folds around his eyes, and thin lips the color of spoiled knockwurst." Amy Sterling Casil, "Chromosome Circus", *Fantasy & Science Fiction*, Jan. 2000.

kobold *n.*

from *Kobold*: a sprite, spirit, brownie or gnome [German *Kobold* < Middle High German *kóbolt, kobólt* "house spirit"]. See also nickel, quartz.

- "The Rooms were cold, the Hearth was grey:/Asleep in the ashes the Kobold lay./The Board-Floor creaked,/The Grey-Mouse squeaked,/And the Kobold dreamed its ear he tweaked." Howard & Katharine Pyle, *The Wonder Clock: Or Four and Twenty Marvelous Tales*, 1887, p. 28.

- "These oppressed yet dreaded fugitives obtained, naturally enough, the character of the German spirits called Kobold, from which the English goblin and the Scottish bogle, by some inversion and alteration of pronunciation, are evidently derived." Sir Walter Scott, *Letters on Demonology and Witchcraft*, 1884, p. 103. Goblin does indeed come from Middle High German *kobold* by way of Middle English and Middle French *gobelin*.

- "There was but one picture -- a magazine color-plate of a steep-roofed village in the Harz Mountains which suggested kobolds and maidens with golden hair." Sinclair Lewis, *Main Street*, 1920, p. 117.

- "Oh, no, cried the host, quite humbly, I will gladly produce everything, only make the accursed kobold creep back into the sack." Jacob & Wilhelm Grimm, *Grimm's Fairy Tales*.

- "May it not be a hint that the traditions are akin, of elfin and kobold races in Europe, and monkeys, actually cognate with them in Hindustan?" Helene Petrovna Blavatsky, *Isis Unveiled: A Master-Key to the Mysteries of Ancient and Modern Science and Theology*, p. 563.

- "The king had seen all kind of gnomes, goblins, and kobolds at his coronation; but they were quite rectilinear figures, compared with the insane lawlessness of form in which the Shadows rejoiced; and the wildest gambols of the former, were orderly dances of ceremony, beside the apparently aimless and wilful contortions of figure, and metamorphoses of shape, in which the latter indulged." George MacDonald, *Adela Cathcart*, 1864.

kohlrabi *n.* [*pl.* **kohlrabies**]

from *Kohlrabi:* a kind of cabbage with an edible, bulbous stem that looks somewhat like a turnip [< Italian *cavolo rapa* "cole rape" < Latin *caulis* "cabbage" + *rapa* "turnip"].

Kommandant *n.*

"commander".

- *Death Dealer: The Memoirs of the SS Kommandant at Auschwitz*, by Rudolf Hoss et al., 1996.

Konzertmeister, Konzert-Meister, Concertmeister, Concert-Meister *n.*

from *Konzertmeister* "concertmaster": leader of the first violins in a symphony orchestra, usually assistant to the conductor [< German *Konzert* < Italian *concerto* "concert, agreement, contract" < *concertare* "make an agreement or contract" + Meister, see -meister].

- "The Konzert-Meister bows to his friend in the third row, as he tucks his violin under his chin." Edna Ferber, *Fanny Herself*, 1917, p. 279.
- "His Concert-Meistership/Was first again." Amy Lowell, *Men, Women and Ghosts*.

kraut *n.*

from *Kraut* "cabbage": sauerkraut.

kraut, Kraut *n.*

from *Kraut* "cabbage": a usually disparaging name used for Germans during World War II [< Old High German *krut*].

- "... the onions and green peppers diced for the breakfast omelets, the electric dicer working like a gem (those crafty Krauts), the Costa Rican coffee freshly dripped ..." Garrison Keillor, "Winthrop Thorpe Tortuga", *The Book of Guys*, 1993.

Krieg *n.*

"war" [German *Krieg* "war" < Middle High German *kriec* "exertion, effort, endeavor, trouble, pains, struggle, strain, competition, quarrel, dispute, fight, combat, (armed) conflict, war" < Old High German *chreg* "doggedness, pertinacity, stubbornness, obstinacy"].

kriegspiel, Kriegspiel, kriegsspiel, Kriegsspiel *n., v.i.*

from *Kriegsspiel* "war game": chiefly British, a game for teaching or practicing military tactics using small figures representing troops, tanks, ships, etc. moved around a large map of the terrain; a form of chess with an umpire, in which each player has only limited information about the opponent's moves [< German *Krieg* "war" + *Spiel* "game"]. This entry suggested by Christiane Leißner.

- "We then proceeded to Kriegspiel, according to the mysterious ideas of those in authority over us." H. G. Wells, *The World Set Free*, 1914, p. 69.

krimmer, crimmer *n.*

from *Krimmer* "Crimean": the lambskin of the karakul sheep from the Crimean region in central Asia, dressed as a fur [< German *Krim* "Crimea"]. This entry suggested by Christiane Leißner.

Kristallnacht *n.*

"night of (broken) glass": the night of Nov. 9, 1938, on which the Nazis coordinated an attack on Jews and their property in Germany and German-controlled lands, referring to the broken glass resulting from the destruction [< German *Kristall* "crystal" < Middle High German *cristalla* < Old High German *cristalle* < Middle Latin *(pl.) crystalla* < Latin *crystallus* < Greek *krýstallos* "ice, mountain crystal" < *krýos* "icy coldness, frost" + *Nacht* "night" < Middle High German *naht* < Old High German *naht* "night"].

- "I mean to say, when the Storm Troopers burned down forty-two of Vienna's forty-three synagogues during Kristallnacht, Waldheim did wait a whole week before joining the unit." Bill Bryson, *Neither Here Nor There: Travels in Europe*, 1991, p. 264.

- "Three years later came the Kristallnacht, on 9 November 1938, when the Nazis went on a rampage against Jewish property and desecrated synagogues in Austria and Germany." Hella Pick, *Simon Wiesenthal: A Life in Search of Justice*, 1996.

krone, kr., K., k., kn. *n.* [*pl.* **kronen**]

from *Krone* "crown": a former German gold coin; the former monetary unit or a silver coin of Austria [< Latin *corona* "crown"].

krummholz *n.*

"crooked wood": stunted forest characteristic of timberline.

- "As we emerged from a zone of krummholz, the stunted trees that mark the last gasp of forest at treeline, and stepped onto the barren roof of Little Haystack we were met by a stiff, sudden wind—the kind that would snatch a hat from your head and fling it a hundred yards before you could raise a hand—which the mountain had deflected over us on the sheltered western slopes but which here was flying unopposed across the summit." Bill Bryson, *A Walk in the Woods*, 1997.

kuchen *n.* [*pl.* **kuchen**]

from *Kuchen* "cake": a kind of German coffeecake [Old High German *kuocho*]. See also <u>lebkuchen</u>.

kultur, Kultur, *Kultur n.*

from *Kultur* "culture": civilization; social organization; culture emphasizing practical efficiency and individual subordination to the state; the highly systematized German culture held to be superior especially by militant Hohenzollern and <u>Nazi</u> expansionists; often used ironically or in a derogatory sense when referring to imperialism, racism, chauvinism, authoritarianism, militarism, terrorism, etc. [< Latin *cultur(a)* "cultivation, care"].

- "Poison gas was one of the first fruits of Kultur." "Boys and Girls Can Help", *The Review Messenger*, Sebeka and Menahga, MN, Jul. 29, 1998, p. B-22, reprinted from Sep. 20, 1918.

- "These were the native guides impressed into the service of Kultur and upon their poor, bruised bodies Kultur's brand was revealed in divers cruel wounds and bruises." Edgar Rice Burroughs, *Tarzan the Untamed*, 1920.
- "Blood hatred of everything German had infected all of Europe and spread to America, where Hollywood produced a string of hate films such as *To Hell with the Kaiser*, *Wolves of Kultur*, and *The Kaiser: The Beast of Berlin*." Kitty Kelley, *The Royals*.

Kulturkampf, Kulturkampf *n.*

"culture battle": the struggle between the Roman Catholic Church and the German government from 1873 to 1887.

- "But even the latest national crisis—over tax reform—was put aside for this summer's great *Kulturkampf*: should *die Flussschifffahrt* (river navigation) be spelled with three *s*'s and *f*'s, or two?" Christopher Ogden, "A War of German Words", *Time*, Sep. 29, 1997.

kümmel *n.*

from *Kümmel* "cumin": a liqueur flavored with cumin, caraway, anise, etc. [Old High German *kumil, kumin*; Latin *cuminum* "cumin"].

Künstlerroman *n.*

"artist novel": a *Bildungsroman* in which the protagonist becomes an artist, musician or poet.

Kursaal, kursaal *n.*

from *Kursaal* "cure hall": a public hall or room for the use of visitors at health resorts or spas in German-speaking countries, a casino [< German *Kur* "cure, (course of) treatment, (medical) care" < Latin *cura* + *Saal* "hall, large room" < Middle and Old High German *sal* "hall, building, temple, church" < Germanic **salaz, *saliz* "one-room house", related to English *salon, saloon*]. This entry suggested by Christiane Leißner.

- "Just before the revolution of 1848, nearly all the watering-places in the Prusso-Rhenane provinces, and in Bavaria, and Hesse, Nassau, and Baden, contained Kursaals, where gambling was openly carried on." Andrew Steinmetz, *The Gaming Table: Its Votaries and Victims, In All Times and Countries, especially in England and in France*, 1870, p. 139. A watering place is (was) a health resort or spa. *Kursaal* is used 23 times in this book.
- "Having brought it to a close, he took his way to the Kursaal. The great German watering-place is one of the prettiest nooks in Europe, and of a summer evening in the gaming days, five-and-twenty years ago, it was one of the most brilliant scenes." Henry James, *Confidence*, p. 1056.
- "Down the road a piece was a Kursaal, – whatever that may be, – and we joined the human tide to see what sort of enjoyment it might afford." Mark Twain, *A Tramp Abroad*, 1879, p. 355.
- "'Yes, said Jill. I heard someone talking about it when I was dining with the Bedells. It sounded priceless. I had a sort of idea it was quite small, and had a prince, but it's really quite big, and it's got a king over it, and they all wear the old picturesque dress, and the scenery's gorgeous. And, if it was wet, we could go to the- the- ' 'Kursaal,' said Berry. 'No, not Kursaal. It's like that, though.' 'Casino?' 'That's it- Casino. And then we could go on to Nice and Cannes, and- '" Dornford Yates, *The Brother of Daphne*.

- "Warrington walked by Mrs. Pendennis's donkey, when that lady went out on her evening excursions; or took carriages for her; or got 'Galignani' for her; or devised comfortable seats under the lime-trees for her, when the guests paraded after dinner, and the Kursaal band at the bath, where our tired friends stopped, performed their pleasant music under the trees." Robert Burns, *The Complete Works of Robert Burns*, 1859, p. 181.
- "Remounting after a time, we sped forward, and sighted in front a dark line, but partially lit up about the flanks, with a brilliant illumination in the centre, the Kursaal of Mr. Hopkins, the local Crockford." Sir Richard Francis Burton, *The City of the Saints: And, Across the Rocky Mountains to California*, 1862, p. 496.

kvell *v.i.*

related to *quellen* "to spring, gush, well (up), swell (up)": to be extraordinarily pleased or proud, rejoice [< Yiddish *kveln* "to be delighted" < Middle High German *quellen* "to well, gush, swell" < Middle High German *quellan*].
- "For one thing, they give parents a chance to *kvell*—to bask in their children's happiness." Anita Diamant, *The New Jewish Wedding, Revised*, 2001, p. 111.
- "... they even poke some friends across the aisle, a couple from Mount Vernon they've just met (the Perls, Sylvia and Bernie), and these two *kvell* also to see a tall, goodlooking, young Jewish lawyer (and single! a match for somebody's daughter!) suddenly begin to weep upon making contact with a Jewish airstrip." Philip Roth, *Portnoy's Complaint*, 1994, p. 244.
- "Mark Rydell (very pre-*On Golden Pond*) kvells all the way through lunch: she walks, she talks, she spins great tales." Julia Phillips, *You'll Never Eat Lunch in This Town Again*, 2002, p. 90.
- "She could have said she bought canned tuna on sale at D'Agostino's and her mother would kvell for hours about what a smart girl Sara was." Caroline Leavitt, *Girls in Trouble*, 2003, p. 186.
- "And my proud mom stood on the sidelines and kvelled." Connie Glaser, *What Queen Esther Knew: Business Strategies from a Biblical Sage*, 2003, p. 223.
- "It was a discreet affair held in the pod clubhouse, where Carol *kvelled* as though she were the mother, not the daughter-in-law, of the bride." Paula Marantz Cohen, *Jane Austen in Boca: A Novel*, 2003, p. 257.
- "Listen to me. I'm *kvelling* about a parakeet." F. Paul Wilson, *All the Rage (Repairman Jack Novels)*, 2001, p. 56.

L

lager beer, lager-beer, lager *n.*

from *Lagerbier* "storehouse or stored beer": a beer which is aged for several months after it has been brewed. See further example under stein.

- "'Now this will be very nice,' he promised and poured me a glass of what turned out to be very warm lager." Bill Bryson, *Neither Here Nor There: Travels in Europe*, 1991, p. 18.
- "The old man munched his sandwich, drank his lager, and watched pretty girls, with a smile of innocent pleasure." Robert A. Heinlein, *Citizen of the Galaxy*, 1982, p. 252.
- "Give an Irishman lager for a month, and he's a dead man. An Irishman is lined with copper, and the beer corrodes it. But whiskey polishes the copper and is the saving of him, sir." Mark Twain, *Life on the Mississippi*.
- "Should he say that the State Constable was enforcing the liquor law on whiskey, but was winking at lager?" Edward Everett Hale, *The Brick Moon and Other Stories*, 1899.
- "The popular notion that lager-beer, ale, wine, or alcohol in any other form, is in any degree necessary or beneficial to a nursing woman, is a great error, which cannot be too often noticed and condemned." John Harvey Kellogg, *Plain Facts for Old and Young: Natural History and Hygiene of Organic Life*, 1877.
- "He catapulted balls of fire across the room that Godzilla would be proud of, but this was not enough to win him first prize since the judgement is made on the quality of flames and the singing, and after fifteen bottles of lager he was badly out of tune." Wendy Northcutt, *The Darwin Awards*, 2000, p. 126.
- "Blackwell hadn't said two words to anybody, drinking lager instead of sake and packing his food away as though he were trying to plug something, some gap in security that could be taken care of if you stuffed it methodically with enough sashimi." William Gibson, *Idoru*, 1997, p. 248.

lammergeier, lammergeyer, lammergeir *n.*

from *Lämmergeier* "lamb vulture": another name for the Bearded Vulture (*Gypaëtus barbatus*), nowadays called *Bartgeier* in German.

- "Lammergeyer of the Alps." Caption of an engraving by Chas. Parsons depicting a man fending off an attacking vulture with a stick. Jacob Abbott, *Aboriginal America*, 1860.
- "Lammergeier *Gypaetus barbatus* in Caucasia", A. Abuladze, in *Journal für Ornithologie 1994, Sonderheft: Research Notes on Avian Biology 1994*. As cited in Aubrecht et al., *Avian Conservation Problems in Central and Eastern Europe and Northern Asia*, BirdLife Austria, Vienna, 1997, p. 8.
- "This bird; u catch eny distinguishin marx on it? It woz a lammergeier, thas oll I no, but ther cant b oll that meny ov them aroun thi norf-west cornir of thi grate hol ½ a our ago. Lammergeiers r a bit funy theez days, but Il ask aroun." Iain M. Banks, *Feersum Endjinn*, 1994, p. 58. This quote suggested by dnh.

lampenflora *n.*

from Lampenflora "lamp flora": algae and mosses which dwell within the artificial lighting of caves that have been opened to the public. This entry suggested by Kristian Koehntopp.

- "Biologically, a common effect is the proliferation of algae and mosses (collectively, termed 'lampenflora') near the light sources." G. Huppert, E. Burri, P. Forti & A. Cigna, "Effects of Tourist Development on Caves and

Karst", *Cave Conservationist: The Newsletter of Cave Conservation and Management*, Jul. 15, 1994.

landau, landaulet, landaulette *n.*

from *Landau*: a type of carriage or automobile, named for Landau, Germany.

- "Away they went, and I was just wondering whether I should not do well to follow them when up the lane came a neat little landau, the coachman with his coat only half-buttoned, and his tie under his ear, while all the tags of his harness were sticking out of the buckles." Arthur Conan Doyle, *A Scandal in Bohemia: Stories from the Adventures of Sherlock Holmes*, 1891.

- "She had something to suffer perhaps when they came into contact again, in seeing Anne restored to the rights of seniority, and the mistress of a very pretty landaulette; but she had a future to look forward to, of powerful consolation." Jane Austen, *Persuasion*, 1818.

- "It was a landaulet, with a servant mounted on the dickey." Washington Irving, *Tales of a Traveller*.

Ländler, ländler, landler, Landler *n.*

"of or from Landl": a slow folk dance in 3/4 time, considered to be the predecessor of the <u>waltz</u>, named for Landl, Austria; the music for this dance [< dim. of *Land* "land, country"].

- "Joseph's cousin, Walpurga Moser, to an orchestra of clarionet and zither, taught the family the country dances, the Steierisch and the Ländler, and gained their hearts during the lessons." Robert Louis Stevenson, *Memoir of Fleeming Jenkin*.

- "Ländler for Piano", *Schroeder's Greatest Hits*, composed by Ludwig van Beethoven, Wolfgang Amadeus Mozart, et al., 1992.

landsknecht *n.*

from *Landsknecht* "servant or soldier of the country or land": a European mercenary foot soldier of the 16th century, armed with a pike or halberd.

- "One Sunday as [Martin] Luther was going out of church he was accosted by a landsknecht, who complained of being constantly tempted of the devil, and told how he often came to him, and threatened to bear him away." M. Michelet, *The life of Martin Luther, gathered from his own writings*, 1858, p. 225.

- "The drill and discipline of these unwieldy landsknecht regiments, which often swelled up from 4,000 to 10,000 men, were suited to the battle-fields of those days." J. G. Heck, *Icenographic encyclopaedia of science, literature & art*, 1860, p. 43.

- "LANSQUENET.[91]
  Lansquenet is much played by the Americans, and is one of the most exciting games in vogue.
  Note: [91] This name is derived from the German 'landsknecht' ('valet of the fief'), applied to a mercenary soldier." Andrew Steinmetz, *Gaming Table: Its Votaries and Victims in All Times and Countries Especially in England and in France*, 1870, p. 242.

Landsturm *n.*

"land storm": in Germany and other countries, a general levy in time of war of men under sixty not already in the armed services or in the reserve.

68

Landtag *n.*

"land day": the legislative assembly of a German state.

- "At this time the future maker of the German Empire rose in the Landtag and made his bow before the world; a young Prussian land-magnate, Otto von Bismarck by name, he shook his fist in the face of the new German liberalism, and incidentally of the new German infidelity:" Upton Sinclair, *The Profits of Religion: An Essay in Economic Interpretation*, 1918.

- "The Landtag, exasperated at his high-handed methods, refused to give him the necessary credits." Hendrik Willem Van Loon, *The Story of Mankind*, 1921.

Landwehr *n.*

"land defense": in Germany and other countries, the military reserve of trained men. See also <u>Wehrmacht</u>.

langlauf, langlauf *n.*

from *Langlauf* "long run": a cross-country ski run.

langläufer, langläufer *n.*

from *Langläufer* "long runner": a participant in a cross-country ski run.

lautverschiebung *n.* [*pl.* **lautverschiebungen**]

from *Lautverschiebung* "sound shift": (linguistics) sound shifting [< German *Laut* "sound" + *Verschiebung* "shift"]. This entry suggested by Marek Roth.

- "Grimm was the first to discover a regular system of displacement of sounds (*lautverschiebung*) pervading the Gothic and Low German languages as compared with Greek and Latin." William Smith, *Dr. William Smith's dictionary of the Bible*, 1868-70, p. 3291.

- "Until a rational account of these changes, comprehended under the name of *Lautverschiebung*, is given, we must continue to look upon them, not as the result of phonetic decay, but of dialectic growth." Max Müller, *Chips from a German workshop*, 1871-1881, p. 101.

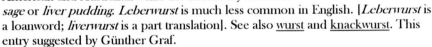

leberwurst, liverwurst, leber wurst *n.*

from *Leberwurst* "liver sausage": a usually spreadable sausage containing liver. Apparently *liverwurst* is chiefly American and Australian while the British say *liver sausage* or *liver pudding*. *Leberwurst* is much less common in English. [*Leberwurst* is a loanword; *liverwurst* is a part translation]. See also <u>wurst</u> and <u>knackwurst</u>. This entry suggested by Günther Graf.

- "Some liverwurst so old and gray/One smelled it from a mile away...." Roald Dahl, *Charlie and the Chocolate Factory*, 1998, p. 117.

- "She sliced an onion and set it out with liverwurst and mustard and a long reddish herring that looked like a person's tongue. Art fixed himself a liverwurst-onion-herring sandwich that made Diana blanch." Garrison Keillor, *Wobegon Boy*, 1997, p. 193.

- "The beer flowed in rivers, and yet the people were always thirsty (the consummation most devoutly wished), or, if not thirsty, huge slices of *leberwurst* soon made them so." W. W. Wright, *Doré. By a stroller in Europe*, 1857, p. 248.

- "The women, health-conscious, ate a sandwich with curd cheese, I had a sandwich with liverwurst." Gert Hofmann, *The Film Explainer*, 1996.

- Walter Matthau as Hamilton Bartholomew: "I've got liverwurst, liverwurst, chicken and liverwurst."
  Audrey Hepburn as Regina Lampert: "No, thank you."
  ...
  Audrey Hepburn: "May I have a sandwich, please?"
  Walter Matthau: "Chicken or liverwurst?"
  Charade, directed by Stanley Donen, 1963.
- "The liverwurst solution", Robert B. Reich, *American Prospect*, Jun. 11, 2000, p. 56.

Lebensraum, *Lebensraum* n.

"living space": living space; territory for political and economic expansion: term of German imperialism.

- "But here they are/With everything they could have wanted:/Beaucoup de Lebensraum/A steamy potpourri of plants." John M. Burns, "Drosophila in Paradise" *BioGraffiti: A Natural Selection*, 1981, p. 67.

lebkuchen, Lebkuchen n.

from *Lebkuchen* "lebkuchen": a Christmas cookie flavored with honey and spices, very similar to gingerbread, also called *Pfefferkuchen* or *brauner Kuchen* in parts of Germany. *Lebkuchen* is used in southern and western Germany and Austria [< Middle High German *lebkuoche, lebekuoche* < perhaps Middle High German *leip*, related to English *loaf* + *kuoche* "cake"]. See further example under <u>gemutlich</u>. See also <u>kuchen</u>.

- "In a series of 65 passion sermons, he elaborated a comparison between Christ and a ginger cake—the German *Lebkuchen*." Philip Schaff, *History of the Christian Church*.
- "Some cookies are so strongly identified with a particular country–German lebkuchen, for example--they're as national as a flag." "Cookies, Spice, and Everything Nice", *Better Homes and Gardens*, Nov. 1999.
- "Classic almond recipes include trout amandine (which means 'with almonds'), marzipan, and German lebkuchen." "Nuts to you", *Better Homes and Gardens*, Feb. 1997.
- "Also bake lebkuchen, pfeffernusse, or other cookies that need a few weeks to soften." Janet Bailey, "30 days to a perfect Christmas", *Ladies' Home Journal*, Dec. 1997.
- "Certainly some of the things the Trapp family does at Christmas are not entirely suited to the Heath family. I know. I know. And some—give me that much—I didn't even try. Like baking the traditional Spekulatius on December 6 (St. Nicholas's Day), for instance; or the traditional Kletzenbrot on December 21 (St. Thomas's Day); or even the traditional Lebzelten, Lebkuchen, Spanish Wind, Marzipan, Rum Balls, Nut Busserln, Coconut Busserln, Stangerln, Pfeffernusse, and Plain Cookies on December 23." Aloise Buckley Heath, "A Trapp Family Christmas: An NR tradition", *National Review*, Dec. 31, 2000.

lederhosen, *Lederhosen n.pl.*

from *Lederhosen* "leather trousers": knee-length leather trousers worn especially in Bavaria and Austria. In contrast to English the singular *Lederhose* in German is one pair of leather trousers while the plural *Lederhosen* is more than one pair. See further example under dirndl.

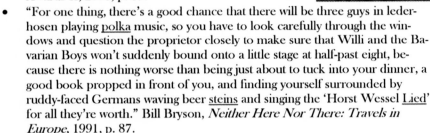

- "General: Who's not on our side yet?
  Captain: Umm ... Switzerland?
  General: Great. We'll kick their little lederhosen butts!" Scott Adams, *The Dilbert Future: Thriving on Business Stupidity in the 21st Century*, 2000, p. 200.
- "After bitter legal proceedings, Uwe of Brandenburg found that he had lost everything but his lederhosen knickerbockers." Wendy Northcutt, *The Darwin Awards II*, 2001, p. 19.
- "For one thing, there's a good chance that there will be three guys in lederhosen playing polka music, so you have to look carefully through the windows and question the proprietor closely to make sure that Willi and the Bavarian Boys won't suddenly bound onto a little stage at half-past eight, because there is nothing worse than being just about to tuck into your dinner, a good book propped in front of you, and finding yourself surrounded by ruddy-faced Germans waving beer steins and singing the 'Horst Wessel Lied' for all they're worth." Bill Bryson, *Neither Here Nor There: Travels in Europe*, 1991, p. 87.
- "In Mariazell, too, I bought *Lederhosen*—Austrian leather shorts—suspenders, and knee socks." George W. Long, "Occupied Austria, Outpost of Democracy", *National Geographic*, Jun. 1951, p. 775.
- "In his locker downstairs he [the tuba player] keeps a pair of lederhosen for freelance jobs." Garrison Keillor, "The Young Lutheran's Guide to the Orchestra", *Lake Wobegon Loyalty Days*, Emd/Angel, 1989.
- "THAT ATTENDANT WAS WEARING LEDERHOSEN", Jim Davis, *Garfield* cartoon.

leitmotiv, leitmotif *n.*

from *Leitmotiv* "leading theme": a clearly defined musical or literary theme.

- "All the early sagas rest on that idea, which continues to be the *Leitmotiv* of the biblical tales dealing with the relation of man to God, to the State, to society." Emma Goldman, *Anarchism and Other Essays*.
- "In Martin Luther's Christmas hymn 'Vom Himmel hoch da komm' ich her [From heaven above to earth I come],' which was to become the leitmotiv in each successive cantata of Johann Sebastian Bach's Christmas Oratorio of 1734-35, another angel was presented as saying, to the shepherds of Bethlehem and through them to all the world, 'Euch its ein Kindlein heut' geborn,/Von einer Jungfrau auserkoren [To you this day is born a Child, from an elect Virgin].'" Jaroslav Pelikan, *Mary Through the Centuries: Her Place in the History of Culture*, 1998.
- "One theme had recurred so frequently in these conversations that it had become the leitmotif of the trip: 'Please, don't think of us as Russians. We are not Russians. We are Estonians [or Latvians or Lithuanians, depending

on the location].'" Jack F. Matlock, Jr., *Autopsy on an Empire: The American Ambassador's Account of the Collapse of the Soviet Union*, 1995.

- "Duchamp introduces these two elements in a note, entitled Preface, that would become a leitmotif in his life and work: Given 1st the waterfall/2nd the lighting gas ..." Calvin Tomkins, *Duchamp: A Biography*, 1998.
- "The word 'power' runs like a leitmotif through other descriptions of Theodore Senior: he was a person of inexorable drive." Edmund Morris, *The Rise of Theodore Roosevelt*, 2001.
- "I suspect it is a whimsical leitmotif she sees, hydrangeas, ponds, rivers suspended idly in fat and fiber, floating serenely." Spencer Nadler, *The Language of Cells: Life As Seen Under the Microscope*, 2001.

lied, *lied,* Lied, *Lied* n. [*pl.* lieder, *lieder,* Lieder, *Lieder*]

from *Lied* "song": a German lyric or song; the major song form in the 19th and 20th centuries, developed in Austria and Germany. See further example under *lederhosen.*

- "Instead, Schumann-Heink sang her *lieder* for them; McCutcheon talked and cartooned for them; Madame Bloomfield-Zeisler played." Edna Ferber, *Fanny Herself,* 1917.
- "If you learn a great many of the *Lieder,* you will know the German language already." Willa Cather, *The Song of the Lark.*
- "That he could play pieces, and difficult pieces, I knew well, because at my request he has played me some of Mendelssohn's Lieder, and other favourites." Arthur Conan Doyle, *A Study in Scarlet,* 1887.

Liederkranz, liederkranz *n.*

"garland of songs": a collection or group of songs; a men's singing society; a soft cheese similar to but milder than Limburger, produced in New York State in 1892: a trademark [< *Lieder* pl. of *Lied* "song" + *Kranz* "wreath, garland"].

- "The Lansing Liederkranz Club, a German-American singing and fellowship society, was founded in 1868." Tim Martin, "German influence strong here", *Lansing State Journal,* Jun. 9, 2002.

loden, *Loden* n.

from *Loden:* a coarse woolen cloth; a coat made of loden; the color of loden.

- "Flannel-like material called *Loden* is trimmed in green; buttons are made from antlers." George W. Long, "Occupied Austria, Outpost of Democracy", *National Geographic,* Jun. 1951, p. 780.

liverwurst *n.*

See leberwurst.

loess *n.*

from *Löß:* a loam deposit resulting from materials finer than sand deposited by the wind [< *lösen* "to loosen, dissolve"].

- "We have evidence in the loess of the Rhine of considerable changes of level in the land within a very recent geological period, and when the surface was peopled by existing land and fresh-water shells." Charles Darwin, *On the Origin of Species by Means of Natural Selection, or the Preservation of Favoured Races in the Struggle for Life,* 1859.

72

- "These dirt-cliffs, or 'loess,' to give them their scientific name, are remarkable banks of brownish-yellow loam, found largely in Northern and Western China, and rising sometimes to a height of a thousand feet." Elbridge Streeter Brooks, *Historic girls; stories of girls who have influenced the history of their times*, 1891.

LSD, LSD-25 *n.*

from *LSD*: a drug that produces states similar to those of schizophrenia, used in medicine and illicitly as a strong hallucinogen [abbr. of *Lysergsäure-Diäthylamid*, not of *lysergic acid diethylamide*, as some dictionaries will have one believe]. This entry suggested by Olaf.

- "A respected Princeton mathematician gets turned on to LSD, takes a several-year sabbatical in the caves of the Himalayas during which he trips his brains out, then returns to the university and dedicates himself to finding equations to map the shapes in his psychedelic visions." Douglas Rushkoff, *Cyberia: Life in the Trenches of Hyperspace*, 1994.

luftmensch, Luftmensch *n.* [*pl.* luftmenschen]

related to *luft* "air" + *mensch* "person": an impractical contemplative person having no definite business or income [< Yiddish *luftmentsch* < *luft* "air" < German *Luft* "air" + *mentsch* "person" < German *Mensch* "person"]. See also Luftwaffe, mensch.

- "Both babas structured their practice as radically disjunctive from the material world through their literal embodiment as luftmenschen." p. 280, "For most old men with access to the rhetorical possibilities of *Sannyasa*, even a partial relocation of their identity from home to interstice was insufficient to transform their relations with family and neighbors from the pathetic request of the old grandfather to the inviolate liminality of the luftmensch." p. 284, Lawrence Cohen, *No Aging in India: Alzheimer's, the Bad Family, and Other Modern Things*, 1998.
- "He is a Luftmensch, a lost soul as adrift as Le Carre's similarly abandoned George Smiley ...." Nicholas Fraser, "Darkness visible: the intrigues of Alan Furst", *Harper's Magazine*, Jul. 2003.
- "Despite Florence Rubenfeld's 1997 biography of [Clement] Greenberg, the story of how this inveterate luftmensch found his way to art criticism and why he was so well prepared for it has been told only sketchily." Raphael Rubinstein, "*The Harold Letters 1928-1943: The Making of an American Intellectual* - Review", *Art in America*, Dec. 2000.
- "[Gene] McCarthy was a charming guy, but a Luftmensch: In the Senate he had been one of LBJ's pocket votes, had planned to nominate Johnson against Kennedy at Los Angeles in 1960, was raised by Hubert Humphrey in the Minnesota Democratic–Farm Labor Party, and resigned from the national board of ADA in 1960 when we endorsed Jack Kennedy!" John P. Roche, "Indochina revisited; the demise of liberal internationalism", *National Review*, May 3, 1985.
- "Sweetness, innocence, violin music and intelligence mingled in his personality. He [Danny Pearl] had something of the luftmensch, the Jewish prince. He did his best thinking, he told his friend Karen Edwards, after he had dropped out of journalism for a while to work at a convenience store in Sun Valley, Idaho, and sat at the counter, bored and lost in thought." Philip

Weiss, "Merrily, He Rolled: Pearl Was Exuberant, Deeply Cultured", *The New York Observer*, Mar. 4, 2002.

- "If it [the Holocaust] ends the possibility of the Jewish luftmensch, living outside of history, it gives us a people returned to land, to power, and the body, faced with the dilemma of balancing survival with the need to be faithful to a reality larger than the self." Judith Plaskow, "The Spirit of Renewal: Crisis and Response in Jewish Life - book reviews", *Tikkun*, Jan.-Feb. 1993.

Luftwaffe, *Luftwaffe* n.

from *Luftwaffe* "air weapon, air force": the German air force. This entry suggested by Fritz Kuhnd. See also luftmensch.

- "Consecrated on the tenth of February in 1185 by Heraclius, Patriarch of Jerusalem, the Temple Church survived eight centuries of political turmoil, the Great Fire of London, and the First World War, only to be heavily damaged by Luftwaffe incendiary bombs in 1940." Dan Brown, *The Da Vinci Code*, 2003, p. 343.
- "Later, Hermann Goering invited him to see the newly-forming Luftwaffe in action." Eloise Engle & Lauri Paananen, *The Winter War: The Soviet Attack on Finland 1939-1940*, 1973, p. 59.
- "Although Britain did not have the air power (brute force) of Hitler's Luftwaffe, England had radar, giving it information." Peter McWilliams, *Ain't Nobody's Business If You Do: The Absurdity of Consensual Crimes in Our Free Country*, 1996.
- "General Loehr, a Luftwaffe officer, had been in command of the Fourth Air Force in Russia before receiving his new appointment as commander in the Balkans; he had also commanded the task force which captured Crete in May 1941." Robert M. Kennedy, *Hold the Balkans!: German Antiguerrilla Operations in the Balkans 1941-1944*, 2001.
- "We got most of the bombs the Luftwaffe hadn't had time to drop on London." Claire Bloom, *Leaving a Doll's House: A Memoir*, 1998.

Machtpolitik, machtpolitik *n.*

from *Machtpolitik* "power politics": international diplomacy in which each nation uses or threatens to use military or economic power to further its own interests. The English term *power politics* is a loan translation of *Machtpolitik*. *Machtpolitik* is sometimes used as a singular noun as it is in German and sometimes in the plural, as *power politics* is. [< German *Macht* "power, might" + *Politik* "politics, policy"]. See also Ostpolitik, *Realpolitik*, Wehrmacht, *Weltpolitik* and *Westpolitik*. This entry suggested by Christiane Leißner.

- "In fact, Nazi Germany was the indomitable enemy of the Western democracies, Soviet Russia was their indispensable ally, while the right of national self-determination was a weapon of Hitler's Machtpolitik only." Stephen Borsody, *The New Central Europe: Triumphs & Tragedies*, 1993.

- "But Machtpolitik, the rule of force, is cruel: with the Kahama out of the way, the Kasekelans' new neighbors were the powerful Kalande -- and now the ranks of the Kasekela started to thin." Mark Ridley, "Going Ape", review of *Demonic Males: Apes and the Origins of Human Violence* by Richard Wrangham & Dale Peterson, *The New York Times*, Oct. 27, 1996.
- "The apparent transformation of New York City Mayor Rudolph Giuliani from ruthless master of metropolitan machtpolitik into compassionate hybrid of Hamlet, the Duke of Windsor and Graham Greene raises a fascinating question. Can a person really, and I mean fundamentally, change?" Mark Leyner, "A Changed Man? No Such Animal", *Time*, Jun. 5, 2000.

mark, -mark *n.*

See deutsche mark, reichsmark.

masochism, masochist *n.*, **masochistic** *adj.*, **masochistically** *adv.*

from *Masochismus* "masochism": getting (sexual) pleasure from being dominated, mistreated or hurt, named for Leopold von Sacher-Masoch, 1835-1895, Austrian writer in whose stories it is described. This entry suggested by Wilton Woods.

- "(Heterosexual) sado-masochism is the enactment of surrender, and demand for such surrender, to sheer overwhelming might instead of the loving request and avid surrender to the power of (mutual) authority which is exercised for the mutual good of the partners." H. Vernon Sattler, *Challenging Children to Chastity: a Parental Guide*, 1991.
- "All other themes for action are, by virtue of their unintended air of masochism, unfit for the calculating citizenry." Adilkno (Foundation for the Advancement of Illegal Knowledge), *Media Archive*, 1998.
- "Late in the film, O burns an 'O' into Sir Stephen's hand, and Ted saw this as the completion of her development, sadism now accompanying masochism." Norman N. Holland, *The Critical I*, 1992, p. 20.
- "Masochism corresponds to the passivism of Stefanowski, and is the opposite of sadism, in which the pleasure is derived from inflicting pain on the object of affection." George Milbry Gould & Walter Lytle Pyle, *Anomalies and Curiosities of Medicine*, 1896, p. 480.
- "The thing itself, indeed, might be reasonably described as a special feminine character; there is in it, in more than one of its manifestations, a femaleness as palpable as the femaleness of cruelty, masochism or rouge." H. L. Mencken, *In Defense of Women*, 1920.
- "But economic masochism is a way of life, as American as Japanese VCRs." Christopher John Farley, *My Favorite War: A Novel*.
- "Beginning with childhood, Kinsey had lived with two shameful secrets: he was both a homosexual and a masochist." James Howard Jones, *Alfred C. Kinsey: A Public/Private Life*.

Mauser *n.*

from *Mauser* "Mauser": a trademark used for a repeating rifle or pistol, named for Peter Paul & Wilhelm Mauser, German weapons manufacturers [< German *Mauser* "mouser, mouse catcher" < Middle High German *mus* < Old High German *mus*].

- "Personal handguns such as Mauser pistols were borrowed from machine-gun companies and anit-panzer units." Eloise Engle & Lauri Paananen, *The Winter War: The Soviet Attack on Finland 1939-1940*, 1973, p. 111.

- "... the workers began to wreck their arms. They did it with practised hands, striking a Mauser with a Browning and a Browning with a Mauser." Leon Trotsky, *My Life*.
- "Across his chest he laid his Mauser rifle, lingering affectionately for a moment to wipe the dampness from the barrel." Jack London, *The House of Pride and Other Tales of Hawaii*.
- "When I can tell at sight a Mauser rifle from a javelin", Gilbert & Sullivan, *The Pirates of Penzance*.
- "I had brought out a shot-gun of my own, and I borrowed a cheap Mauser sporting rifle from the store." John Buchan, *Prester John*.
- "Sin Sin Wa, crooning his strange song, came in carrying a coil of rope--and a Mauser pistol!" Sax Rohmer, *Dope*.
- "And he has two Mauser holes in him." Richard Harding Davis, *Lion and the Unicorn*, 1899, p. 95.

meerschaum *n.*
from *Meerschaum* "sea foam": a light, heat-resisting, hydrous magnesium silicate, sepiolite.

Mein Herr *n.*
from *mein Herr* "Sir, My Lord": [< German *mein* "my" + *Herr* "lord, master, Mr."]. See also <u>Herrenvolk</u>.
- "Consider yourself under arrest, Mein Herr." Ian Fleming, *From Russia with Love: A James Bond Novel*, 2002, p. 162.

-meister *n. suffix*
"master" often slang or humorous, one who is renowned for, has expertise in, or is a connoisseur of, for example <u>angst</u>meister, cartelmeister, chatmeister, dietmeister, dramameister, grungemeister, mediameister, schlockmeister, shlockmeister, spinmeister, talkmeister, wordmeister [< German *Meister* < Middle High German *meister* < Old High German *meistar* < Latin *magister* "chairman, leader, teacher"]. See also <u>Kapellmeister</u>, <u>Konzertmeister</u>, <u>waldmeister</u>.
- "Thousands of Indians around and I get paired with the wackomeister of the wigwams", Tom K. Ryan, *Tumbleweeds*, Jul. 1, 2004.
- "You're a Harvard historian, for God's sake, not a pop schlockmeister looking for a quick buck." Dan Brown, *The Da Vinci Code*, 2003, p. 163. [*schlock* "damaged or shoddy merchandise" possibly < Yiddish *shlak* "apoplexy, stroke, wretch, evil, nuisance" < Middle High German *slag, slak* "stroke" < *slahen* "to strike" < Old High German *slahan*, related to Modern German *Schlag* "a hit, blow, stroke"]
- "Last week the company scored a coup by landing a deal to co-produce English-lingo series 'Queen of Swords' for powerhouse telco-turned-mediameister Telefonica Media and Canada's Fireworks Entertainment (see separate story on this page)." John Hopewell, "Morena toppers take global view", *Variety*, May 1, 2000.
- "Demos holds seminars at 11 Downing Street, Mulgan has become a member of Blair's 'policy unit,' and Leadbeater, who was rumored last year to be the prime minister's very favorite political thinker, boasts blurbs from Blair as well as Peter Mandelson, the notorious 'New Labour' spinmeister, on the

dust jacket of his book." Thomas Frank, "Connexity", *Harper's Magazine*, May 2000.

- "But when [Microsoft chairman Bill] Gates called [Senate Judiciary Committee chairman Orrin] Hatch on Feb. 12, the Softmeister was anything but restrained." Steven Levy, "Microsoft vs. the World", *Newsweek International*, Mar. 9, 1998, p. 36.
- "It is this arcane legal regime, more than cultural differences, that keeps U.S. businessmen from acting like Japanese *keiretsu* lords or European cartelmeisters, who often casually fix industry prices in their stagnant economies." Michael Hirsch, "The Feds' Case Against Bill Gates", *Newsweek International*, Mar. 9, 1998, p. 41.
- "Sure! 'Bearmeister'! 'Bunny Boy'! 'Antler Guy'!" G. B. Trudeau, *Doonesbury*, Apr. 3, 2002.

Meistersinger *n.*

"master singer": a member of the German guilds for poets and musicians of the 14th, 15th, and 16th centuries.

- "The other night, when we were heading off a steamer and firing six-pounders across her bows, the band was playing the 'star' song from the Meistersinger." Richard Harding Davis, *Adventures and Letters of Richard Harding Davis*, 1917, p. 230.

Meistersinging *n.*

the act of performing as a Meistersinger.

mensch *n.*

related to *Mensch* "person, human being": a person of integrity and honor [< Yiddish *mentsh* < Middle High German *mensch*, from Old High German *mennisco*; akin to Old English *man*]. See also luftmensch.

- Robin Gorman Newman, *How to Meet a Mensch in New York: A Decent, Responsible Person Even Your Mother Would Love.*

mesmerism, mesmerist, mesmerizer, mesmeriser, mesmerization, mesmerisation *n.*, **mesmeric** *adj.*, **mesmerize, mesmerise** *v.t.*

from *Mesmerismus*: animal magnetism, hypnotism, compelling attraction, fascination, named for Franz or Friedrich Anton Mesmer, 1733-1815, German or Austrian physician [Swiss German *Mesmer, Messmer* "sexton, sacristan, verger" < German *Mesner, Messner* < Old High German *mesinari* < Middle Latin *masionarius, mansionarius* "sexton; building caretaker" < Latin *mansio* "place one stays or lives", related to English *mansion*].

- "Normally I would have considered this [medical] exam a joke, but instead I found myself totally mesmerized." Fran Drescher, *Cancer Schmancer*, 2002, p. 179.
- "They felt underdressed in the lobby and in the bar, where they sat mesmerized by the people who were clearly more at ease about simply being in Le Bristol than they were." John Irving, *The Fourth Hand*, 2001, p. 22.
- "At first, when as a young man he began to dip into the secrets of mesmerism, his mind seemed to be wandering in a strange land where all was chaos and darkness, save that here and there some great unexplainable and disconnected fact loomed out in front of him." Arthur Conan Doyle, *The Captain of the Polestar and other Tales*, 1894, p. 84.

- "He engaged a bright little girl who was exceedingly susceptible to such mesmeric influences as he could induce." Joel Benton, *The Life of Hon. Phineas T. Barnum*, 1891, p. 138.
- "Many persons affirmed that the history and elucidation of the facts, long so mysterious, had been obtained by the daguerreotypist from one of those mesmerical seers, who, now-a-days, so strangely perplex the aspect of human affairs, and put everybody's natural vision to the blush, by the marvels which they see with their eyes shut." Nathaniel Hawthorne, *The House of Seven Gables*, 1851, p. 243.
- "I resolved to try on Winters, silently, and unconsciously to himself a mesmeric power which I possess over certain kinds of people, and which at times I have found to work even in the dark over the lower animals." Mark Twain, *Roughing It*, 1871, p. 587.
- "Dislocate your spine if you don't sign, he says, 'I'll have you seeing double.' Mesmerize you when he's tongue-tied simply with those eyes. Synchronize your minds and see the beast within him rise." Queen, "Flick of the Wrist", *Sheer Heart Attack*, words and music by Freddie Mercury, 1974.

milch *adj.*

related to *Milch n.* "milk": giving milk, kept for milking. [English *milch* does not derive from German *Milch* but rather from Middle English *-milche*, Old English *-milc(e)* and Anglo-Saxon *-milce, -meolc*, but is included here due to common spellings and origins. The common Indo-European root **melg-* meant "to stroke, press out, wipe off, milk". Therefore the verb *to milk* originally had nothing to do with the noun *milk* and is etymologically earlier, and the adjective *milch* is derived from the verb meaning *to milk*.] A *milch cow, milk cow* in Modern English is a *Melkkuh, Milchkuh* in Modern German.

- "The little milch beasts had been caught by it, too." Anne McCaffrey, *The Renegades of Pern*, Del Rey, New York, 1990, p. 132.

minnesinger *n.*

from *Minnesänger* "singer of love songs": a German lyric poet-composer of the 12th to the 14th century.

mogul *n.*

from *Mugl* (Austrian dialect): a bump on a ski slope.

- "At the 1992 Olympics, where moguls skiing was first included as an official Olympic sport, Weinbrecht won the gold medal." "Weinbrecht, Donna", *Microsoft® Encarta® 98 Encyclopedia*.

mol, mole *n.*

from *Mol* "mol": in chemistry, a gram molecule, molecular weight of a substance in grams. The German *Mol* is an abbreviation of *Molekulargewicht* "molecular weight" or *Grammolekül* "gram molecule".

- "In 1971 the mole was defined as the amount of substance of a system that contains as many elementary entities as there are atoms in 0.012 kilogram of carbon-12." "International System of Units", *Microsoft® Encarta® 98 Encyclopedia*, 1998.

muesli *n.*

from *Müesli, Müsli* "muesli": a breakfast cereal of Swiss origin consisting of untoasted, rolled oats, nuts and dried fruit; granola [< Swiss German dialect dim. of

German *Mus* "mush" < Middle High German *muos* "meal" < Old High German *muos*; related to Old English *mōs* "food"]. This entry suggested by Aldorado Cultrera.

- "Somebody *did* own that view, could sit there every morning with his muesli and orange juice, in his Yves St Laurent bathrobe and Gucci slippers, and look out on this sweep of Mediterranean heaven." Bill Bryson, *Neither Here Nor There: Travels in Europe*, 1991, p. 187.

- "It is primarily confectionery, chocolates and muesli products that Aldi has decided to drop from its assortment, as well as products supplied by US food group Kellogg." "Aldi slashes sale of brands", *Eurofood*, Mar. 11, 1999.
- Mary Riddell, "The reporting of the story of Cook, his wife and his lover makes it plain that affair-speak is still as mealy-mouthed as dry muesli." *New Statesman*, Aug. 8, 1997.

Munchausen, Munchhausen, Münchhausen, Münchausen, Munchausen syndrome *n.*
from *Münchhausen*: fantasist, somebody who makes up fantastic stories in order to impress others; tall story, a fantastic story full of exaggeration, told to impress people [< Baron Karl Friedrich Hieronymus von Münchhausen (1720-1797), of a book of impossible adventures written in English by the German author Rudolf Eric Raspe < the German town of Münchhausen < German *Mönch* "monk" + -*hausen* "settlement" < *Haus* "house"].

- "What about exposing a fraud–a modern Munchausen–and making him rideeculous [*sic*]?" Arthur Conan Doyle, *The Lost World*, 2004, p. 11.

N

Nazi, nazi, NS *adj., n.*
from *Nationalsozialist* "National Socialist": the German fascist political party; a member or supporter of this party [shortened from the first two syllables of *Nationalsozialist*, spelled with -*zi*, because -*tion* in German is pronounced <tsi-on> while *Nati would be pronounced with a <t> sound; the -*zi* is not from the middle of *Sozialist* as some dictionaries will have one believe]. The entire name of the party was *Nationalsozialistische Deutsche Arbeiterpartei (NSDAP)* "National Socialist German Worker's Party". See further examples under <u>Anschluss</u>, <u>Gestapo</u>, <u>Gleichschaltung</u>, <u>Machtpolitik</u>, <u>Reich</u>, <u>Sturm und Drang</u>, and <u>Zeitgeist</u>.

- "Knowledge of man's inhumanity to man became more real as the newspapers and radio hinted at unspeakable horrors perpetrated on the Jews of Europe and the cruelties of Hitler's Nazi regime." Jane Goodall, *Reason for Hope*, 1999.
- "Spectre also suggests you rope in the local news media by getting publicity out of using a quitclaim deed to provide some bogus or unpopular charity with ownership of some valuable piece of property sure to stir up the public

unrest, e.g. deeding the town square of Skokie, Ill., to the American Nazi party." George Hayduke, *Getting Even 2: More Dirty Tricks from the Master of Revenge*, 1981.

- "I lowered my window to tell the Nazi, I mean, guard, 'Hi, I'm Fran Drescher.'" Fran Drescher, *Enter Whining*, 1996, p. 161.
- "Halfway through the week Elaine was referring to her [health spa] counselor as 'the Nazi' while I was blessing mine." Fran Drescher, *Enter Whining*, 1996, p. 252.
- "Nazi creep. Murderer." Garrison Keillor, "Norman conquest", *The Book of Guys*, 1993.
- "French Prime Minister Lionel Jospin lamented the rise of a party [the Freedom Party] 'which had not dealt with its Nazi past,' while Nicole Fontaine, head of the European Parliament, said it would be 'intolerable' for a party that 'negates the fundamental principles of respect for human rights' to take power in a member state [Austria]." Andrew Purvis, "Forward into the Past", *Time*, Feb. 7, 2000.

Neanderthal man, Neanderthal, Neanderthaler, Neandertal *n.*
from *Neanderthal(er), Neandertal(er)* "(one from) the Neander Valley": an extinct species of man.

- "The man was stocky and dark, almost Neanderthal, dressed in a dark double-breasted suit that strained to cover his wide shoulders." Dan Brown, *The Da Vinci Code*, 2003, p. 19.
- "Neanderthal man (or Homo sapiens neanderthalensis) was very different from modern man." Bill Bryson, *The Mother Tongue: English and How it Got that Way*, 1990, p. 21.
- "Neandertals were those stout, football-headed, muscular people who inhabited Europe and the Mediterranean for a couple hundred thousand years during the Ice Ages and died out about 32,000 years ago. They used to be spelled with an *h* but aren't any more." Jonathan Marks, *What It Means to Be .98% Chimpanzee*, 2003, p. 95.
- "Until this decade scientists knew little about humans in Europe before the Neandertals appeared about 230,000 years ago." Rick Gore, "The First Europeans", *National Geographic*, July 1997.

nicht wahr?, nicht?
"not true?": isn't it so?, *n'est-ce pas?*

- "Nicht wahr, Monsieur, 'twas that you meant?" Henrik Ibsen, *Peer Gynt*.
- "If he tries to climb out into the air as inexperienced people endeavour to do, he drowns – nicht wahr?" Joseph Conrad, *Lord Jim*, 1900.
- "It seems such a pity that you should have to spend the day at the hotel, and also a little uncomfortable ... in a strange place. *Nicht wahr?*" Katherine Mansfield, *Bliss and Other Stories*.
- "Oh, look, Herr Professor, there are swallows in flight; they are like a little flock of Japanese thoughts–*nicht wahr?*" Katherine Mansfield, *In a German Pension*.

nickel *n.*

from *Nickel* "nickel; originally a nix, devil, <u>kobold</u>": shortened from German *Kupfernickel* or Swedish *kopparnickel*, so-called because the ore looks like copper ore, but does not contain the valuable metal. A modern English translation might be "copper trickster, fool's copper". *Nickel* was and is a diminutive of *Nikolaus*, "Nicholas". *(Old) Nick* is a name for the Devil in English. The U.S. and Canadian five-cent pieces are called nickels because they are made of an alloy of nickel and copper. See further examples under <u>cobalt</u> and <u>zinc</u>.

- "Last week, he went to battle with a handful of quarters, a couple of five dollar bills, three rolls of nickels, an Indian head penny, six canceled stamps and an I.O.U. for $6.67 that he'd been carrying in his back pocket from the last Friday night poker game he played in." Robert M. Renneisen, *How to Be Treated Like a High Roller: ... Even Though You're Not One*, 1996.

- "A recent study found the nickel content in two of the new euro coins going into circulation in January may cause skin irritation or eczema in 10% of the population", "Omen", *Time*, Dec. 10, 2001.

NS *n., adj.*

See <u>Nazi</u>.

O

ohm *n.*

from *Ohm* "ohm": in electricity a unit of measurement for resistance, named for Georg Simon Ohm, 1787-1854, German physicist [German *Ohm, Oheim* "mother's brother, uncle, any relative"]. This entry suggested by Wilton Woods.

- "By increasing the battery from eight to twelve cells we get a spark when the vibrating magnet is shunted with 3 ohms." Frank Lewis Dyer & Thomas Commerford Martin, *Edison, His Life and Inventions*, 1910, p. 824.

- "The high tension voltage of that bright blue current felt like ohm sweet ohm, but Aubrey dared not risk too much of it at once." Christopher Morley, *The Haunted Bookshop*, 1918, p. 91.

- "Exclusive features include MASS (Magnetic Apex Symmetrical Stasis) inverted, long magnetic 'gap' motor with single or dual 4-ohm, aluminum voice coils on a Kapton former." "MASS", *European Car*, Nov. 2000.

- "This low reading (28.4 ohms) indicates a good switch." Bruce Clark, "Troubleshooting with a Multimeter", *Family Handyman*, Apr. 2000.

Ouija *n.*

from French *oui* "yes" + German *ja* "yes": a trademark for a board with letters and a pointer by which answers to questions are spelled out, supposedly by spiritual forces, also called talking board or spirit board [German *ja* "yes" < Middle and Old High German *ja*, related to English *yea* and *yes*, originally *ja so*].

- "If you have messed around with Ouija boards, you know there are malicious spirits floating around, liable to tell you anything, and you shouldn't believe them." Kurt Vonnegut, *A Man Without a Country*, 2005, p. 34.
- "She asks (big surprise) who likes her; the Ouija spells out R, I, C, K." Audrey Niffenegger, *The Time Traveler's Wife*, 2004, p. 62.

Ostpolitik *n.*

"politics toward the East": in the following example *Ostpolitik* refers to politics toward Eastern Europe. See also <u>Machtpolitik</u>, <u>*Realpolitik*</u>, <u>*Weltpolitik*</u> and <u>*Westpolitik*</u>.

- "Clinton's Ostpolitik", Christopher Ogden, *Time*, May 26, 1997, p. 24.

P

panzer *adj., n.*

from *Panzer, Panzer-* "armor, armored": armored, belonging to an armored division; a vehicle, especially a tank, in a panzer division [German *Panzer* "armor" < Middle High German *panzier* "breast armor" < Old French *pancier, panciere* "coat of mail, literally belly piece", *pance* "belly" < Italian *panzia, pancia* "belly" < Latin *pantex, panticis* "belly", related to *paunch*].

- "Intelligence reports had indicated that the Finns had only a few old lightweight tanks and probably fewer than 100 small-caliber anti-panzer guns." Eloise Engle & Lauri Paananen, *The Winter War: The Soviet Attack on Finland 1939-1940*, 1973, p. 4.
- "By 4 February, however, it was seen that this reinforcement was not enough to crush the Anzio beachhead and General Jodl asked Hitler for permission to move in the 9th <u>SS</u> Panzer Division, the only fully combat ready armored division in France." Gordon A. Harrison, *European Theatre of Operations: Cross-Channel Attack*, 1993, p. 234.
- "Heinrich Jäger stuck his head and torso up through the open cupola of his Panzer V for a look around, then ducked back down into the turret of the panzer." Harry Turtledove, *Upsetting the Balance (Worldwar Series, Volume 3)*, 1996.
- "In the spring of 1940, when Germany was making its lightning strikes into the Netherlands, Belgium, and Luxembourg, the <u>Nazis</u> had 2.2 million troops in uniform, nine motorized divisions, and ten panzer divisions protected by 3,500 combat aircraft." Tom Brokaw, *An Album of Memories: Personal Histories from the Greatest Generation*, 2001.
- "Stalingrad's five-month trial by fire began on August 23, 1942, when the first panzer grenadiers of the German Sixth Army reached the Volga on the city's northern outskirts." David L. Robbins, *War of the Rats: A Novel*, 2000.

patzer *n.*

probably from *Patzer* "bungler": a poor or amateurish chess player [German *patzen* "to blunder"]. This entry suggested by Andreas Kempf.

- "I'm a 'patzer,' a chess player who knows how to move the pieces fairly well but is forever doomed to mediocrity." Mike Adams, "Check mate; Game brings out the best and the worst in many players", *The Baltimore Sun*, Jan. 11, 1999.

Pez, PEZ *n.*

short for *Pfefferminz* "peppermint" (the first, middle and last letters): a brand of candy invented by the Edward Haas company of Vienna, Austria, in 1927, originally with peppermint flavor as an alternative to smoking, now sold with plastic dispensers that have heads of familiar characters and are collectors' items [German *Pfefferminz* "peppermint" < *Pfeffer* "pepper" + *Minze* "mint"]. See also <u>hasenpfeffer</u>.

- "'They collect Elvis everything--plates, towels, napkin holders, we even have an Elvis Pez dispenser.' 'They have Elvis Pez heads?' 'Some lunatic collector in Alabama put sideburns on a Fred Flintstone Pez, filed down the nose, and painted on sunglasses.'" Brad Meltzer, *The Tenth Justice*, 1997.
- "Wesley collected PEZ dispensers, and she mentioned that since they had moved from Boston to Silicon Valley, she was having trouble finding fellow collectors to trade with." Adam Cohen, *The Perfect Store: Inside eBay*, 2002.
- "He realizes he's a lucky monkey, someone who made an accidental $50,000 guessing that eBay, a Web site designed for buying and selling Pez dispensers, would emerge with a market capitalization comparable to General Motors." Thomas A. Bass, "Don't Quit the Night Job", *The New York Times*, Apr. 23, 2000, review of *Dumb Money: Confessions of a Day Trader*, by Joey Anuff & Gary Wolf.
- "WHEN THE WEB WAS really young, cyberspace was dominated by academia and personal home pages were dedicated to pressing topics like spelunking and Pez dispensers, the online community's response to proposals of governmental regulation was a consistent and resounding 'hands off.'" Justin Oppelaar, "Sign on the Dot-Com Line", *Variety*, Dec. 18, 2000.
- "4th Annual Los Angeles PEZ-A-THON/MAR. 26-27. Twenty-five hundred Pezheads gather to buy and sell thousands of Pez dispensers and search for the long-lost '63 Bullwinkle Mom tossed aeons ago." Gia Gittleson, "the guide", *Los Angeles Magazine*, Apr. 1999.
- "Simple bead kits, a deck of cards, a Pez candy dispenser - all will be received as cherished treasure by the child who keeps asking, 'When are we going to get there?'" "Destinations & detours: California family travel planner", *Sunset*, May 1996.

pils, pilsner, Pilsner, pilsener, Pilsener *n., adj.*

from *Pils, Pilsner, Pilsener* "of Pilsen": a pale, light <u>lager</u> beer originally brewed in Pilsen, Bohemia, Czech Republic; Pilsner glass, a tall glass tapered at the bottom used especially for beer [German *Pils* shortened from *Pilsner, Pilsener* < German *Pilsen* < Czech *Plzen*].

- "I believe I may even have failed to notice them edging away when, emboldened by seven or eight glasses of Jupiler pils or the memorably named Donkle Beer, I would lean towards one of them and say in a quiet but friendly voice, 'Je m'appelle Guillaume. L'habite Des Moines.'" Bill Bryson, *Neither Here nor There: Travels in Europe*, 1991, p. 20.

- "NATASHA LYONNE: What kind of beer do you have? CHLOE SEVIGNY: A Pilsner." Gus Van Sant, "The Bonnie and Clyde of Indie Film", *Interview*, Nov. 1999.
- "Today the spectrum of beer flavors runs from the crisp, slightly hoppy freshness of pale, European-style pilsners to the creamy-sweet maltiness of an English-style brown ale." Jeff Phillips, "Beer! And the foods that love it", *Sunset*, Oct. 1996.
- "When the project is done, fill your 'window sill' with technicolor flowers, such as these gerber daisies lined up in pilsner glasses." Rebecca Jerdee, "Weekend decorating", *Better Homes and Gardens*, Aug. 1996.
- "If Eloise had made it past adolescence, she might well have been smoking Marlboro Lights, drinking Pilsner beer and belching freely, as Ms. Roi was on a recent evening as she sat on a couch in her mother's hotel, next to her boyfriend of four months, Marc Beckman." Alexandra Jacobs, "Alice Roi, the 25-Year-Old Designer, Is Thinking Girl's Anti-Shoshanna", *The New York Observer*, May 7, 2001.

pinscher *n.*

from *Pinscher* "terrier": a breed of dog [origin unclear but probably from *Pinzgauer* "from the region of Pinzgau in the province of Salzburg in Austria"]. See also <u>Doberman pinscher</u>.

- *The Miniature Pinscher: Reigning King of Toys*, by Jacklyn E. Hungerland, 2000.

plattenbau *n.*

from *Plattenbau* "panel building": a building whose facade is constructed of large, prefabricated concrete slabs, often found in eastern Europe [German *Platte* "panel, plate, sheet" + *Bau* "building, construction"]. This entry suggested by Christiane Leißner. See also <u>Bauhaus</u>.

- "For a generation of West Germans, to whom East Germany was synonymous with ugly, old-fashioned and second-rate, nothing symbolized that inferiority better than plattenbaus, the high-rise apartment buildings from the postwar period that sprawled endlessly over the Communist landscape." Alisa Roth, "In Chic New Berlin, Ugly Is Way Cool", *The New York Times*, Jan. 24, 2002.
- "Plattenbau (Bosna), 2000, is an exact copy of an entrance to a government-planned high-rise apartment block that had been built using prefabricated panels." Harald Fricke, "Sabine Hornig", *ArtForum*, Apr. 2000.

polka *n., adj., v.i.*

from *Polka*: a fast dance for couples developed in Bohemia, Czech Republic; music for this dance; to dance the polka; of the polka, as in *polka dots* [< German *Polka* & French *polka* < Czech *polka* "Polish dance" < Polish *Polka* "a Polish woman"]. See further example under <u>lederhosen</u>.

- "My great-grandfather John Tollefson was not a pietist, he was one of the Happy Lutherans: he loved to dance the polka, which is a Norwegian martial art, and to drink beer and tell jokes." Garrison Keillor, *Wobegon Boy*, 1997, p. 46.
- "Thalassa's leading composer had contrived a witty musical score beginning with a slow pavane and culminating in a breathless polka—slowing down to

84

normal speed again at the very end as the final block of ice was jockeyed into position." Arthur C. Clarke, *The Songs of Distant Earth*, 1986, p. 282.

- "The hall was empty, and they had a grand polka, for Laurie danced well, and taught her the German step, which delighted Jo, being full of swing and spring." Louisa May Alcott, *Little Women*, 1869.

- "When they reached the ballroom the band was striking up a polka, and presently Mr Bunker, with his accustomed grace, was tearing round the room with Lady Muriel, while the Baron -- the delight of all eyes in his red waistcoat -- led out her sister." J. Storer Clouston, *The Lunatic at Large*, 1905, p. 103.

- "She picked out some things by Caruso and Tetrazzini and piled them on a chair, but James had things to himself up there, and played The Spring Chicken through three times during dinner, with Miss Cobb glaring at the gallery until the back of her neck ached, and the dining-room girls waltzing in with the dishes and polka-ing out." Mary Roberts Rinehart, *Where There's a Will*, 1912, p. 178. *Polka-ing* can also be spelled *polkaing*.

- "Fluffy polka-dots of white cotton had been sewed to it generously; also it was ornamented with a large cross of red flannel, suggested by the picture of a Crusader in a newspaper advertisement." Booth Tarkington, *Penrod*, 1914, p. 24.

- "And now we began with waltzes, which passed into polkas, which subsided into other round dances; and then in very exhaustion we fell back in a grave quadrille." Edward Everett Hale, *The Brick Moon and Other Stories*, 1809, p. 353.

poltergeist *n.*

from *Poltergeist* "noisy ghost": a spirit reputed to make much noise [< German *poltern* < *boldern* "to be noisy, make noise" (onomatopoeic) + German *Geist* < Middle High German *geist* < Old High German *geist* "ghost, spook, spirit, essence"]. See also <u>hopfgeist</u>, <u>zeitgeist</u>.

- "The room was clean and passably swank, but the television didn't work, and when I went into the bathroom to wash my hands and face, the pipes juddered and banged like something from a poltergeist movie and then, with a series of gasps, issued a steady brown soup." Bill Bryson, *Neither Here Nor There: Travels in Europe*, 1991, p. 301.

- "And finally I made a list of beliefs about which I hold no opinion, either because evidence is lacking, or because the issue seems to me fundamentally a matter of faith. These beliefs include reincarnation, past lives, entities, poltergeists, ghosts, the yeti, the Loch Ness monster, and the power of crystals." Michael Crichton, *Travels*, 1988, p. 384.

- "Nearly Headless Nick was always happy to point new Gryffindors in the right direction, but Peeves the poltergeist was worth two locked doors and a trick staircase if you met him when you were late for class." Joanne K. Rowling, *Harry Potter and the Philosopher's Stone (Book 1)*, 1997, p. 145. This is one of only two German words mentioned in this book. The other is <u>rucksack</u>.

- "Peeves was the school poltergeist, a grinning, airborne menace who lived to cause havoc and distress." Joanne K. Rowling, *Harry Potter and the Chamber of Secrets (Book 2)*, 1999, p. 126. This is one of only two German words mentioned in this book. The other is <u>waltz</u>.

- "He led them along the deserted corridor and around a corner, where the first thing they saw was Peeves the poltergeist, who was floating upside-down in mid-air and stuffing the nearest keyhole with chewing gum." Joanne K. Rowling, *Harry Potter and the Prisoner of Azkaban (Book 3)*, 1999, p. 99. This is the only German word mentioned in this book.
- "Harry looked up, and saw, floating twenty feet above them, Peeves the poltergeist, a little man in a bell-covered hat and orange bow-tie, his wide malicious face contorted with concentration as he took aim again." J. K. Rowling, *Harry Potter and the Goblet of Fire* (Book 4), 2000, p. 152. This is one of four German words mentioned in this book. The others are <u>*burger*</u>, <u>*rucksack*</u> and <u>*waltz*</u>.
- *Poltergeist*, starring JoBeth Williams, Heather O'Rourke, et al., 1982.

pretzel *n.*

from *Brezel, Bretzel, Pretzel* "pretzel": a bakery product in a particular shape; this shape [< Middle High German *prezel, prezile, brezel* < Old High German *brezzila, brezitel, brezitella* < Middle Latin *bracellus* "bracelet" or Latin *brachiatus* "having branches like arms" < Latin *brachium, bracchium* "arm"].

- "Along Getreidegasse, the site of Mozart's birthplace, every shop had one of those hanging pretzel signs above the door, including, God help us, the local McDonald's (the sign had a golden-arches M worked into its filigree), as if we were supposed to think that they have been dispensing hamburgers there since the Middle Ages." Bill Bryson, *Neither Here Nor There: Travels in Europe*, 1991, p. 252.
- "Aside from an occasional visit to the Loewen Garden 'over the Rhine,' with a glass of beer and a few pretzels, consumed while listening to the excellent music of a German band, the theatre was the sum and substance of our innocent dissipation." Frank Lewis Dyer and Thomas Commerford Martin, *Edison: His Life and Inventions*, 1910.
- "'I 'spect the tickets cost a heap,' he thought ruefully, as he drew himself up into a regular pretzel of a boy; 'but, then, she never does have no fun, an' never gits a thing fer herself.'" Alice Caldwell Hegan, *Mrs. Wiggs of the Cabbage Patch*, 1902.

pumpernickel *n.*

from *pumpern* "to break wind" + <u>*Nickel*</u> "a goblin; devil; <u>kobold</u>": a coarse, dark bread reputed to be hard to digest.

- "The devil take you, and your Westphalian ham, and pumpernickel!" Henry Wadsworth Longfellow, *Hyperion*.

Q

quartz *n.*

from *Quarz* "quartz": a common mineral, silicon dioxide [probably diminutive of Middle German *querch* "dwarf", so-called because dwarves were supposedly responsible for relatively worthless minerals. English *Quartz* and *dwarf* and German *Zwerg* "dwarf" probably all come from a common root.] See also cobalt and nickel.

- "'No, the exterior lights are a hundred-fifty-watt quartz halogen,' Edmunds was saying." Michael Crichton, *Sphere*, 1987, p. 58.
- "And primitive quartz tools found at a lower level of the dig proved older still, dating back to about a million years ago." Rick Gore, "The First Europeans", *National Geographic*, Jul. 1997, p. 104.

quartzite *n.*

a granular metamorphic rock consisting essentially of quartz in interlocking grains.

- "There are the granites, quartzite schists, gneisses, and other igneous and metamorphic rocks which were formed in pre-Cambrian times." Fred Singleton, *A Short History of Finland*, 1989, p. 5.

R

Rassenhygiene *n.*

"race hygiene": racial cleansing [< *Rasse* "race" < French *race* "race" < Italian *razza* "race" + *Hygiene* "hygiene" < Greek *hygieinós* "promoting health" < *hygiés* "healthy, good"].

- "To cite only the most flagrant example, the Third Reich's policy of *Rassenhygiene* offered what purported to be a rational, scientific solution to the problem of large numbers of inferior and undesirable people." Jonathan Marks, *What It Means to Be 98% Chimpanzee*, 2003, p. 277.

Realpolitik, realpolitik *n.*

"realistic politics": practical politics, usually a euphemism for Machtpolitik. See also Ostpolitik, *Weltpolitik* and *Westpolitik*.

- "Realpolitik, however, was the principal reason for Constantinople's variety of nationalities." Philip Mansel, *Constantinople: City of the World's Desire 1453-1924*, 1998.
- "That's how it looks to Moscow because the *realpolitik* is simple: Russia is weak; the new Eastern and Central European democracies are fragile; Russia has the size, resources and, historically, the inclination to rise and threaten again." Christopher Ogden, *Time*, May 26, 1997, p. 24.

Reich *n.*

"empire" (< Middle High German *rich, riche* < Old High German *rihhi,* related to English *-ric* in *bishopric*]. See further example under <u>Gleichschaltung</u>.

- "The leaders of Rome, Greece, the Third Reich, the British Empire, never saw the onset of decadence and internal rot in time; we can, and we must, if the United States is not to succumb to its internal hatreds and moral excesses, to be consumed by its own self-destruction." Carl Thomas Rowan, *The Coming Race War in America: A Wake-Up Call.*
- "His [Bullock's] dramatic reconstruction of the high-stakes maneuvering for the Reich chancellorship, which brought Hitler to power in 1933, subverts the notion of some profound historical inevitability of Hitler by emphasizing the degree to which pure luck and shabby backstage scheming played a role in bringing him to office." Ron Rosenbaum, "Explaining Hitler", *The New Yorker,* May 1995.
- "In temperament and outlook [German chancellor Helmut Kohl] is plainly not a Bismarck, whose Prussian blood-and-iron politics forged the Second Reich (the first was the Holy Roman Empire, long lost in medieval mists but not formally declared dead till 1806)." James Walsh, *Time,* Dec. 30, 1996-Jan. 6, 1997.
- "'The story has nothing which makes the rightest fringe happy, nothing that is anywhere near a positive view of Hitler and the Third Reich,' comments Friedman." Ursula Sautter, "Can Der Führer Be Funny?", *Time,* Aug. 17, 1998.
- "Then, as now, Austria had not fully come to terms with its role in the crimes of the Third Reich." Andrew Purvis, "Forward into the Past", *Time,* Feb. 7, 2000.

reichsmark, Reichmark, RM., r.m. *n.* [*pl.* reichsmarks, reichsmark, Reichmarks] from *Reichsmark* "imperial mark".

- "Suddenly, a barter economy based more on cigarettes and candy that [*sic*] on the nearly worthless Reichmarks left over from Hitler's Germany, was transformed into a throbbing industrial engine." Jordan Bonfante, "A German Requiem", *Time,* July 6, 1998, p. 21.

Reichstag *n.*

"imperial assembly": the former German assembly or parliament, the building in Berlin where it met [< *Reich* "empire" + *Tag* "day (of assembly)" < Middle High German *tac* < Old High German *tag* "daytime, time during which the sun shines", related to English *diet* meaning "assembly"].

- "In an avowed protest against the new dome on the Reichstag, the fiend had attached an explosive device to the dog's collar." John Irving, *The Fourth Hand,* 2001, p. 55.
- "Admiral Prince Henry of Prussia did likewise, and the first act of the Reichstag, after reassembling on Tuesday, was to pass a standing vote of condolence with the British people in their distress." Logan Marshall, *The Sinking of the Titanic & Great Sea Disasters: Thrilling Stories of Survivors with Photographs and Sketches,* 1912, p. 228.
- "In Germany the Socialist party became the strongest faction of the Reichstag, and, in spite of differences of opinion among its members, it preserved its

formal unity with that instinct for military discipline which characterizes the German nation." Bertrand Russell, *Proposed Roads to Freedom*, 1918, p. 56.

- "The writer sat in the visitors' gallery of the Reichstag when the Socialists were protesting against the torturing of miserable Herreros in Africa, and he heard the deputies of the Holy Father's political party screaming their rage like jaguars in a jungle night." Sinclair Upton, *The Profits of Religion*, 1918, p. 154.
- "In addition, it was suspected that construction was being started in advance of the dates scheduled by the German Navy Law—in advance even of the authorization of funds by the Reichstag." Jeffrey T. Richelson, *A Century of Spies: Intelligence in the Twentieth Century*, 1997.
- "In his Reichstag speech of 6 October 1939, Hitler reminded his audience that in 1919 Poland had taken German lands developed over many centuries." Deborah Dwork & Robert Jan van Pelt, *Auschwitz: 1270 to the Present*, 1996.
- "In 1911 a measure to repeal paragraph 175 came to a floor vote in the Reichstag but was defeated." Somin LeVay, *Queer Science: The Use and Abuse of Research into Homosexuality*, 1996.

rinderpest *n.*

from *Rinderpest* "cattle plague": an acute infectious disease of cattle, cattle plague.

- "At very long intervals a species may have to face the onslaught of some entirely new menace, such as the introduction into Africa of rinderpest in the last decade of the nineteenth century, or the Black Death in Europe." Leslie Brown, "Population Control among Large Mammals", in Anthony Allison (Ed.), *Population Control*, 1970, p. 93.
- "As a veterinarian formerly involved [in the Serengeti] in the annual vaccination of cattle against rinderpest (cattle plague), I would point out that distemper, rinderpest, and human measles, among others, are believed to be closely related viruses, capable of jumping from species to species." John F. Callear, Letter to the Editor, *National Geographic*, May 1995, unpaged.

rollmops, rollmop *n.*

from *Rollmops* "rollmops": marinated herring fillet rolled around a pickle or onion as an hors d'oeuvre [< German *rollen* "to roll" < Old French *roller, roler* < Latin *rotulare* "roll a wheel or disk" < *rotulus* + German *Mops* "pug dog" < Low German-Dutch *mops* < Low German *mopen* "to open or twist the mouth", Dutch *moppen* "to grumble, to be bad-tempered"]. This entry suggested by Britta.

- "now the woman who's invited me, this donna, she's leaning against an amp, smoking one of these rollmop constructions/smiles through the hit, and I smile right back when she holds out the joint to me", Jeff Noon, *Needle in the Groove*.

rottweiler *n.*

from *Rottweiler* "from Rottweil": a breed of dog named for the German town of Rottweil.

- *The Rottweiler: Centuries of Service*, by Linda Michels & Catherine M. Thompson, 1998

rucksack *n.*

from *Rucksack* "back sack": backpack. Incidentally, *knapsack* is from the Dutch *knapzak* and has nothing to do with the German *Knappe.*

- "He carried a rucksack slung over one shoulder." W. R. Thompson, *Infiltrator (Star Trek: The Next Generation)*, 1996, p. 14.
- "Sessine was dressed in plain, utilitarian clothes and carried a light rucksack across his shoulder." Iain M. Banks, *Feersum Endjinn*, 1994, p. 179.
- "Harry watched, careful not to blink in case he missed it—but just as the boy reached the divide between the two platforms, a large crowd of tourists came swarming in front of him, and by the time the last rucksack had cleared away, the boy had vanished." J. K. Rowling, *Harry Potter and the Philosopher's Stone* (Book 1), 1997, p. 103.
- "Mrs Weasley was still glowering as she kissed Mr Weasley on the cheek, though not nearly as much as the twins, who had each hoisted their rucksacks onto their backs and walked out without a word to her." J. K. Rowling, *Harry Potter and the Goblet of Fire* (Book 4), 2000, p. 65.
- "I lugged my rucksack over to find a young couple arguing in the front seat." Bill Bryson, *Neither Here Nor There: Travels in Europe*, 1991, p. 16.
- "A tan rucksack hung from his shoulder." Walter Mosley, *Gone Fishin': An Easy Rawlins Novel*, 1997.
- "It was by sheer habit and inadvertency that he permitted Firmin, who had discovered a rucksack in a small shop in the town below, to carry both bottles of beer." H. G. Wells, *The World Set Free*, 1914.

sauerbraten, sauer-braten, sourbraten *n.*

from *Sauerbraten* "sour roast": beef marinated in vinegar and seasonings before roasting.

sauerkraut, sauer-kraut, kraut, sourkraut, sourkrout, sour-krout, saur kraut, sourcrout, sour croute *n.*

from *Sauerkraut* "sour cabbage": cut cabbage fermented in brine, often for several months, before cooking. See also kraut. See further examples under bratwurst and knackwurst.

- "In some places long rows of tables were placed, surrounded by broad, good-natured faces, more fleshly than spiritual, and groaning (not the faces) under jugs, mugs, bottles, bowls, and any thing else that would hold the national beverage; while the interstices were filled with bread, rolls, *petzkuchen* (a pet cake in Frankfort), *boobies' shanks* (I spell it phonographically; there may be an error of a letter or two), *brödchen mit umsständen,* saur kraut, cold puddings, and the ubiquitous *würst.*" W. W. Wright, *Doré. By a stroller in Europe*, 1857, p. 248.

- "He burst out indignantly, 'Was I to let that sauerkraut-eating civilian wipe his boots on the uniform of the 7th Hussars?'" Joseph Conrad, *A Set of Six*, 1906.
- "So I'd say then: 'Run along, you old goose! You'll be suggesting sauerkraut and <u>wieners</u> next.'" Edna Ferber, *Buttered Side Down*, 1911.
- "I was just getting up steam to pray as hard as ever I could; for days I'd been thinking of it, and I was nearly to the point where one more killdeer crying across the sky would have sent me headlong from the schoolhouse anywhere that my feet were on earth, and the air didn't smell of fried potatoes, kraut, sweat, and dogs, like it did whenever you sat beside Clarissa Polk." Gene Stratton Porter, *Laddie: A True Blue Story*, 1913, p. 271.
- "He [Captain Bligh] took up a glass of the reeking ship's water, rinsing his mouth preparatory to an attack on the sourcrout." Charles Nordhoff & James Norman Hall, *Mutiny on the Bounty*, 1932, p. 45.

schadenfreude, Schadenfreude *n.*

"joy of harm": the malicious pleasure one feels at someone else's misfortune.

- Lisa: Dad, do you know what schadenfreude is?
  Homer: No, I do not know what schadenfreude is. Please tell me, because I'm dying to know.
  Lisa: It's a German term for shameful joy, taking pleasure in the suffering of others.
  Homer: Oh, come on Lisa. I'm just glad to see him fall flat on his butt! He's usually all happy and comfortable, and surrounded by loved ones, and it makes me feel... What's the opposite of that shameful joy thing of yours?
  Lisa: Sour grapes.
  Homer: Boy, those Germans have a word for everything!
  "When Flanders Failed" episode of *The Simpsons* season 3, written by John Vitti, directed by Jim Reardon, 1991.
- "Like Adolf Hitler, Springer is easily tickled by what the Germans call Schadenfreude, the feeling of joy at another's misfortune." Thomas Pynchon, *Gravity's Rainbow*, 1995, p. 526.
- "So when my friend John called a few minutes later from L.A. and mentioned that a mutual friend of ours, whose first book was out (for which he had been grossly overpaid, if you ask me), had gotten a not-very-good review in *Newsweek* recently, all of a sudden, talking on the cordless phone and nursing my baby in the moonlight, I had a wicked, dazzling bout of schadenfreude." Anne Lamott, *Operating Instructions: A Journal of My Son's First Year*, 1994, p. 120.
- "*Schadenfreude* was not peculiar to the Middle Ages, but it was a dark variety indeed, induced by plague and successive calamities, the found expressions in gruesome scenes of the tortures on the cross, with the soldiers shown spitting on the Redeemer of man." Barbara W. Tuchman, *Distant Mirror: The Calamitous Fourteenth Century*, 1987, p. 312.
- "Never underestimate the power of *schadenfreude!*" Marian Salzman, Ira Matathia & Ann O'Reilly, *Buzz: Harness the Power of Influence and Create Demand*, 2003, p. 79.
- "Nothing raises the spirits like a little *schadenfreude*." Evan Morris, *The Book Lover's Guide to the Internet*, 1998, p. 260.

- "*Schadenfreude* is the preeminent pastime among journalists." Jonah Goldberg, "Mr. Kurtz, He Alive & Well", *National Review*, May 5, 2000

scheisse, scheiss, sheisse, sheiss, shice *n., v.i.*

from *Scheiße* "excrement": droppings [< German *Scheiße* "dung", perhaps by way of Yiddish, related to English *shit* and *to shed*]. See further example under schmier. See also shicer, shyster.

- "*Scheisse!*' the driver yelled. A pedestrian had suddenly darted in front of the Mercedes, and the driver jammed on the brakes to avoid hitting him." Sidney Sheldon, *Are You Afraid of the Dark?*, 2005, p. 339.
- "The transport officer stared at the mess and said *scheiss* through clenched teeth." Alan Furst, *Night Soldiers: A Novel*, 2002, p. 309.
- "I told you before, I'm bored by all that philosophy *sheisse*... I can't relate to- -to esoteric discussions." Carl Shapiro, *Slayer of the Sacred Cow: A Contemporary Freethought Novel*, 1986, p. 86.
- "Thirty-five thousand feet up a fountain pen sheisses into a shirt pocket a purplish black gush that can now never become one of the great elemental words – *fire night wind shit*." Galway Kinnell, *Imperfect Thirst*, 1996, p. 65.
- "We had words. He gave me some *sheiss*." William Diehl, *Hooligans*, 1985, p. 75.

scheister *n.*

See shyster.

schicer *n.*

See shicer.

schiller *n.*

"luster, splendor, iridescence": a bronzy iridescent luster (as of a mineral).

schillerize *v.t.*

give schiller to.

schilling, S., Sch. *n.*

from *Schilling* "shilling": the standard monetary unit of Austria before the euro; a coin of this value; a former minor coin of Germany [< German *Schilling* < Middle High German *schillinc* < Old High German *scilling*; English *shilling* <  Middle English *schilling* < Anglo-Saxon *scylling*; the basic sense of the Indo-European root may have been "that which is cut off from a piece of metal for use as money" or "a small shield"].

- "The entrance charge was twenty schillings, two-thirds as much as the Kunstmuseum, but it was hardly two-thirds as good." Bill Bryson, *Neither Here Nor There: Travels in Europe*, 1991, p. 258.
- "Saggy midsection, that loses the thread in too much uninteresting talk, takes some of the shine off the picture but this could still pull in a few schillings in select European markets." Derek Elley, "Hold-Up", *Variety*, Sep. 4, 2000.
- "ERWIN SCHRODINGER (1887-1961) CURRENCY: Austrian, 1,000 schillings ($57 when last issued, in 1983)", Edward F. Redish, "Cold, Hard Proof that Science Has Cultural Currency", *Discover*, Nov. 1999.

to **schlepp,** to **schlep** *v.i., v.t.*

    related to *schleppen* "tow": drag, lug, tote; move slowly or tediously [Yiddish *shlepn* < Middle High German *sleppen* < Middle Low German *slepen*]. (A laptop computer in German is humorously called a *Schlepptop.*)

- "And show the goddam daughters a good time—all the daughters, even the dogs. Schlepp 'em out to the terrace. Show 'em the stars. Romance 'em any way you want." *Dirty Dancing,* starring Patrick Swayze & Jennifer Grey, 1987.
- "My mom schlepped her watermelon breasts to the doctor at once." Fran Drescher, *Enter Whining,* 1996, p. 40. This book mentions *to schlepp* seven times.
- "You talk about schlepping peppers with a girl named Debra, I think, or perhaps you are escaping from leopards across the sea." Garrison Keillor, "Buddy the Leper", *The Book of Guys,* 1993.

schlieren *n.pl.* (*sing.* **schliere**)

    from *Schlieren* "streaks": small streaks or masses in igneous rocks.

schlockmeister *n.*

    See -meister.

schmaltz, schmalz *n.*

    related to *Schmalz* "rendered fat": sentimental or florid music or art; unctuous sentimentalism [Yiddish *shmalts* < German *Schmalz* < Middle High German *smalz*].

- "On a radio dial full of headbanger music and honkytonk and religious schmaltz and the steady whanging of commercials, public radio brings you worthwhile and even beautiful things." Garrison Keillor, *Wobegon Boy,* 1997, p. 127.
- "It's ['Angie'] quite a straight, schmaltzy pop tune, with the piano and string arrangement so prominent, which is probably why it was so popular in Latin countries at the time." Mick Jagger, insert in *Jump Back: The Best of the Rolling Stones,* CD, 1997.

schmier, shmier, shmir, schmear, shmear, schmeer, shmeer *n., v.t.*

    related to *Schmiere, schmieren* "ointment, salve, smear, grease, lubricant, greasy dirt, bribe, scrawl, scribble": a mass or group of related things ("the whole schmear"); a spread, often cream cheese on a bagel; to spread; a bribe; to bribe [< Yiddish *shmir, shmeer* "smear, smudge" < *shmirn, shmiren, schmeeren* "to smear, grease" < Middle High German *smiren* < Old High German *smirwen,* related to Pennsylvania German *schmear* "fat, grease"]. This entry suggested by Christian Macho. See also schmierkase.

- "If the first or the last fiddle, the timpani or horn, the flute or oboe takes off with his own interpretation, the result will be not only anarchy, but such a schmier, such a mishmash that the audience will run away in horror!" Uta Hagen, *Respect for Acting,* 1973, p. 198. This is a meaning I have not found in dictionaries as it appears to mean a group of unrelated things rather than similar things.
- "You eat usually eggs and toast mit raspberry shmier for breakfast, ze garbage fast food for lunch, maybe ze wiener made from pig balls or a slice of Scheisse you call pizza." David Ives, *Time Flies and Other Short Plays,* 2001, p. 45. This is a German character speaking in a play.

- "'Was your son given free rein to access whatever web sites he liked, including, say, violent or pornographic ones?' 'Oh, we did the whole parental-controls schmear, but Kevin cracked it in a day.'" Lionel Shriver, *We Need to Talk About Kevin: A Novel*, 2003, p. 45.
- "Try '99 bagels with schmear on the wall, 99 bagels with schmear' to kill even the strongest bagel cravings." Cameron Tuttle, *The Bad Girl's Guide to the Open Road*, 1999, p. 1.
- "They are high-class, high-performance mostly Stratocaster-like guitars, available in spectacular custom colors including 'psychedelic vomit' and even 'hazmat-sewage-fiasco shmear.'" Tony Bacon, *Electric Guitars: The Illustrated Encyclopedia*, 2000, p. 203.
- "'How about an extra five over the meter?' 'You're on. Get in.' Ah, the power of the schmeer." Steve Karmen, *Me and Bobby D.: A Memoir*, 2003, p. 351.
- "'That's fine,' said Boaz. 'Only wear a broad-brimmed hat and shmeer yourself with lotion. Otherwise you'll get red as a tomato, and they'll pick you by mistake.'" Erich Segal, *Acts of Faith*, 2003, p. 202.

Schmierchemie *n.*

from *Schmierchemie* "messy chemistry": a derisive term for biochemistry [< German *Schmierchemie* < *schmieren* (see <u>schmier</u>) + *Chemie* "chemistry"].

- "No wonder 'real' chemists sneered at biochemistry, called it 'Schmierchemie', which they continued to do until much more recently than 1859!" (p. 22), "All animal chemistry used to be disparaged by the dictum, 'Tierchemie ist Schmierchemie'." (p. 261) Charles Tanford & Jacqueline Reynolds, *Nature's Robots: A History of Proteins*, 2001.
- "'This heralds the end of organic chemistry: let's finish off the terpenes, and only the smears ('Schmieren') will be left!' [the derisive term *Schmierchemie* was used by organic chemists to denote physiological chemistry, or biochemistry as it is now known]." Walter Gratzer, *Eurekas and Euphorias: The Oxford Book of Scientific Anecdotes*, 2002, p. 134.
- "No one knew how to purify, isolate, synthesize, or identify their huge and immensely complicated structures. German chemists condescendingly referred to organic chemistry as 'Schmierchemie,' or grease chemistry, and no large university in the United States devoted a department to large polymers." Sharon Bertsch McGrayne, *Prometheans in the Lab*, 2002, p. 120.
- "It was grueling, unglamorous work. *Tierchemie*, runs an old German expression, *ist nur Schmierchemie* (Animal chemistry is just the chemistry of slimes and messes)." Barry Werth, *Billion Dollar Molecule: The Quest for the Perfect Drug*, 1995, p. 66.

schmierkase, Schmierkaese, shmierkase, smierkase, smiercase, smearkase, smearcase *n.*

related to *Schmierkäse* "soft cheese, cheese for spreading": chiefly North Midland U.S., any cheese suitable for spreading or eating with a spoon, especially cream cheese or (a sour) cottage cheese, therefore a synonym for <u>schmier</u> [< Pennsylvania German *Schmierkees* < German *Schmierkäse* < *schmieren* (see <u>schmier</u>) + *Käse* "cheese" < Middle High German *kaese* < Old High German *kasi* < Latin *caseus*]. See also <u>schweizerkäse</u>.

- "This cheese [cottage cheese] goes by many other names: **clabber, pot, Dutch, farmer's, Schmierkaese** and **bakers'**." Irma S. Rombauer & Marion Rombauer Becker, *Joy of Cooking*, 1964, p. 513. In the 1997 edition of the same book, the word is spelled *Schmierkase* (p. 536).
- "Pork and <u>sauerkraut</u>, chicken soup with saffron, *schmierkase* (similar to cottage cheese) with apple butter, and the vast array of pickles and pies that made up the famous 'Seven Sweets and Seven Sours' seem to have been exotic enough for the average American's taste." David J. Walbert, *Garden Spot: Lancaster County, the Old Order Amish, and the Selling of Rural America*, 2002, p. 87.
- "They wandered like children on a school trip, listening to the strange Germanic inflections of the farm wives who sold them such exotica as cup cheese, shmierkase, sause, meringue kisses, and eggs boiled in beet juice." Leslie Chang, *Beyond the Narrow Gate: The Journey of Four Chinese Women from the Middle Kingdom to the Middle America*, 2000, p. 113.
- "smierkase > cottage cheese", index entry, Alan Davidson, *The Oxford Companion to Food*, 1999, p. 891.
- "The meal typically involves slices of bread, peanut butter, smearcase (cheese spread), pickled vegetables, snitz (dried apple) pie, and coffee." Donald B. Kraybill, *The Riddle of Amish Culture*, 2001, p. 352.
- "She fed her little turkeys with boiled egg or smearcase, as my Grandmother Milhous always called clabber cheese (cottage)." Jessamyn West, *Hide And Seek: A Continuing Journey*, 1987, p. 261.
- "*Schmierkäse* has become *smearkase*, and the *sauer* in *sauer-kraut* and *sauerbraten* is often spelled *sour*." H. L. Mencken, *The American Language*, 1936, p. 411. Mencken may have meant *smearcase* here since he spelled it that way at two other points in the book. Besides he is trying to emphasize the American spelling of foreign words.

schmuck, shmuck, schmo, schmoe, shmo *n.*

probably not related to *Schmuck* "jewelry, decoration, adornment": a jerk, oaf, fool. This word would normally not be included here because it probably does not come from German, but so many people have asked me about it that I am including an explanation. The mildly offensive English word *schmuck* is from the very offensive Yiddish word *schmock, shmok* "fool, penis." This much is certain. Most dictionaries say the Yiddish word probably comes from Polish *smok* "snake, tail," although at least one says it probably comes from Slovenian, which, like Polish, is Slavic, not Germanic. The problem is that *schmuck* looks German, and there is even a German word *Schmuck*. One could even draw a connection between the Yiddish and German meanings ("penis" and "jewelry" respectively) with the expression "family jewels," but this is probably pure coincidence.

To complicate matters, at least one dictionary says the literal meaning of the Yiddish word is "a pendant" (which again could be a connection to jewelry) and that it is related to Old High German *smocko*, from which we get *smock*, a garment that hangs around one's neck.

It gets worse: One dictionary I found said the Yiddish word does indeed come from German *Schmuck* (without even a "probably"). Go figure.

Many dictionaries avoid the question altogether (or are extremely honest) and say "origin unknown" or leave it at "Yiddish" (if they include the entry at all).

schnapps, schnaps *n.*

from *Schnaps* "spirits, brandy, gin". See also kirschwasser.

- "Larry had lives in a house that reeked of garbage; he was addicted to crème de banana and licorice schnapps." Garrison Keillor, *Wobegon Boy*, 1997, p. 17.

- "Only the old war-horses in Finland sometimes reminisce about it over a late-night schnapps." Eloise Engle & Lauri Paananen, *The Winter War: The Soviet Attack on Finland 1939-1940*, 1973, p. viii.

- "A pigtailed Tyrolese, seen at a celebration in Jochberg, carries a cask of Enzian schnapps, a liquor made from roots of the gentian, an Alpine wildflower." George W. Long, "Occupied Austria, Outpost of Democracy", *National Geographic*, Jun. 1951, p. 780.

- "'Rum is warm,' mumbled the old man, rocking to and fro in his chair, 'and schnapps is warm, and there's 'eat in soup, but it's a dish o' tea for me.'" Arthur Conan Doyle, *Round the Red Lamp*, 1894.

- "You would let a good man die sooner than give him a drop of schnapps. That's what you Germans call economy." Joseph Conrad, *Lord Jim*, 1900.

schnauzer *n.*

from *Schnauzer* "moustache": a breed of rough-haired terrier. See further example under affenpinscher.

- "It was some kind of miniature schnauzer with a silver-gray beard, like its master's." John Irving, *The Fourth Hand*, 2001, p. 225.

schnitzel *n.*

See Wiener schnitzel.

to schnorr *v.i., v.t.,* **to be on the schnorr** *v.i.*

related to *schnorren* "(colloquial) to beg": (colloquial) to beg. See also schnorrer. This entry suggested by Brian.

schnorrer, shnorrer *n.*

related to *Schnorrer* "(colloquial) beggar": (colloquial) beggar, cadger, moocher, sponger, chiseler, scrounger, bum, parasite [Yiddish *schnorrer, shnorer* "beggar" < German *Schnorrer* "beggar" < *schnorren* "to beg" < *schnurren* "to whir, purr" (because of the musical instruments carried by the beggars) < Middle High German *snurren* (of echoic origin)].

- "Here comes Captain Spaulding, the African explorer—did someone call me, schnorrer?", Groucho Marx in *Animal Crackers*, 1930.

- "He was speaking figuratively, the way a person might call even a rich fundraiser a 'schnorrer' (Yiddish for beggar), despite the literal incongruity of such an appellation.", Philip Greenspun, *Philip and Alex's Guide to Web Publishing*, 1999.

- "'That's Shnorrer, the beggar,' he says, indicating an aged man whose glazed eyes are always zeroing in on leftovers.", Ed Leibowitz, "Market Watch" *Los Angeles Magazine*, Oct. 2001.

schottische, schottish *n.*

from *(der) schottische (Tanz)* "(the) Scottish (dance)": a round dance similar to but slower than the polka; music for the schottische.

- "I attended private parties in sumptuous evening dress, simpered and aired my graces like a born beau, and <u>polked</u> and schottisched with a step peculiar to myself—and the kangaroo." Mark Twain, *Roughing It*, 1871.
- "He taught certain uncouth lads, when they were of an age to enter society, the intricacies of contra dances, or the steps of the schottische and mazurka, and he was a marked figure in all social assemblies, though conspicuously absent from town-meetings and the purely masculine gatherings at the store or tavern or bridge." Kate Douglas Smith Wiggin, *Rebecca of Sunnybrook Farm*, 1903.
- "During the whole evening the bands of the Préobrajensky and Paulowsky regiments had played without cessation polkas, mazurkas, schottisches, and waltzes from among the choicest of their repertoires." Jules Verne, *Michael Strogoff: A Courier of the Czar*, 1911.
- "Flying Cloud Schottische", *Come and Trip It - Instrumental Dance Music 1780s-1920s*, composed by Gilles Jullien, Traditional, et al., 1994
- "Rainbow Schottisch", "Jennie's own Schottische", *By The Old Pine Tree*, composed by Stephen Foster and Sidney Lanier, 1996

schtoom, schtum *adj.*

See <u>shtum</u>.

schuss *n., v.i.*

from *Schuß* "a shot": in skiing, a straight descent with no attempt to decrease speed; to execute a schuss.

- "For communications junkies who dread the thought of losing touch while schussing down the Swiss Alps or hiking the Himalayas, one word: relax." William Reiser, *Time*, Dec. 2, 1996.
- "Whether harmless dribbles or million-ton masses more than a mile wide, avalanches tend to schuss down the same runs year after year." Sharon Begley, "Taming the White Dragon", *Newsweek*, Mar. 8, 1999.

Schutzstaffel, S.S., SS., SS *n.*

"protective rank, defense corps": the personal bodyguard of Adolf Hitler; later, the Elite Guard of the <u>Nazi</u> militia, the Black Shirts. See also <u>Waffen SS</u>. See further examples under <u>Gestapo</u> and <u>Kommandant</u>.

- "Since 1995, when [Jörg] Haider last spoke of the SS, his popularity has grown dramatically." Andrew Purvis, "Forward into the Past", *Time*, Feb. 7, 2000.

schvitz *n., v.i.*

See <u>shvitz</u>.

schwa *n.*

from *Schwa*: weak, neutral vowel sound found in most unstressed syllables in English, e.g. the *a* in *alone*, the *e* in *happen*, the *i* in *easily*, the *o* in *gallop* and the *u* in *circus*, represented by an upside-down *e* [< German *Schwa* < Hebrew *sh'wa, shewa*, the name of a diacritic mark used instead of a vowel].

- "On the other hand, we more freely admit a dead schwa into *-ile* words such as *fragile, hostile*, and *mobile* (though not, perversely, into *infantile* and *mercantile*) where the British are, by contrast, scrupulously phonetic." Bill Bryson, *The Mother Tongue: English and How it Got that Way*, 1990, p. 89.

- "The glyph /*/ is used for the 'schwa' sound of unstressed or occluded vowels (the one that is often written with an upside-down 'e')." Eric S. Raymond, *The New Hacker's Dictionary.*

schweizerkäse, *Schweizerkäse* *n.*
from *Schweizer Käse* "Swiss cheese". See also schmierkase.

- "He had an engagement to take supper with several of his intimates at the Irving Place café, where he could throw aside the heaviest parts of his pose and give way to his appetite for beer and *Schweizerkäse* sandwiches." David Graham Phillips, *Fortune Hunter*, 1906.

sheiss, sheisse *n.*
See scheisse.

sheister *n.*
See shyster.

shice *n.*
See scheisse.

shicer, schicer *n.*
probably from *Scheißer* "contemptible person, coward": Australian English, an unproductive mine or claim; slang, a swindler, welsher or cheat; an unscrupulous person; a worthless thing; a failure [German *Scheißer* literally "one who moves one's bowels" < *scheißen* "to move one's bowels" < Middle High German *schizen* < Old High German *scizen, skizzan* + *-er* "-er"]. See also shyster, scheisse.

- "One such [term from goldfields slang] was SHICER (from British slang for someone considered worthless) and applied in Australia to a worthless mine. By the 1890s SHICER had come to mean a criminal type of person, surviving into the present as SHYSTER." Graham Seal, *The Lingo: Listening to Australian English*, 1999, p. 142.
- "Millie heard the name as Shickster, but that couldn't be the case because this nattily dressed pillar of the community was beyond reproach. Glory heard Shice, or Shicer, but that couldn't have been correct either, because the lady in question religiously attended church each and every Friday and alternate Sundays." Theodore L. Kloski, *Winter Quarter for Bees*, 2005, p. 309.

shiseter *n.*
See shyster.

shlockmeister *n.*
See -meister.

shmier, shmir, shmear, shmeer *n., v.t.*
See schmier.

shmierkase *n.*
See schmierkase.

shnorrer *n.*
See schnorrer.

shtum, schtum, shtoom, schtoom, stumm *adj.*
related to *stumm* "silent": quiet, silent, secretive, unwilling to give information or details about something [Yiddish *shtum*, related to German *stumm* "silent, dumb (unable to speak)"]. This entry suggested by Sarah Hart.

- "No opportunity to spread bug awareness should be missed, even when protocol demands you keep shtum", Karl Feilder, "Not so presidential but a class act anyway", *Computer Weekly*, Jun. 24, 1999.

shvitz bod, shvitz, schvitz *n., v.i.*

related to *Schwitzbad* "steam bath, sauna": a steam bath, to take a steam bath; to sweat, therefore *shvitzing* means "extremely hot" [Yiddish *shvitz bod*, related to German *Schwitzbad* < German *schwitzen* "to sweat" + *Bad* "bath"]. This entry suggested by Sarah Hart.

- "A no-frills bath in the old style, a shvitz, a place where we sit in steam, in wet heat, in dry heat, in a room that sounds like something from the Arabian Nights: the Radiant Room." Mary Gordon, "Still Life", *Harper's Magazine*, Dec. 1998.

- "So, Shvitz City it may be, but wipe your eyes and remember what you came looking for." Hal Rubenstein, "Why August in New York might just be heaven on earth", *Interview*, Aug. 1996.

- "You may feel you've spent the plays [sic] brief running time on a sort of intellectual Stairmaster, panting to keep up with all the smart talk. And when you get off, you may wonder if all that schvitzing was worth it." Charles Isherwood, "Honour", *Variety*, Apr. 27, 1998.

- "There–dazed, daunted and schvitzing–we immediately found ourselves amidst Hammocks, a magnanimous installation by the American artist Patrick Killoran, of approximately 20 modified but perfectly functional string beds attached to pillars, in the shade of the pier's lovely old industrial arcade." Lisa Liebmann, "A Summer Place", *Art in America*, Jun. 1999.

- "'All I know is that in high school, you know, I was always kind of a tense person,' she said. 'A schvitzer, you might say.'" Ian Blecher, "Acid Reflux, Chic Gastric Ailment, Replaces the Ulcer--Ask Gandolfini", *The New York Observer*, Mar. 12, 2001.

shyster, sheister, scheister, shiseter, shyseter *n.*

probably from *Scheißer* "contemptible person, coward": slang or informal insult, an unscrupulous, dishonest, underhanded, unethical or questionable practitioner, especially a lawyer or politician, a pettifogger. [Some dictionaries say *shyster* comes from *Scheißer* without mentioning *shicer*; others, including Merriam-Webster, say it comes from *Scheißer* through *shicer*. One says it may come from *shy*, but that this is dubious. Many say, "origin unknown", and some say it may come from the name of a disreputable 19th-century New York lawyer called Scheuster, but none of them seem to know his first name. Many other origins have been conjectured.] See also shicer, scheisse.

- "Next we come to His Excellency the Prime Minister, a renegade American from New Hampshire, all jaw, vanity, bombast, and ignorance, a lawyer of 'shyster' caliber, a fraud by nature, a humble worshiper of the scepter above him, a reptile never tired of sneering at the land of his birth or glorifying the ten-acre kingdom that has adopted him—salary, four thousand dollars a year, vast consequence, and no perquisites." Mark Twain, *Roughing It*, 1994, p. 362.

- "They are the epitome of stability in a fast shifting culture full of shifty shiftless sheisters." Stephen Powers, *The Art of Getting Over: Graffiti at the Millennium*, 1999, p. 113.

- "I left them with the parting shot that they should have their scheister call my lawyer, when convenient." Tony & Sandra Midea, *A Fool's Guide To Landlording*, 2004, p. 115.

sitz bath, sitz-bath *n.*

from *Sitzbad* "seat + bath; sitting bath": a bath one takes in a sitting position; a tub or basin used for such a bath.

- "Sitz Bath & Heat Treatment", sign on a spa door in *Thunderball*, a James Bond movie starring Sean Connery, 1965.
- "So he sat on the floor, and lit a pipe which I gave him, threw one of my red blankets over his shoulders, inverted my sitz-bath on his head, helmet fashion, and made himself picturesque and comfortable." Mark Twain, "A Ghost Story", *Sketches New and Old*, 1903.
- "She added hot baths, sitz baths, shower baths, and plunges." Mark Twain, *The Adventures of Tom Sawyer*, 1876.
- "The cool air above, and the continual bathing of our bodies in mountain water, alternate foot, sitz, douche, and plunge baths, made this walk exceedingly refreshing, and we had travelled only a mile or two, after leaving the torrent, before every thread of our clothes was as dry as usual, owing perhaps to a peculiar quality in the atmosphere." Henry David Thoreau, *The Maine Woods*, 1858.
- "The medical staff X-rayed the patient's scrotum to locate the staples, and gave him tetanus antitoxin, broad-spectrum antibiotics, and a hexachlorophene Sitz bath prior to surgery the next morning." Wendy Northcutt, *The Darwin Awards*, 2000, p. 266.

sitzmark *n.*

from *Sitzmarke* "seat + mark; mark made by sitting": a depression left in the snow by a skier falling backward.

smierkase, smiercase, smearkase, smearcase *n.*

See schmierkase.

sourbraten *n.*

See sauerbraten.

sourkraut, sourkrout, sour-krout *n.*

See sauerkraut.

spiegeleisen *n.*

from *Spiegeleisen* "mirror iron": a pig iron containing manganese and carbon.

- *The 2000 World Forecasts of Pig Iron, Cast Iron and Spiegeleisen in Pigs and Blocks Export Supplies (World Trade Report)*, 2000.

spiel *n., v.i., v.t.*

from *Spiel; spielen* "game, play; to play": voluble, mechanical, often extravagant talk, especially a sales pitch.

- "I mean, I didn't want to sound difficult, but they did give Twiggy the same spiel." Fran Drescher, *Cancer Schmancer*, 2002, p. 105.

100

- "WHEN YOU TALK TO A PROSPECTIVE CUSTOMER, DO YOU HAVE A RE-HEARSED SPIEL?" Chris Cassatt & Gary Brookins, *Shoe* comic strip, Aug. 23, 2003.
- "Then, remembering her position, she gave me a little bit of the official line—a brief, practised, articulate spiel to the effect that one should never forget that the [Appalachian] trail is not insulated from the larger ills of society but that statistically it remains extremely safe compared with most places in America." Bill Bryson, *A Walk in the Woods*, 1997.
- "He sat there and doodled with his blue pencil on a tablet, listening to me spiel to him for three or four minutes before he got a word in." Malcolm X & Alex Haley, *The Autobiography of Malcolm X*, 1992.
- "You should have heard the spiel he gave her on how they'll be living back on a 'civilized' planet and all the advantages of same." Anne McCaffrey, *The Chronicles of Pern: First Fall*, 1994.
- "Heaven's a *joke*, the kind of thing your Reverend Martin would spiel happily on about for hours, if you kept buying him shots and beers—it's no more real than Tom Billingsley's fishes and horses!" Stephen King, *Desperation*, 1996.
- "Joe was giving him the whole spiel about static electricity and was doing it well." Nicholas Evans, *The Horse Whisperer*, 1995, p. 375.

spieler *n.*

from *Spieler* "player": one who does the above.

- "You're a fair spieler, child." Sinclair Lewis, *Main Street*, 1920.

Sprechgesang *n.*

from *Sprechgesang* "speaking song": a vocal style between singing and speaking, speech-song [German *sprechen* "to speak" + *Gesang* "song, singing"]. See also Sprechstimme. This entry suggested by Christiane Leißner.

- "To signify Moses' inability to articulate God's inexpressible nature, Schoenberg wrote this role using Sprechgesang, a combination of song and speech that British bass John Tomlinson navigates with powerful finesse." Charles Isherwood, "Moses und Aron", *Variety*, Feb. 22, 1999.

Sprechstimme, sprechstimme *n.*

from *Sprechstimme* "speaking voice": a voice part employing Sprechgesang [German *sprechen* "to speak" + *Stimme* "voice"].

- "In works such as the 1912 Pierrot lunaire, Arnold Schoenberg invented the device of sprechstimme, or speech-song; in The Cave Reich has perfected the principle and built an entire work upon it." Michael Walsh, "Music: Words Sliced And Diced", *Time*, May 31, 1993, p. 69.
- "When the men vocalize-Ewan McGregor in more than mezza voce, and Jim Broadbent in spunky sprechstimme-I suspect that the two masculine names billed in the credits as 'vocal doubles' deserve the applause." John Simon, "Nic & J-Lo", *National Review*, Jun. 11, 2001.

spritz *v.i., v.t., n.*

from *spritzen* "to squirt, spray, sprinkle, spatter; inject".

- "While packing it for the plane ride home, she insisted that the mirror was dirty and spritzed it with Windex." Fran Drescher, *Enter Whining*, 1996, p. 31.
- "Soon I had met beetles that move through water by walking on the under-side of the surface as though it were a glass ceiling and beetles that jet ski on

top with the aid of compounds spritzed from their abdomens ...." Douglas H. Chadwick, "Planet of the Beetles", *National Geographic*, Mar. 1998.

spritzer *n.*

from *Spritzer* "a splash, spatter, rain shower, spritzer": a beverage of usually white wine and soda water [perh. < Pennsylvania German < German *Spritzer* < *spritzen* "to spray"].

- "The combination of a white-wine spritzer and a tilted bladder put me badly in need of a bathroom, but oddly enough, it was always occupied, and there seemed to be several voices coming from behind the locked door." Fran Drescher, *Enter Whining*, 1996, p. 48.

- "Eh, no big loss, I can't be charming and keep my lipstick on with a rumaki in one hand and a spritzer in the other anyway." Fran Drescher, *Enter Whining*, 1996, p. 224.

SS, S.S., SS. *n.*

See *Schutzstaffel*.

stalag, Stalag *n.*

from *Stalag* short for *Stammlager* "main camp": a German camp for prisoners of war, especially in World War II.

- "'Welcome to the Stalag,' said a man with an ironic smile and an English accent." Bill Bryson, *A Walk in the Woods*, 1997.

- *Hogan's Heroes: Behind the Scenes at Stalag 13*, by Brenda Scott Royce & Werner Klemperer, 1998.

stark *adj.*

related to *stark* "strong": stiff, rigid, standing out, bleak, desolate, barren, sheer, utter, downright, hard, harsh, severe, strong, powerful [Middle English *starc* < Anglo-Saxon *stearc*]. *Stark* doesn't come from Modern German but rather from Middle English and Anglo-Saxon and therefore has common roots with Modern German. The spelling and meaning are so similar that I have included it here. This entry suggested by Brigitte.

- "'What have I been all this time?' she asked herself, and answered, 'Just stark egotism, crude assertion of Ann Veronica, without a modest rag of religion or discipline or respect for authority to cover me!'" H. G. Wells, *Ann Veronica: A Modern Love Story*, 1909.

Stasi *n.*

the internal security force or secret police of the former German Democratic Republic (East Germany) [short for German *Staatssicherheitspolizei* or *-dienst* "State security police or service" < *Staat* "State" + *Sicherheit* "security, safety"].

- "They're the perpetrators of the Stasi secret police—who like the Nazis before them feel no remorse." Stefan Thiel, "Old Stasi Never Die", *Newsweek*, Dec. 10, 2001, p. 39.

- "This time the artists shot in the abandoned Berlin headquarters of the East German secret police, known as the Stasi, and the results are spectacular." Brooks Adams, "Jane and Louise Wilson at 303", *Art in America*, Oct. 1998.

- "Interviewees run an intriguing gamut, from an East Berlin minister to a former Stasi official and Bavarian entrepreneur whose longtime dream to 'recycle the Wall' (literally, as road and building-foundation raw material) duly came true." Dennis Harvey, "After the Fall", *Variety*, May 8, 2000.

stein *n.*

from *Stein* "stone": a large (earthenware) mug used especially for beer; the quantity of beer that a stein holds; in mining, stone-work used to secure the sides of a shaft. See further example under <u>lederhosen</u>. See also <u>Ehrenbreitstein</u>, <u>Frankenstein</u>, <u>stein</u>.

- "We camped together in a high Alpine pass, somewhere along the road between Salzburg and Klagenfurt, and in the evening walked into the nearest village, where we found awaiting us a perfect inn, full of black panelled wood and a log fire with a sleeping dog before it and ruddy-faced yeoman customers swinging steins of beer." Bill Bryson, *Neither Here Nor There: Travels in Europe*, 1991, p. 250.

- "When I returned for breakfast, local families were already eating big platters of goulash, <u>Wiener Schnitzels</u>, and *Würstel* (page 766), and drinking tall steins of beer." George W. Long, "Occupied Austria, Outpost of Democracy", *National Geographic*, Jun. 1951, p. 771.

- "They went to the balcony of a big, noisy restaurant and had a shore dinner, with tall steins of beer." Willa Sibert Cather, *Youth and the Bright Medusa*, 1920.

- "Steins of <u>lager</u> beer were ventured upon." Frances Hodgson Burnett, *The Shuttle*, 1907.

steinbock, steinboc, steinbok, steinbuck, stonebock, stonebuck *n.*

from *Steinbock* "stone buck": a type of wild goat in Europe, the European, Capra, Stone or Alpine Ibex (*Capra ibex*); a type of antelope in Africa, the Steenbok (*Raphicerus campestris*) [< German *Stein* "stone" + *Bock* "male deer, goat or sheep", some of the spellings above no doubt influenced by the Dutch *steenbok*]. See also <u>Ehrenbreitstein</u>, <u>Frankenstein</u>, <u>stein</u>.

- "In the Alps the Steinbock or stone ibex and chamois are common, scrambling with ease over precipitous rocky hillsides, while marmots emerging from holes in the ground make a screeching sound to warn their mates at the first signs of danger." Michael Hambrey & Jürg Alean, *Glaciers*, 2004, p. 221.

- "You may also see deer, chamois (Gemse), and an occasional Steinbock (bouquetin), a mammal that is larger than a deer." Marcia & Philip Lieberman, *Walking Switzerland, the Swiss Way: From Vacation Apartments, Hotels, Mountain Inns, and Huts*, 1997, p. 51.

- "It amounted to 2430 zebra, 967 wildebeeste, 846 Coke's hartebeeste, 932 Grant's gazelle, 546 Thomson's gazelle, 146 impala, 8 steinbock, 2 duiker, 46 eland, 19 giraffe, 1 rhinoceros, 86 ostrich, 1 cheetah, 5 hyena and pack of 7 hunting dogs." Rick Ridgeway, *The Shadow of Kilimanjaro*, 1999, p. 54.

Steppenwolf *n.*

from *Steppenwolf* "steppe wolf": a U.S. rock band founded by German American John Ray (born Joachim Fritz Krauledat), named for the book *Steppenwolf* by German author Hermann Hesse [< German *Steppe* "steppe" + *Wolf* "wolf"].

- "Then they would either explode and separate forever, and there would be no more Steppenwolf, or else they would come to terms in the dawning light of humor." Hermann Hesse, translated by Basil Creighton, *Steppenwolf: A Novel*, 2002, p. 56.

- "The Sunday morning kickoff featured Jay Leno as the grand marshal and Peter Fonda as the honorary grand marshal (this town ain't big enough for two marshals), while John Kay and Steppenwolf got up god-awful early Sunday morning to play 'Born to Be Wild' at Harley-Davidson of Glendale for the thousands who turned up to take part in the 50-mile 'motorcycle caravan' that chugged along L.A. freeways to Castaic Lake Recreation Center in Santa Clarita." Paul Garson, *Born to Be Wild: A History of the American Biker and Bikes 1947-2002*, 2003, p. 144.

strand *n., v.i., v.t.*

related to *Strand* "beach": shore, especially the ocean shore, that is, beach. *Strand* doesn't come from Modern German but rather from Middle English, Old English and Anglo-Saxon and therefore has common roots with Modern German. The spelling and meaning are so similar that I have included it here.

- "A viewing of those gallant whales/That blew at every strand." Herman Melville, *Moby Dick*, 1851, p. 174.

- "Far below us was the beach, from half a dozen to a dozen rods in width, with a long line of breakers rushing to the strand." Henry David Thoreau, *Cape Cod*, 1865.

- "He gazed with eyes that dared not focus too long on the human jetsam and the wreckage flung up on the long narrow strand that was the nearest landfall." Anne McCaffrey, *The Chronicles of Pern: First Fall*, 1994.

streusel *n.*

from *Streusel* "sweet crumbly topping": mainly U.S., a crumbly topping or filling for cakes, breads and muffins made of sugar, flour, butter, and often cinnamon and chopped nuts. The resulting cake is called a streusel, streusel cake, coffeecake or coffee cake. [< German *Streusel* "something strewn" < Middle High German *ströusel* < *ströuwen* "to strew, sprinkle" < Old High German *strouwen, strewen*].

- "A related cooking term [to the *straw* in *strawberry*] is *streusel*, an informally scattered topping on baked goods." Harold McGee, *On Food and Cooking: The Science and Lore of the Kitchen*, 2004, p. 265.

- "To add cold roux to a simmering liquid, work the roux to break it up into small pieces, like a streusel topping, and then scatter it into the simmering cooking liquid." Culinary Institute of America, *The Professional Chef*, 2001, p. 536.

- "The audience held its breath, hoping they made it back across the ring without the owner falling and turning her hip into streusel." Emily Yoffe, *What the Dog Did: Tales from a Formerly Reluctant Dog Owner*, 2005, p. 112.

- "Use your hands for mixing doughs, streusel toppings and very thick mixtures, such as meat loaf." Betty Crocker, *Betty Crocker's Cookbook: Everything You Need to Know to Cook Today*, 2000, p. 6.

- "Combine oats (set aside 1 tablespoon), GrapeNuts, and jam in a food processor and process until jam is evenly distributed and mixture has a streusel-like feel." Dean Ornish, *Everyday Cooking with Dr. Dean Ornish: 150 Easy, Low-Fat, High-Flavor Recipes*, 1997, p. 263.

- "Alyssa grabbed two small plates and put one of the blueberry streusel muffins on each dish." Carly Phillips, Janelle Denison & Jacquie D'Alessandro, *Stroke of Midnight*, 2004, p. 207.

- "'Our former secretary,' Jo snapped and rustled one hand into the bag from the Leaf and Bean before pulling out a cinnamon-streusel-topped muffin." Maureen Child, *And Then Came You: Sam's Story*, 2004, p. 7.

strudel *n.*

from *Strudel* "whirlpool": a kind of pastry. See further example under <u>bratwurst</u>.

- "Thus when Prodi visited Bonn last month to lobby for his EMU bid, he wasn't exactly the contrite vassal seeking approval from the masterful lord, and it was the unemployment-plagued Kohl who had to eat humble strudel." Jay Branegan, *Time*, Mar. 17, 1997.

stumm *adj.*

See <u>shtum</u>.

Sturm und Drang, *Sturm und Drang*, sturm and drang *n.*

from *Sturm und Drang* "storm and stress": actually a movement in 18th-century German literature but often used today simply to mean "turmoil".

- "'Durmstrang,' the name of the wizarding school that admits only full-blooded wizards and has questionable links to Lord Voldemort, comes from a German artistic style called *Sturm und Drang*, which was a favourite of <u>Nazi</u> Germany. As well, Durmstrang students arrive at Hogwarts in a ship like the one featured prominently in a famous *Sturm und Drang* opera." David Colbert, *The Magical Worlds of Harry Potter: A Treasury of Myths, Legends and Fascinating Facts*, 2001, p. 15.

- "So dawned the time of *Sturm und Drang*: storm and stress to-day rocks our little boat on the mad waters of the world-sea; there is within and without the sound of conflict, the burning of body and rending of soul; inspiration strives with doubt, and faith with vain questionings." W. E. Burghardt DuBois, *The Souls of Black Folk*, 1903.

- "After six months of sturm and drang she had to let him go." Bennet Cerf, Ed., *Laughing Stock*, 1945.

T

taler, thaler, dollar *n.* [*pl.* **taler, talers, thaler, thalers, dollars**]

from *Taler, Thaler* "from the valley": any of several former German silver coins [*dollar* < Late German *daler* < German *Thaler* shortened from *Joachimsthaler* "from Joachim Valley" < *St. Joachimsthal* (town in Bohemia where silver for the coin was mined); *Tal, Thal* "valley" is related to English *dale*].

- "'Miss Sieppe, Miss Sieppe, your ticket has won five thousand dollars,' cried Maria. 'Don't you remember the lottery ticket I sold you in Doctor McTeague's office?' 'Trina!' almost screamed her mother. 'Five tausend thalers! five tausend thalers!'" Frank Norris, *McTeague: A Story of San Francisco*, 1899, p. 81.

- "Therefore it was droll in the good Riemer, who has written memoirs of Goethe, to make out a list of his donations and good deeds, as, so many hundred thalers given to Stilling, to Hegel, to Tischbein: a lucrative place found for Professor Voss, a post under the Grand Duke for Herder, a pension for Meyer, two professors recommended to foreign universities, &c. &c." Ralph Waldo Emerson, *Essays: Second Series*, 1844, p. 502.

- "Egad, what a spendthrift I shall be this night; pence, shillings, thalers, marks, francs, dollars, sovereigns – they are the same to me!" Eugene Field, *The Love Affairs of a Bibliomaniac*, 1896, p. 213.

- "He was regarded as a brilliant ornament to Germany; and a paltry Duke of Brunswick thought a few hundred thalers well spent in securing the glory of having such a man to reside at his provincial court." John Fiske, *The Unseen World, and Other Essays*, 1876, p. 147.

- "It may be all as thou sayest, and inevitable, but I dare not mention the thing to mother, and five thalers is all I can spare out of my own wages." Bayard Taylor, *Beauty and the Beast: and Tales of Home*, 1872, p. 146.

- "And he took his money out of his pocket and counted out the seven talers, always reckoning four and twenty groschen to a taler." Jacob & Wilhelm Grimm, *Grimm's Fairy Tales*, 1909.

- "The worker who owns a little house to the value of a thousand talers is certainly no longer a proletarian, but one must be Dr. Sax to call him a capitalist." Frederick Engels, *The Housing Question*, 1872-1873.

thaler *n.*

See taler.

traumkeller *n.*

from *Traum + Keller* "dream + cellar, basement": no doubt made up by the author of the following example.

- "He cast his regard farther afield, and was briefly in the mind of a scape-scrounge haunting the quiet ruins of Manhattan, then looked through the eyes of a wild chimeric condor, high above the southern Andes, then in the mind of a young woman surfing at dawn off New Sealand, before becoming part of a chimeric triple-mind within a sounding humpback in mid-Pacific, then joining a chanting priestess in some midnight temple in Singapore, followed by a drunken night-guard at an ovitronics plant in Tashkent, an insomniac agronometricist in Arabie, a spanceled Resiler preaching unheeded in the smoky chaos of a traumkeller in old Prag, and finally a sleepy balloonist descending through the dusk above Tammanrusset." Iain M. Banks, *Feersum Endjinn*, 1994, p. 77.

U

über-, uber-, über *prefix, adj.*

"over-, super-": Used like *wunder-* as in <u>*wunderkind*</u> [< German *über* "over" < Middle High German *über* < Old High German *ubar*]. Interestingly German-speakers often prefer Anglicisms and would therefore prefer, for example, *Superhacker* to *Überhacker*, although they would understand both to mean the same thing. In the same vein the word *superman* in English originates as a direct translation (loan translation) of the German *Übermensch*, but one hears *Superman* much more often in German. See also <u>"Deutschland über alles"</u>.

- "ÜBER BERMUDA, DAD." Jerry Scott & Jim Borgman, *Zits* comic strip, Jun. 16, 2004.
- "This all sounds *über-*romantic." Adele Parks, *Larger than Life*, 2002, p. 11.
- "Two years ago, when the capture of America's best-known computer criminal, Kevin Mitnick, was front-page news, it was Littman who got the *über-*hacker's inside story and wrote a book, *The Fugitive Game*, that was sympathetic to Mitnick." Joshua Quittner, *Time*, May 5, 1997, p. 48.
- "Frazier asked *über-*agent Amanda Urban to put up his book for auction so early because he wanted to choose an editor carefully." Malcolm Jones, "King of the Mountain" (review of *Cold Mountain* by Charles Frazier), *Newsweek*, Apr. 22, 2002, p. 65.
- "Uber-Guber Goes Multimedia" (filmmaker Peter Guber), Charles Lyons, *Variety*, Aug. 23, 1999.
- "Uber-skate journalist Jacko Weyland checks in on the state of the nation ..." "Skaters eye", *Thrasher Magazine*, May 2002.
- "Uber-ISP AOL has teamed up with mobile phone king Nokia to produce a cut-down version of the Netscape browser for WAP devices." "Uber-ISP AOL", *Internet Magazine*, Mar. 2001.

... über alles, ... uber alles

"... over everything": When used in phrases like "now he's become the boss über alles" or "it seems like its Shaq and the Lakers über alles", "... über alles" is derived from <u>"Deutschland über alles"</u>, which see. This entry and examples suggested by Wilton Woods.

- "Distribution Uber Alles" (German giant Bertelsmann's digital distribution plans), Brad King, *Variety*, Dec. 18, 2000.

U-boat *n.*

from *U-Boot* "submarine": submarine [short for German *Unterseeboot* "undersea boat"].

- "The road felt frictionless, as if I were at the wheel of a destroyer on the North Atlantic, and the shapes in the mist off to starboard weren't farmhouses but cargo ships in the convoy, and the windshield wiper was a sonar antenna tracking German U-boats." Garrison Keillor, *Wobegon Boy*, 1997, p. 164.
- "On January 13, 1940, Hitler ordered a military committee to research the feasibility of military action in the north, with an eye to the Norwegian ports of Narvik and Trondheim for use by Admiral Karl Dönitz's U-boat force." Eloise Engle & Lauri Paananen, *The Winter War: The Soviet Attack on Finland 1939-1940*, 1973, p. 120.
- "You have a long coast line and you may need the U-boat yourself some day." Henry Morgenthau & Ara Sarafian, *Ambassador Morgenthau's Story*, 1918.
- "Ever since entering the U-boat zone we had been on the lookout for periscopes, and children that we were, bemoaning the unkind fate that was to see us safely into France on the morrow without a glimpse of the dread marauders." Edgar Rice Burroughs, *The Land That Time Forgot*.

umlaut *n., v.t.,* **umlaut-mark** *n.*

from *Umlaut* "change of sound": also called vowel modification, mutation or inflection; the change of a vowel sound (e.g., *mouse–mice, goose–geese, langlauf–langläufer*); the vowel altered in this way; the diacritical mark consisting of two dots (¨) over a modified vowel; to modify by umlaut; to write an umlaut over. [German < *um-* "about, changed" < Middle High

From a book published in 1732. One can see the superscript "e" used as an umlaut in *Gärtlein* "little garden" and *schönen* "beautiful".

German *umbe* < Middle High German *umbi* + *Laut* "sound" < Middle High German *lut*, coined by Jacob Grimm of the Brothers Grimm.] This entry suggested by Aldorado Cultrera.

The diacritic marks *umlaut* and *dieresis* [chiefly Am.] (also spelled *diaeresis* [chiefly Br.]) are identical in appearance but different in function. The dieresis (Greek "to take apart") indicates that the vowel so marked is to be pronounced separately from the one preceeding it (e.g., *naïve, Noël*) or that the vowel should be sounded when it might otherwise be silent (e.g., *Brontë*).

The origin of the German umlaut is an abbreviated "e", i.e. the vowel is influenced by the following (semi-)vowel "e" in a process called apophany, therefore the correct transliteration of an umlaut is to use an "e" after the vowel. Umlauts occur mostly in Germanic languages but also for example in Finnish. When German words with umlauts are assimilated into the English language, they sometimes keep their umlauts (e.g., *doppelgänger, Flügelhorn, föhn, Der Freischütz, führer, jäger, kümmel, Künstlerroman, schweizerkäse, über-*), but often are simply written without the diacritic (e.g., *doppelganger, flugelhorn, Der Freischutz, yager*), and less often are correctly transliterated using an "e" (e.g., *foehn, fuehrer, jaeger, loess*). Of course, sometimes more than one spelling makes its way into

English. _Muesli_ could have originated from _Müesli_ or _Müsli_, so it's not clear if the umlaut was lost or transliterated.

- "Simeon Potter believed that English spelling possessed three distinguishing features that offset its other shortcomings: The consonants are fairly regular in their pronunciation, the language is blessedly free of the diacritical marks that complicate other languages—the umlauts, cedillas, circumflexes, and so on—and, above all, English preserves the spelling of borrowed words, so that people of many nations 'are immediately aware of the meanings of thousands of words which would be unrecognizable if written phonetically.'" Bill Bryson, _The Mother Tongue: English and How It Got that Way_, 1990, p. 121.

- "Now you look like a German in American clothes. I don't know—I do believe it's your face, Ted. I wouldn't have thought that ten years or so in any country could change the shape of one's nose, and mouth and cheekbones. Do you suppose it's the umlauts?" Edna Ferber, _Fanny Herself_, 1917.

- "Because of my frequent need to use the Umlaut (ve must have capitals for a noun, pleess), my face has become so distorted and angry-looking and I might immediately be found out to be a German!" "Umlaut and about", _The Dominion_, Sep. 9, 2000.

- "The Department of Internal Affairs is sticking by its decision which effectively changes the surname of a a [_sic_] Swiss family who gained New Zealand citizenship last week. The [Yvonne] Kuenzi family's correct name has no letter e but an umlaut—two dots above the u—which is used in Germanic languages to indicate a change of vowel or sound." Anonymous, "Change of family's name is 'policy'", _Nelson Mail_, Nov. 9, 1998.

Unruhe _n._

from _Unruhe_ "unrest, restlessness, commotion": the title of season 4, episode 2 of the TV series _The X-Files_ [< German _un-_ "un-" + _Ruhe_ "rest" < _ruhen_ "to rest" < Middle High German _ruon, ruowen_ < Old High German _ruowen, ruowon_]. This entry suggested by CauNo.

ur-, Ur- _prefix_

"original, primitive, ancient" [< German _ur-_ "the original condition or first representative of a thing" < Middle & Old High German _ur-_ "out (of)"].

- "They certainly looked like Ur-bats, the original bats, the bats of prehistory, their slow, labored flapping interspersed with ungainly glides, and indeed perhaps they were a species of leaf-nosed bat, not much altered from their fossil ancestors of sixty million years ago and probably earlier–seventy to 100 million years ago–early enough to have been catching insects in the evening over a shallow lake full of dinosaurs." Redmond O'Hanlon, _No Mercy: A Journey Into the Heart of the Congo_, 1998.

- "I know what he did to the first author, the ur-Horace Jacob Little." David Czuchlewski, _The Muse Asylum_, 2001, p. 79.

- "He was holding up a steaming coffee cup, white and smoothly iconic, in a big, white-gloved, three-fingered ur-Disney hand." William Gibson, _Idoru_, 1997, p. 34.

- "Trevor-Roper was not writing fiction, of course, but his spellbinding, cinematic vision of Hitler, Rosenfeld argues, became the defining image, the ur-

Hitler for the decades of pulp fiction and film that followed." Ron Rosenbaum, "Explaining Hitler", *The New Yorker*, May 1995, p. 60.
- "Even the 'Ur-Alphabet', namely the Phoenician, developed from several sources." Niklaus Shaefer, "Spelling Systems have always been mixes and have drawn ideas from multiple sources", *Journal of the Simplified Spelling Society*, 2001/2.

verboten *adj.*

from *verboten* "forbidden": forbidden [< German *verbieten* "to forbid" < Middle High German *verbieten* < Old High German *farbiotan*]
- "Smoking around this gas is expressly verboten, as these girls learned to their dismay." Wendy Northcutt, *The Darwin Awards II*, 2001, p. 180.
- "What Charlie Chaplin did more than 60 years ago with 'The Great Dictator' and 'Hogan's Heroes' did with its POW antics in the 1960s--playing the <u>Nazis</u> for onscreen laughs--has always been verboten in Germany." Ed Meza, "'Goebbels' guffaws target Teuton taboo. (Der Furor)", *Variety*, Nov. 25, 2002. ("Der Furor" is a play on <u>der Führer</u>.)
- "News, after all, frequently covers violent, adult-oriented subjects, which puts many news stories into the same verboten range as porn." Joshua Quittner, "Unshackling Net Speech", *Time*, Jul. 7, 1997, p. 31.
- "The cache is important; it can store immense volumes of your surfing history including images, some of which may be verboten." Thomas C. Greene, "Data security for Linux power users", *The Register*, Jul. 11, 2002.

Volkswagen, VW *n.*

"people's car": a German automobile manufacturer; an automobile made by this manufacturer [< German *Volk* "folk, people" < Middle High German *volc* "folk, people; troop of warriors" < Old High German *folc* "pile; folk, people; troop of warriors" + *Wagen* "automobile, car, wagon" < Middle High German *wagen* < Old High German *wagan* "that which moves, vehicle"]
- "In response to the oil shocks of the 1970s, Japanese carmakers and Germany's Volkswagen introduced small, fuel-efficient cars that appealed to young buyers." Peter McWilliams, *Ain't Nobody's Business If You Do: The Absurdity of Consensual Crimes in Our Free Country*.
- "Mercedes-Benz, BMW, and Volkswagen are at the forefront of ecological design in car production ...." Deanna J. Richards, *The Industrial Green Game: Implications for Environmental Design and Management*, 1997, p. 213.
- "Having written 'Cadillac' and 'Volkswagen' in the neat block capitals that are actually taught in education courses, the teacher asks the student which of those brands they 'identify with' and to get up and move to the corresponding side of the room." Richard Mitchell, *Less Than Words Can Say*.

- "They were ordinarily transported in two vehicles, a Volkswagen Jetta and a minibus." Alison Liebhafsky Des Forges, *Leave None to Tell the Story: Genocide in Rwanda*, 1999.
- "You say to someone 'I saw a Volkswagen Beetle today with a vanity license plate that read FEATURE'. If he/she laughs, he/she is a geek." Eric S. Raymond, *The New Hacker's Dictionary*.
- "So expect the already crowded radio spectrum that accommodates wireless communications to be jammed more tightly than a Volkswagen at a clown convention, as the air around us fills with data." Steven Levy, "The Next Big Thing", *Time*, Dec. 17, 2001, p. 62.

Vorsprung durch Technik, Vorsprung durch ..., Vorsprung *n.*

"advantage through technology": used by Audi in a 1986 advertising campaign in the UK, no doubt in order to emphasize German quality [< German *Vorsprung* "advantage, lead, leading edge, start, head start" + *durch* "through" + *Technik* "technology"]. This entry suggested by ngi99178. See also <u>Fahrvergnügen</u>.

- "Following directions conveyed by Ned Capel's solicitors they left the village and continued on into the dark, turning off at last up a steep drive which proved to be more like a cart-track, their rough passage shaking the Audi until its Vorsprung seemed to come unsprung." Jan Siegel, *Prospero's Children*, 2001, p. 19.
- "Vorsprung durch Anglistik", sidebar describing English loan words used in German car advertising, David Crystal, *The Cambridge Encyclopedia of the English Language*, 1995, p. 114.
- "Despite a unified Europe, political correctness, *Vorsprung durch Technik* and Jürgen Klinsmann, national prejudice remains a real issue and many people hold strong negative stereotypes about Germany." Norbert Pachler (editor), *Teaching Modern Foreign Languages at Advanced Level*, 1999, p. 295.
- "This latter development was, moreover, accompanied by advertising initiatives which, in Audi's case, made play with the phrase *Vorsprung durch Technik* (Progress through Technology) in a British campaign that was no less astute than Volkswagen's earlier American one (Bayley 1986: 93-100)." Nick Perry, *Hyperreality and Global Culture*, 1998, p. 54.
- "In the automotive industry German manufacturers such as Mercedes, BMW and Audi have successfully positioned their offerings at the high quality end of the spectrum through superior design, technical engineering skills ('Vorsprung durch Technic [*sic*]' - leading through technology) and attention to quality control through the manufacturing process." Colin Egan & Michael J. Thomas (editors), *CIM Handbook of Strategic Marketing*, 1998, p. 136.
- "Zooropa ... Vorsprung durch Technik/Zooropa ... Be all that you can be/Be a winner/Eat to get slimmer", U2, *Zooropa*, 1993.

111

Waffen SS *n.*

"weapon SS". See also *Schutzstaffel*.

- "When Austria's Jörg Haider commended Hitler's 'orderly' employment policies and praised former members of the Waffen SS as 'decent men of good character' he was an ambitious outsider from Austria's rural Carinthia province looking for a way to broaden his appeal to older voters." Andrew Purvis, "Forward into the Past", *Time*, Feb. 7, 2000.

waldmeister, Waldmeister *n.*

from *Waldmeister* "forest master": an Old World flower and herb, sweet woodruff, *Galium odoratum*, an operetta by Johann Strauss II, 1895 [< German *Wald* "woods, forest" < Middle High German *walt* < Old High German *walt* + *Meister*, see -meister].

- "There are many classic and traditional 'bowlen' in Germany, and peaches, pineapple, or 'waldmeister' (woodruff) may be used instead of strawberries." Katherine Burton & Helmut Ripperger, *Feast Day Cookbook*.

Waldsterben *n.*

"forest death": the dying of forest ecosystems by acid rain or other forms of pollution, first described in Germany and the former Czechoslovakia.

- "Waldsterben—the death of forests from air pollution—is costing Europe (including Russia) at least $29 billion annually in lost timber, tourism, manufactured goods and other social benefits—losses that may continue for the next century." Don Hinrichsen, "Computing the Risks: A Global Overview of our Most-pressing Environmental Challenges", *International Wildlife*, Mar.-Apr. 1996, p. 28.

waltz *n., v.i., v.t., adj.*

from *walzen* "to roam, travel around, waltz": a certain dance, to do the dance, to cause to do the dance, pertaining to the dance, also figuratively. A **waltzer** is one who waltzes, although in German *Walzer* is the dance itself. See further examples under schottische and polka.

- "On the third day of my hospital stay, my surgeon came waltzing into my room, all chipper and smiles, followed by Doctor #8, the gynecologist who'd finally diagnosed me." Fran Drescher, *Cancer Schmancer*, 2002, p. 132.
- "The dungeon was full of hundreds of pearly-white, translucent people, mostly drifting around a crowded dance floor, waltzing to the dreadful, quavering sound of thirty musical saws, played by an orchestra on a raised, black-draped platform." Joanne K. Rowling, *Harry Potter and the Chamber of Secrets* (Book 2), 1999, p. 132.
- "Neville and Ginny were dancing nearby – he could see Ginny wincing frequently as Neville trod on her feet – and Dumbledore was waltzing with Madame Maxine." J. K. Rowling, *Harry Potter and the Goblet of Fire* (Book 4), 2000, p. 365.
- "Ten minutes after that she would be home, and the husband would be there to greet her; and even a man like Cyril, dwelling as he did in a dark phlegmy

world of root canals, bicuspids, and cares, would start asking a few questions if his wife suddenly waltzed in from a week-end wearing a six-thousand-dollar mink coat." Roald Dahl, "Mrs Bixby and the Colonel's Coat", *Kiss Kiss*, 1959, p. 91.

- "Hector was doing obese male exhibitionists who enjoy putting on organdy tutus and dancing to the 'Waltz of the Sugarplum Fairy' in public and were pleased to do so on his show ...." Garrison Keillor, "The Chuck Show of Television", *The Book of Guys*, 1993.
- "If the Cardassians waltz away with the photonic pulse cannon, do you think they're going to admit to us that it's a piece of junk?" Dafydd ab Hugh, *Balance of Power (Star Trek: The Next Generation)*, 1995.
- "The risk was too great: could you imagine yourself waltzing into the Mem outpatient clinic and waltzing out with a box of morphine bottles under your arm?" Michael Crichton writing as Jeffery Hudson, *A Case of Need*, 1968.
- "I jumped around for several minutes doing the *Nutcracker Waltz* while simultaneously singing the lost lyrics, which go something like this: 'EEYOWWW!!! OUCH OUCH OUCH AAAUUUAAAAHHH!!!'." Scott Adams, *The Joy of Work: Dilbert's Guide to Finding Happiness at the Expense of Your Co-workers*, 1999.

wanderlust *n.*

from *Wanderlust* "desire to wander": strong longing to travel. *Wandern* more often means "to hike" than "to wander" in German; to emphasize the difference a German-speaker will say *herum wandern*, literally "to wander around".

- "Here was another man who didn't share my wanderlust." Fran Drescher, *Cancer Schmancer*, 2002, p. 52.
- "I look behind me/And I see there's just/Me and the wanderlust." Mark Knopfler, "Wanderlust", *Sailing to Philadelphia*, 2000.
- "His sense of wonder and awe, his gentle encouragement toward 'direct experience,' and his simple yet graphic prose will stir the wanderlust in many a reader." Booklist, a review in: Michael Crichton, *Travels*, 1988, p. i.
- "Like humans, wolves possess associative minds and wanderlust." Mark Derr, *Dog's Best Friend: Annals of the Dog-Human Relationship*, 1997.
- "The Wonderlust—probably it's a worse affliction than the Wanderlust." Sinclair Lewis, *Main Street*, 1920.
- *Wanderlust*, Danielle Steel, 1986.
- *Wanderlust*, magazine.

wedeln *n.*

from *wedeln* "to wag": a skiing technique first developed in Austria in the 1950s that consists of high-speed turns made in succession with both skis parallel while not noticeably setting the ski edges on a slope. Using this technique one's rear end wags like a dog's tail [< German *wedeln* "to wag (the tail), fan" < Middle High German *wadelen, wedelen* < *wadel, wedel* "fan, tuft of hair" < Old High German *wadal, wedil*].

- "Then, between bouts with tomato sauce, cheese and toppings, he was yodeling and wedeln-ing his way down the slopes." Jay Lloyd, "Getting job at ski area can help you get more time on the slopes", *Lancaster (PA) Sunday News*, Dec. 19, 1999.

Wehrmacht, *Wehrmacht n.*

"defense force": the German armed forces before and during World War II [< German *Wehr* "defense" < Middle High German *wer, were* < Old High German *weri, wari* "defense" + *Macht* "force, might" < Middle and Old High German *maht* "ability", related to English *might*]. See also <u>Landwehr</u>, <u>Machtpolitik</u>.

- "In the back seat, reading some papers, was – I swear to God – the famous Dr Kurt Waldheim, the aforementioned Wehrmacht officer and now president of Austria." Bill Bryson, *Neither Here Nor There: Travels in Europe*, 1991, p. 264.
- "During World War II, the Soviet Union began to build what Soviet sources refer to as history's first coalition of a progressive type when it organized or reorganized the armies of Eastern Europe to fight with the Red Army against the German Wehrmacht." Stephen R. Burant, *East Germany, a Country Study*, 1987.
- "Incorporated into the Wehrmacht, the corps was composed largely of anti-Soviet émigrés who had served in the armies of the Czar; many of the personnel were incapable of extended field service, and the Germans generally restricted them to such security duties as the protection of the vital Belgrade-Nish railroad line." Robert M. Kennedy, *Hold the Balkans!: German Antiguerrilla Operations in the Balkans 1941-1944.*
- "One of them was Lieutenant-General Kurt Dittmar, a fifty-seven-year-old Wehrmacht officer who had made a name for himself broadcasting communiques from the front and was known everywhere as the 'voice of the German High Command'." Ada Petrova & Peter Watson, *The Death of Hitler: The Full Story With New Evidence from Secret Russian Archives*, 1995.
- "The entire Western campaign of 1940 had cost the Wehrmacht only 156,000 casualties (with 30,000 dead)." Howard Andrew G. Chua-Eoan, "War in Europe", *Time*, Dec. 2, 1991, p. 62.

Weihnachtsbaum, Der *n.*

from *Der Weihnachtsbaum* "The Christmas Tree": set of 12 piano pieces by Liszt, composed 1874-1876 [< German *der* "the" + *Weihnacht* "Holy Night, Christmas Eve" + *Baum* "tree"].

- "She hesitated, searching her memory for a good Liszt; then softly she began to play one of the twelve pieces from *Der Weihnachtsbaum*." Roald Dahl, "Edward the Conqueror", *Kiss Kiss*, 1959, p. 171.

Weismannism, weismannism, Weissmannism, Weismann's theory *n.*

from *Weismannismus* "Weissmannism": the theory that the contents of ova and sperm are not affected by other changes in the body, thus ruling out the possibilty of inheriting acquired characteristics from one's parents, a key element of neo-Darwinism [August Friedrich Leopold Weismann (1834–1914), the German biologist who propounded this principle < German *weise* "wise" + *Mann* "man"].

- "*Publications* [of the fictitious George Challenger]: 'Some Observations Upon a Series of Kalmuck Skulls'; 'Outlines of Vertebrate Evolution'; and numerous papers, including 'The Underlying Fallacy of Weissmannism,' which caused heated discussion at the Zoological Congress of Vienna." Arthur Conan Doyle, *The Lost World*, 2004, p. 12.

Weltanschauung, Weltansicht *n.*

"world view": one's philosophy or conception of the universe and of life, a particular attitude toward life and reality. The difference between *Anschauung* and *Ansicht* is the same as that between *look* and *see*. This entry suggested by David.

- "The ideological school plumbed the equally murky depths of his [Hitler's] prose and claimed to find in his feverishly logorrheic discourse an intellectual coherence, a serious Weltanschauung that was the true engine of his murderous acts." Ron Rosenbaum, "Explaining Hitler", *The New Yorker*, May 1995.

Weltpolitik *n.*

from *Weltpolitik* "global politics": the theory that politics is global in scale [< German *Welt* "world" + *Politik* "politics, policy"]. See also <u>Machtpolitik</u>, <u>Ostpolitik</u>, *<u>Realpolitik</u>* and *<u>Westpolitik</u>*. This entry suggested by Richard Hartzell.

- "Germany's *Weltpolitik* was an implicit threat to the hegemony of Great Britain, which at the turn of the century was still the pre-eminent imperial power." Misha Glenny, *The Balkans: Nationalism, War & the Great Powers, 1804-1999*, 2001, p. 309.

Weltschmerz, weltschmerz, Weltschmerz *n.*

from *Weltschmerz* "world pain": sorrow which one feels and accepts as his necessary portion in life; mental depression or apathy caused by comparison of the actual state of the world with an ideal state; sentimental pessimism or sadness. This entry suggested by Frank Weller. See also <u>angst</u>.

- "Carol was plunged back into last night's *Weltschmerz*." Sinclair Lewis, *Main Street*, 1920.

Westpolitik *n.*

from *Westpolitik* "western politics": a policy of a Communist country of adopting trade and diplomatic relations with non-Communist nations [< German *West* "west" + *Politik* "politics, policy"]. See also <u>Machtpolitik</u>, <u>Ostpolitik</u>, *<u>Realpolitik</u>* and *<u>Weltpolitik</u>*.

- "He [German chancellor Konrad Adenauer] had to show the West German public that a policy of cooperation with Europe and the United States—a *Westpolitik*—had clear benefits for them." William I. Hitchcock, *The Struggle for Europe: The Turbulent History of a Divided Continent 1945-2002*, 2003, p. 148.

wiener, wienie, wienerwurst *n.*

from *Wiener Wurst* "Viennese (sausage)": a kind of sausage used in hotdogs, a <u>frankfurter</u>, not to be confused with what Americans call *Viennese sausages*, which are pretty much the same thing but smaller and canned in liquid. Austrians call wieners *Frankfurter (Würste)*. I've never seen Viennese sausages in Vienna. See further example under *<u>sauerkraut</u>*. See also *<u>Wiener schnitzel</u>* and *<u>wurst</u>*.

- "He bought one and it didn't taste like dog meat at all; it reminded him, instead, of a cross between salami and a German wiener." Rosario Ferre, *The House on the Lagoon*, 1995.

- "He seemed to tower over the pitcher—Red was six feet one—and he scowled and shook his bat at Wehying and called, 'Put one over—you wienerwurst!'" Zane Grey, *The Redheaded Outfield*, 1915.
- "Cooking chicken thighs recently, I caught the exact aroma of a Balboa wienie roast, when the fire was ready and the first wienies were deployed above it on long forks with wooden handles." Paul Fussell, *Doing Battle: The Making of a Skeptic*, 1998.
- "In Austria, noted for its tasty sausages (*Würstel*), the word for Vienna is *Wien*, and for Viennese, *Wiener*. It is easy to see where 'wienie' comes from." George W. Long, "Occupied Austria, Outpost of Democracy", *National Geographic*, Jun. 1951, p. 766.
- "Author Frederick Simpich was aghast at buildings shaped like 'owls, derby hats, shoes, airships, dogs, teakettles, windmills, mosques, wienerwursts, zeppelins, and igloos.'" "From our Archives: Dog Gone" *National Geographic*, Nov. 2000, p. 135. Original quote from 1934.
- "With Casey prostrate in the dirt amid the screams and jeers/We threw wieners down at him and other souvenirs." Garrison Keillor, "Casey at the Bat (Road Game)", *The Book of Guys*, 1993.

Wiener schnitzel, Wiener Schnitzel, schnitzel *n.*
from *Wiener Schnitzel* "Viennese cutlet": a thin breaded cutlet traditionally of veal but more usually of pork and sometimes turkey. See further examples under *bratwurst* and *stein*.

- "Dirndls, Mozart, The Sound of Music—genug! Enough already. It gets cloying, like being presented with an extra-large Salzburger Nockerln after too much Wiener schnitzel." Roger Kimball, "Salzburg, for Real", *National Review*, Sep. 17, 2001.
- "With the increasing interest in beef and other meats, Wiener Schnitzel and other veal dishes are in demand." Florence Fabricant, "As German and Austrian cuisines gain in popularity, schnitzel waltzes onto menus", *Nation's Restaurant News*, Mar. 6, 2000.

Wirtschaftswunder *n.*
from *Wirtschaftswunder* "economic miracle": the fast rise of the economy in West Germany in the fifties and sixties [< German *Wirtschaft* "economy" + *Wunder*, "miracle, wonder"]. See also Frauleinwunder and wunderkind. This entry suggested by Bastian Sick.

- "Ruff's photographs from the 1980s of corporate and industrial architecture in Germany's Ruhr area were already mediated by other depictions of such buildings: picture postcards from the fifties and sixties, with which companies advertised their prosperity of the Wirtschaftswunder (industrial miracle, or boom) years." Sven Lutticken, "Haunted space", *Afterimage*, Sep.-Oct. 2002.
- "The German population is rapidly aging, the country's wage bargaining, labor rules, and product market regulations came from another era, and Germany's days as a Wirtschaftswunder are long gone." Donna Harsch, review of *From Rags to Riches: Housework, Consumption and Modernity in Germany* by Jennifer A. Loehlin, *Journal of Social History*, Spring 2002.
- "Postwar Germany, absorbed in rebuilding and mesmerized by its prodigious Wirtschaftswunder, deliberately forgetful of both the horrors it had caused

(Auschwitz, etc.) and those it had suffered (Dresden, etc.), was unthinkable as a homeland." Peter Heinegg, "Memory's martyr", *Cross Currents*, Spring 2002.

- "They regard the old <u>D-mark</u> as the creator of dos [*sic*] Wirtschaftswunder (the economic boom) and question whether it is any accident that monetary union has coincided with Germany experiencing economic decline of a type that has left it struggling to comply with EU rules on debt as a proportion of national income." Tim Luckhurst, "A reluctant people see the bigger picture", *New Statesman*, Jan. 7, 2002.
- "It has also, along with the Bundesverfassung (the Federal Constitution), been one of the few acceptable tokens of national pride, as the emblem and motor of the Wirtschaftswunder, the 'economic miracle' that saw Germany become the most powerful economy in Western Europe." Jonathan Williams & Andrew Meadows, "Europe's national currencies: Jonathan Williams and Andrew Meadows review the history of the various currencies being replaced by the Euro", *History Today*, Jan. 2002.
- "The German population is rapidly aging, the country's wage bargaining, labor rules, and product market regulations came from another era, and Germany's days as a Wirtschaftswunder are long gone." Adam S. Posen, "Who's the comeback kid? France, Germany, and Italy are struggling to recover. Who'll come out on top?" *The International Economy*, Fall 2003.
- "Walther Groz belonged to the large number of entrepreneurs who were the driving force of Germany's Wirtschaftswunder in the 1950s and 1960s." Jurgen Hambrecht, as quoted in "Gaining executive mindshare: US and European chemical CEOs", by Cynthia Challener, *Chemical Market Reporter*, May 26, 2003.

wrack *n., v.t.*

related to *Wrack* "wreck": ruin; destruction, now chiefly in the phrase *wrack and ruin*; wreck; wreckage; seaweed or other marine plant life cast up on shore. One of the several meanings of Modern English *wrack* comes from Low German *wrak* and is similar in spelling, meaning and origin to Modern German *Wrack*.

- "From the fabric of the beach, wrack and wreckage of the world before things changed." William Gibson, *Idoru*, 1997.

wunderkind, wunderkid *n.*

from *Wunderkind* "miracle or wonder child". See also <u>Frauleinwunder</u>, <u>über-</u> and <u>Wirtschaftswunder</u>.

- "Harry? Harry, 19, wunderkind!" Liev Schreiber as Ted Fielding in *Sphere*, produced by Michael Crichton, 1998.
- "Classmates Shamed By Wunderkid's Incredible Talent", Bill Watterson, *Calvin and Hobbes* comic strip, May 6, 1993.
- "When the half-year hazing was over, Lovell, it was announced, had finished first in his class, edging out even such Pax River wunderkinder as Wally Schirra and Pete Conrad." Jim Lovell & Jeffrey Kluger, *Apollo 13*, 1995. This example illustrates the correct German plural of the word.

wurst *n.*

from *Wurst* "sausage": often in compounds such as <u>*bratwurst*</u>, <u>*liverwurst*</u>, <u>*knackwurst*</u>, etc.

- "Then those of my dear neighbors nearest my heart decided to prevent a lonely Christmas for me, so on December 21st came Mrs. Louderer, laden with an immense plum pudding and a big '*wurst*,' and a little later came Mrs. O'Shaughnessy on her frisky pony, Chief, her scarlet sweater making a bright bit of color against our snow-wrapped horizon." Elinore Pruitt Stewart, *Letters of a Woman Homesteader*, 1847.
- "Winnies! *Here's* your hot winnies! Hot winny-*wurst!*" Booth Tarkington, *Penrod*, 1914.
- *The Wurst of PDQ Bach*, P. Schickele (P. D. Q. Bach), 1992.

yager *n.*

See jäger.

yammer *v.i., n.*

related to *jammern* "to whine, whimper, complain, lament, groan": *To yammer* actually comes from Anglo-Saxon *geomerian*, Old English *geomrian* and Middle English *yameren* but was influenced by Middle Low German *jammeren* and is so similar in spelling, pronunciation and meaning to Modern German *jammern* that I have included it here. See also Katzenjammer.

- "When I got my first sight of a Bug, my mind jumped right out of my skull and started to yammer." Robert A. Heinlein, *Starship Troopers*, 1959, p. 136.
- "I don't understand that yammer [foreign language]." Robert A. Heinlein, *Citizen of the Galaxy*, 1982, p. 61.
- "Standing inside the huge wooden shrines with the rain beating down was like being held captive in a primitive, drumlike wooden instrument with the prevailing, high-pitched yammer of rampant schoolgirls surrounding you." John Irving, *The Fourth Hand*, 2001, p. 81.
- "His work—one farmer he pulls through diphtheria is worth all my yammering for a castle in Spain." Sinclair Lewis, *Main Street*, 1920.
- "There's a muckle ship gaun ashore on the reef, and the puir folks are a' yammerin' and ca'in' for help—and I doobt they'll a' be drooned." Arthur Conan Doyle, *The Captain of the Polestar and other Tales*, 1894.
- "The President, a devoted dog man, wasn't interested in trying collie haunches or wearing Hun outfits, but he decided not to interfere with the takeover attempts in the savings-and-loan industry—sure, there were these pesky yammering voices in the press about how he ought to step in, etc., etc., as if it were that *simple*." Garrison Keillor, "George Bush", *The Book of Guys*, 1993, p. 281.

to **yodel** *v.i., v.t., n.*

from *jodeln* "to yodel": a melody or refrain sung to meaningless syllables, with abrupt changes from chest to falsetto tones, common among Swiss and Tyrolese mountaineers [literally to call the syllable "jo", pronounced "yo" in English].

- "Some three hours later, Mr. Samuel Williams, waxen clean and in sweet raiment, made his reappearance in Penrod's yard, yodelling a code-signal to summon forth his friend." Booth Parkington, *Penrod*, 1914.
- "The playful yodeling of many voices in chorus was heard at the close of each song." Charles Alexander Eastman, *Old Indian Days*, 1907.
- "It was still continuing after dinner that evening, when an oft-repeated yodel, followed by a shrill-wailed, 'Jane-ee! Oh, Jane-nee-ee!' brought her to an open window down-stairs." Booth Tarkington, *Seventeen*, 1915.
- "During intermissions young blades danced the high-kicking, heel-and-thigh-slapping *Schuhplattler*, yodeled, or flirted with the pink-cheeked girls in fetching <u>dirndls</u>." George W. Long, "Occupied Austria, Outpost of Democracy" *National Geographic*, Jun. 1951, p. 775.

Z

zaftig, zoftig *adj.*

related to *saftig* "juicy": full-figured, full-bodied, full-bosomed, buxom, having a full rounded figure, pleasingly plump, well-propotioned, slightly fat [Yiddish *zaftik* "juicy, succulent" < *zaft* "juice, sap" < Middle High German *saftec* "juicy" < *saf, saft* "juice" < Old High German *saf* "sap", related to English *sap*].

- "If you're over forty or fat, stay away from numbers. Euphemisms are your friends. Use terms like *boomer babe, sexy senior, ample, voluptuous, zaftig* or *BBW* (Big Beautiful Woman) instead." Myreah Moore, *Date Like A Man: What Men Know About Dating and Are Afraid You'll Find Out*, 2001, p. 135.
- "The new coffee table and my beautiful Bolero [statue] in all her zaftig bronze glory were a welcoming sight." Fran Drescher, *Cancer Schmancer*, 2002, p. 106.

ZDF *n.*

short for *Zweites Deutsches Fernsehen* "Second German Television": a public TV broadcasting company in Germany.

- "For example, Korinna Horta, an economist working for the Environmental Defense Fund, was in a similar manner thwarted—'banned' is the word she used—from traveling into the region; Dr. Birgit Hermes of ZDF television in Germany was denied permission to bring in a crew that would document the bushmeat situation within the CIB concession; and Gary Streiker of CNN asked for similar permission and was likewise turned away." Dale Peterson, *Eating Apes*, 2003, p. 170.
- "Barbara Frei anchored the morning news for ZDF." John Irving, *The Fourth Hand*, 2001, p. 59.

- "A veteran of Germany's ZDF, one of Europe's largest TV stations with an annual budget of 1.8 billion [euro] ($1.5 billion), has been elected to the pubcaster's top job -- ending months of uncertainty about its future head." Christian Kohl, "ZDF ups 20-year vet to its top job", *Variety*, Mar. 25, 2002.
- "The two German public TV channels, ARD and ZDF, both have exclusive broadcasting rights to the new DTM." Greg N. Brown, "AMG Mercedes-Benz CLK55", *European Car*, Nov. 2000.

zeitgeber *n.*

from *Zeitgeber* "timer": an environmental agent or event such as light or temperature that provides the stimulus setting or resetting a biological clock of an organism [German *Zeitgeber* "time giver" < *Zeit* "time" + *Geber* "giver" < *geben* "to give"]. This entry suggested by Richard Harvey. See also zeitgeist.

- "This power to determine emotion is akin to what is called in biology a *zeitgeber* (literally, 'time-grabber'), a process (such as the day-night cycle or the monthly phases of the moon) that entrains biological rhythms." Daniel Goleman, *Emotional Intelligence: Why It Can Matter More Than IQ*, 1997, p. 117. *Geber* does not in any sense mean "grabber", as stated here, but rather "giver".

zeitgeist, zeitgeist, Zeitgeist *n.*

from *Zeitgeist* "time spirit": the spirit of the times; the intellectual, moral and cultural state of a period. See also hopfgeist, poltergeist, zeitgeber.

- "I'm not saying that these are today's Nazis - God forbid. I only wondered whether they might not, back in those days, have been equally well suited to be the embodiment of a ruthless, glacial *Zeitgeist*." Norbert & Stephan Lebert, *My Father's Keeper: Children of Nazi Leaders--An Intimate History of Damage and Denial*, 2001.
- "In declaring war on cancer, President Nixon was no more than iterating the zeitgeist of popular medical and lay opinion." Frank Ryan, M.D., *Virus X: Tracking the New Killer Plagues Out of the Present and Into the Future*, 1998.
- "Plain it is to us that what the world seeks through desert and wild we have within our threshold,—a stalwart laboring force, suited to the semi-tropics; if, deaf to the voice of the Zeitgeist, we refuse to use and develop these men, we risk poverty and loss." W. E. Burghardt Du Bois, *The Souls of Black Folk*, 1903.
- "Or to an Old World zeitgeist so catastrophically hidebound that a few economic reforms won't remedy it?" Michael Krantz, *Time Digital*, Mar. 17, 1997, p. 27.
- "Like a tripwire on the zeitgeist, the novel provided the first glimmer of the public's fresh hunger for a franchise that had hardly lain dormant since the mid-80s." Bruce Handy, *Time*, Mar. 17, 1997, p. 80.
- "Densely riffing on the signifiers and striations of the English class system, lit crit, the PRification of America, marriage, fatherhood, and oral sex, The Information is as zeitgeisty, as technically dazzling, and as laugh-out-loud funny as Money and London Fields (1989)." Graham Fuller, "The prose and cons of Martin Amis", *Interview*, May 1995.

- Google Zeitgeist, search patterns, trends, and surprises according to Google, www.google.com/zeitgeist

zigzag, zig-zag, zig and zag, zig, zag *n., v.i., v.t., adv., adj.*

from *Zickzack*: (to move in) a line or course that moves back and forth to form a series of sharp angles [French *zic-zac* < German *Zickzack*, perhaps reduplication of the interjection *zack!*, perhaps < *Zacke* "tooth, cog" < Middle High German *zacke* "point, nail"].

- "Down from vague and vaporous heights, little ruffled zigzag milky currents came crawling, and found their way to the verge of one of those tremendous overhanging walls, whence they plunged, a shaft of silver, shivered to atoms in mid-descent and turned to an air puff of luminous dust." Mark Twain, *A Tramp Abroad*, 1879, p. 359.

- "So that Monsoons, Pampas, Nor-Westers, Harmattans, Trades; any wind but the Levanter and Simoom, might blow Moby Dick into the devious zig-zag world-circle of the Pequod's circumnavigating wake." Herman Melville, *Moby-Dick, or, The Whale*, 1851, p. 198.

- "We had entered the outskirts of the forest of Zenda, and the trees, closing in behind us as the track zigged and zagged, prevented us seeing our pursuers, and them from seeing us." Anthony Hope, *The Prisoner of Zenda: being the history of three months in the life of an English gentleman*, 1894, p. 76.

- "In a sudden pause of the talk the game would recommence with a sharp click and go on for a time in the flowing soft whirr and the subdued thuds as the balls rolled zig-zagging towards the inevitably successful cannon." Joseph Conrad, *An Outcast of the Islands*, 1896, p. 6.

zinc *n.*

from *Zink*: a metal, element and nutrient [German *Zink, Zinken* prob. < German *Zinke, Zinken* "spike" (so called because it becomes jagged in the furnace) < Middle High German *zinke* < Old High German *zinko*, possibly related to *tooth* and *tin*].

- "In addition to the copper ores, the Outokumpu deposits yield iron, zinc, cobalt, nickel, tin, gold, silver and sulphur." Fred Singleton, *A Short History of Finland*, 1989, p. 5.

- "'Ah, one-horse dentist,' he muttered between his teeth. 'Ah, zinc-plugger, cow-killer, I'd like to show you once, you overgrown mucker, you -- you -- COW-KILLER'" Frank Norris, *McTeague: A Story of San Francisco*, 1899, p. 169.

- "They would also use mercury for bullets in their rifles, just as inhabitants of the intra-Vulcan planets at the other extreme might, if their bodies consisted of asbestos, or were in any other way non-combustibly constituted, bathe in tin, lead, or even zinc, which ordinarily exist in the liquid state, as water and mercury do on the earth." John Jacob Astor, *Journey in Other Worlds*, 1894, p. 392.

- "There, as in all Latin America, marginalized and dispossessed immigrants from the countryside lived in houses made of cardboard and zinc." Jorge G. Castaneda, *Companero: The Life and Death of Che Guevara*, 1997.

- "But Uncle Esteban also took it upon himself to carry out certain more humble tasks which later proved to be the best example he could have given Estefania, such as merely cleaning the gums of the wounded or washing their bodies with ointment of zinc and castor oil when they soiled themselves in bed or picking lice from their heads with infinite patience." Fernando Del Paso, *Palinuro of Mexico*, 1977.

- "Zinc absorption is also enhanced by other factors in human milk." Martha Sears & William Sears, *The Breastfeeding Book: Everything You Need to Know About Nursing Your Child from Birth Through Weaning*, 2000.
- "The prostate's fluid is clear and mildly acidic, and contains many ingredients, most of them designed to sustain sperm outside the body for as long as possible. (These include citric acid, acid phosphatase, spermine, potassium, calcium, and zinc.)" Patrick C. Walsh & Janet Farrar Worthington, *Dr. Patrick Walsh's Guide to Surviving Prostate Cancer*, 2001.

zoftig *adj.*

See zaftig.

zugzwang *n., v.t.*

from *Zugzwang* "compulsion to move": (in chess) a situation in which one is forced to make a disadvantageous move, a no-win situation; to force into a bad (chess) position [German *Zug* "pull, move" < Middle High German *zuc* "pull" < Old High German *ziohan* "to pull" + *Zwang* "compulsion" < Middle High German *zwanc, twanc, dwanc* < Old High German *thwanga*]. This entry suggested by Alfred Pfeiffer.

- "*Zugzwang*—that's what they call it in chess. He had to make a move he didn't want to ...." Emil A. Draitser, "Zugzwang" *Kenyon Review*, 1999.
- "Zugzwang a good thing, if it's not your move." Tal Shaked, *The Arizona Daily Star*, Jan. 18, 1998.
- "(White: Ka7,Qg3,Nc5,Nh7; Black: Kh1,Nb4,Nh2,P:g2): 1.Ne4! Nd3! (On 1...g1Q 2.Nf2+ wins.) 2.Qf2!! Nxf2 (On 2...g1Q 3.Ng3+ or 2...Nf1 3.Qh4+ wins.) 3.Ng3+! Kg1 4.Ng5, black is in zugzwang and is mated either on f3 or h3." Lubomir Kavalek, "Solution to today's composition by A. Gurvich" *The Washington Post*, Dec. 25, 2000.

zwieback *n.*

from *Zwieback* "twice baked": bread which is first baked then toasted.

- "I got to the point where Mr. Moody feeding nickels into the slot-machine with one hand and eating zwieback with the other made me nervous. After a while he went to sleep over it, and when he had slipped a nickel in his mouth and tried to put the zwieback in the machine he muttered something and went up to the house." Mary Roberts Rinehart, *Where There's a Will*, 1912.

zwischenzug *n.*

from *Zwischenzug* "between + move": a determining chess move.

Picture Credits

All pictures copyright Robbin D. Knapp except the following:

angst: detail of the painting "The Scream" by Eduard Munch.

Baedeker: cover of the book *Russia: A Handbook for Travelers* (A facsimile of the original 1904 edition) by Karl Baedeker.

Beck's: magazine advertisement.

dirndl: image of Sandra Bullock from the film *Miss Congeniality*, directed by Donald Petrie, 2000.

Ehrenbreitstein: detail from the book *The Elements of Drawing* by John Ruskin, 1876.

flugelhorn: cover of the CD *Feels So Good* by Chuck Mangione, 1977.

Der Freischütz: cover of the CD *Der Freischütz* by Carl Maria von Weber, 1998.

katzenjammer: U.S. Postage stamp "Katzenjammer Kids".

lederhosen: the author in lederhosen, copyright Gerti Knapp, 2002.

Ouija: photograph by Zaid Zolkiffli.

sitz bath: from the film *Thunderball*, directed by Terence Young, 1965.

steinbock: photo taken by Ferkelparade and released under the GNU Free Documentation License.

umlaut: detail from the book *Der Grosse Neu-Gepflanzte Myrrhen-Garten* by P. Martini von Cochem, 1732.

ZDF: detail from *Tele: Das österreichische Fernsehmagazin.*

Sources and Further Reading

Books and Articles

Associated Press, "Census Shows More in U.S. Identify Themselves as 'American'", *The New York Times*, Jun. 9, 2002.

Aurand, A. Monroe, Jr., *Quaint Idioms and Expressions of the Pennsylvania Germans*, 1939, The Aurand Press, Lancaster, Pa., 32 pages.

Bahlow, Hans, *Deutsches Namenslexikon: Familien- und Vornamen nach Ursprung und Sinn erklärt*, 1991, Gondrom Verlag, Bindlach, 576 pages.

Beale, Paul, *Partridge's Concise Dictionary of Slang and Unconventional English: From the Work of Eric Partridge*, 1989, Macmillan, New York, 534 pages.

Bluestein, Gene, *Anglish/Yinglish: Yiddish in American Life and Literature*, 1998, University of Nebraska Press, Lincoln, 164 pages.

Brockhaus Illustrated Dictionary, English-German, German-English, Eighth Edition, 1978, F. A. Brockhaus, Wiesbaden, 1453 pages.

Bryson, Bill, *The Mother Tongue: English and How It Got that Way*, 1990, Harper-Collins, New York, 270 pages.

Buchanan-Brown, John, et al. (eds.), *Le Mot Juste: A Dictionary of Classical and Foreign Words and Phrases*, 1991, Vintage Books, New York, 170 pages.

Bush, George W., "Proclamation 7481—German American Day, 2001", *Weekly Compilation of Presidential Documents*, Oct. 15, 2001.

Crystal, David, & Linda Wertheimer, "English Helps Itself to Other Tongues at Language Buffet", *All Things Considered*, National Public Radio, Jun. 7, 1996, transcript.

Duden, Band 7, Etymologie: Herkunftswörterbuch der deutschen Sprache, 1997, Dudenverlag, Vienna, 840 pages.

Funk & Wagnalls Standard Desk Dictionary, 1979, Funk & Wagnalls Inc. New York, 878 pages.

Hornblower, Margot, "Roots Mania: Spurred by new resources on the Internet, the ranks of amateur genealogists are growing, and millions of family trees are flourishing", *Time*, Apr. 19, 1999.

Jucker, Andreas H., "Das Fremde in der eigenen Sprache: Fremdwörter im Deutschen und im Englischen", in: *Begegnungen mit dem Fremden*, Lothar Bredella & Herbert Christ (eds.), Verlag der Ferber'schen Universtitätsbuchhandlung, Gießen, 1996, pages 233-247.

Martin, Tim, "German Influence Strong Here", *Lansing State Journal*, Jun. 9, 2002.

Parshall, Gerald, "A 'glorious mongrel': The language that some Americans want to defend against foreign invasions is itself a multicultural smorgasbord of borrowed words", *U.S. News & World Report*, Sep. 25, 1995, page 48.

Random House Dictionary of the English Language, The, College Edition, 1968, Random House, New York, 1568 pages.

Stanforth, A. W., "The semantic assimilation of German loan material in British English", *German Life and Letters*, 1990, pages 153-167.

Stiberc, Andrea, *Sauerkraut, Weltschmerz, Kindergarten und Co.: Deutsche Wörter in der Welt*, 1999, Herder, Vienna, 184 pages.

Stubbs, Michael, "Angst and the Zeitgeist: Notes on German words in English", in: *British Studies in Germany: Essays in Honour of Frank Frankel*, Wolfgang Mackiewitz & Dieter Wolff (eds.), Wissenschaftlicher Verlag Trier, 1997, pages 127-145.

Stubbs, Michael, "Collocations and Cultural Connotations of Common Words", *Linguistics and Education*, 1995, pages 379-390.

Stubbs, Michael, "German Loanwords and Cultural Stereotypes", *English Today*, Jan. 1998, pages 19-26.

Tolzmann, Don Heinrich, "The German-American Legacy", *German Life*, Jul. 31, 1994.

Webster's New Encyclopedic Dictionary, 1993, Könemann, Cologne, Germany, 1787 pages.

Webster's New World Dictionary of the American Language, College Edition, World, 1722 pages.

Internet Links

Amazon.com, www.amazon.com
American Fact Finder, U.S. Census Bureau, factfinder.census.gov
Electronic Text Center, University of Virginia, etext.lib.virginia.edu
FindArticles.com, www.findarticles.com
Google Print, print.google.com
Merriam-Webster OnLine, www.m-w.com
OneLook® Dictionaries, www.onelook.com
Robb's language links, www.robbsnet.com/rclinksc.htm#language
Washingtonpost.com Style Chapter One, www.washingtonpost.com/wp-srv/style/books/chapterone.htm
Wikipedia, www.wikipedia.org

Bibliography

Though not used as sources you may also want to try the following books:

Adams, Willi Paul, Lavern J. Rippley, & Eberhard Reichmann, *The German-Americans: An Ethnic Experience*, 1993, Indiana University Press, Bloomington.

Adeleye, Gabriel, *World Dictionary of Foreign Expressions: A Resource for Readers and Writers*, 2000, Bolchazy-Carducci, Wauconda, Ill.

Ayto, John, *Dictionary of Word Origins*, 1993, Arcade, New York.

Bliss, Alan, *Dictionary of Foreign Words and Phrases in Current English*, 1992, Warner Books, New York.

Bryson, Bill, *Made in America: An Informal History of the English Language in the United States*, 2001, Perennial, New York, 417 pages.

Ehrlich, Eugene, *You've Got Ketchup on Your Muumuu: An A-To-Z Guide to English Words from Around the World*, 2001, Owl Books, New York.

Flippo, Hyde, *The German Way: Aspects of Behavior, Attitudes, and Customs in the German-Speaking World*, 1996, McGraw-Hill, 144 pages.

Frost, Helen. *German Immigrants, 1820-1920: Coming to America*, 2001, Blue Earth Books, Mankato, Minn.

Galicich, Anne, *The German Americans: The Immigrant Experience*, 1996, Chelsea House Publishing, Broomall, Pa.

Guinagh, Kevin (ed.), *Dictionary of Foreign Phrases and Abbreviations*, 1983, H. W. Wilson, New York.

Metcalf, Allan A., *The World in So Many Words: A Country-by-Country Tour of Words That Have Shaped Our Language*, 1999, Houghton Mifflin, Boston.

McKean, Erin (ed.), *Weird and Wonderful Words*, 2002, Oxford University Press, New York.

Pfeffer, J. Alan, *Deutsches Sprachgut im Wortschatz der Amerikaner und Engländer: Vergleichendes Lexikon mit analytischer Einführung und historischem Überblick*, 1986, M. Niemeyer, Tbg.

Pfeffer, J. Alan, & Garland Cannon, *German Loanwords in English: An Historical Dictionary*, 1994, Cambridge University Press, 415 pages.

Phythian, B. A. (ed.), *A Concise Dictionary of Foreign Expressions*, 1984, Rowman & Littlefield, Lanham, Md.

Speake, Jennifer (ed.), *The Oxford Dictionary of Foreign Words and Phrases*, 2000, Oxford University Press, New York.

Swiderski, Richard M., *The Metamorphosis of English*, 1996, Bergin & Garvey, Westport, Conn.

Tolzmann, Don Heinrich, *The German-American Experience*, 2000, Humanity Books, Amherst, N.Y.

Urdang, Laurence (ed.), *Loanwords Index: A Compilation of More Than 14,000 Foreign Words*, 1983, Gale Group, Farmington Hills, Mich.

Urdang, Laurence, & Frank R. Abate (eds.), *Loanwords Dictionary*, 1988, Gale Group, Farmington Hills, Mich.

Zug, John D., & Karin Gottier (eds.), *German-American Life: Recipes and Traditions*, 1991, Penfield Books, Iowa City, Iowa.

ABOUT THE AUTHOR

Robbin D. Knapp is an American who was born in Denver, Colorado, and has been living in the German-speaking country of Austria since 1984 with his Austrian wife. Therefore, he speaks German fluently. He studied Latin, German, and French in high school and at the University of Virginia (Bachelor of Arts in Biology), where he financed his education by working in the university library and hospital. Since 1985, he has been translating a wide variety of texts between German and English. While in the Peace Corps in Tanzania, he learned Swahili and spoke it fluently. He has held a wide variety of jobs, including cab driver, assistant English teacher, computer programmer, and most recently IT manager. He has been an enthusiastic amateur linguist since high school.

Besides managing his own linguistics Web site (HumanLanguages.com), he has also translated many other Web sites from German to English and *vice versa*, for example the Bird Names Translation Index (www.mumm.ac.be/~serge/birds), the City of Linz Web cam project (www.linz.at), and the Biology Center of the Upper Austrian Provincial Museum (www.biologiezentrum.at). On another Web site of his (RobbsBooks.com), he writes book reviews.

Printed in the United States
70643LV00004B/244